A Spiritual Odyssey

The Unfoldment of a Soul

By the same author
Alchemy of Awareness
The Spiritual Journey of Joel S Goldsmith

A Spiritual Odyssey

The Unfoldment of a Soul

by Lorraine Sinkler

The Valor Foundation
in association with
L.N. Fowler and Company Limited
Chadwell Heath   Romford
Essex   England

© Copyright 1991. The Valor Foundation
Paperback edition
ISBN 0-9629119-0-9
Library of Congress Catalog Card No 91-65446

First published in the USA in 1991
by The Valor Foundation
in association with

L.N. Fowler and Company Limited
1201 High Road
Chadwell Heath
Romford
Essex RM6 4DH
England

Cover design by Susan Melrath West Palm Beach Florida
Typeset in New Century Schoolbook 11/14 point by
Swift Typesetting Limited Dagenham Essex England
Printed in the USA by Thomson-Shore Inc. Dexter Michigan.

Dedicated to the Unfolding Soul Within You

"Eye hath not seen,
Nor ear heard,
Neither have entered
Into the heart of man,
The things which God hath prepared
For them that love him."

I Corinthians 2:9

CONTENTS

A Spiritual Odyssey
The Unfoldment of a Soul

So It Began

At some time or other in a person's ongoing, there comes a special moment when one reaches a turning point, a fork in the road. That special moment came to me on September 28, 1949, my spiritual birthday, when I first met Joel Goldsmith, the person who was to open the door of my awareness. It was my great good fortune and blessing to have this twentieth-century mystic and master teacher as a guide to reveal to me the Guide within. What that moment meant to me and the tremendous impact it was to have on my life, I could not then foresee, but the joy that bubbled over in me at having found my own, was so evident that even the waitress who served dinner to my sister and me commented on it. "A birthday celebration?" When I disclaimed any such thing she added, "But there is such a feeling of happiness and gladness here." As I think of it now, I know she was right. It was a real birthday—a time of coming alive and feeling some tremendous force stirring within me. Until then I had not read a single word Joel had written, so I had no idea of the treasure awaiting me....

All my life I had been searching for something I knew existed but could not define or find. That irrepressible urge led me to read innumerable books on metaphysics, philosophy, theosophy, occultism, and religion, both Western and Eastern. From them, I learned that many paths could take me on that long journey within, a number of which I explored. Later, I discovered that although there are innumerable ways, for each of us there is one especially adapted to our temperament and to the degree of preparation undergone in this and in previous lifetimes.

Few records exist to illustrate how a disciple works with a spiritual master. In my correspondence with my teacher, which encompassed a period of fifteen years and during which time hundreds of letters were exchanged—at first infrequently, later sometimes everyday, and even twice a day—considerable light is thrown on such a relationship, as well as the very perceptible change that took place in the character and experience of the disciple.

My letters provide insight into the invaluable instructions given the disciple, although the deepest instruction was always given and received in the silence. Established in that one Consciousness, there was no separation, whether the master and disciple were together or separated by thousands of miles. Nevertheless, the letters indicate the direction the work took in awakening the disciple to the mystical consciousness. They give the day-to-day account of an all-absorbing happening, containing all the spontaneity of the nowness of the happening rather than mere reminiscence.

Some may question the apparent emphasis placed on the practice of spiritual healing and wonder what it has to do with the goal of conscious union with the Source. But, in that practice, the aspirant was forced to see through the appearance-world to the ever present Reality, thereby pushing aside every barrier to total oneness that lifetimes of a sense of separation had imposed. The ability to do that was a *sine qua non* for the Soul to come to its full flowering.

Many of my inner struggles came and went unnoted, for I did not keep a day-by-day account of them for myself. The record contained in my letters to my spiritual teacher, however, gives some clue as to the steps an aspirant may have to take. The letters also reveal that, as the relationship of teacher and student deepened and became a permanent one, the attitude and consciousness of this serious aspirant shifted from a wordy, intellectual, and formal approach to a simple, unvarnished revelation of her innermost thoughts.

In the years that have followed, many students have come to me, seeking to be taught and wanting to know if the many rocks they found along the way were an inevitable concomitant of the spiritual path. Having learned to live in the nowness of spiritual fulfillment, I have usually answered in the negative. It is difficult for me to recall the many spiritual crises that may or may not have been a necessary part of my unfoldment. My letters, however, unmistakably point up those periods of inner struggle.

At my first meeting with Joel Goldsmith, I spoke of feeling the need for a teacher to guide me along the way. He assured me that he would accept me on that basis and that, even though I might not be in his physical presence, the teaching would go on. And all these years, silently and sacredly, that teaching has continued.

The relationship between teacher and student is reciprocal, the teacher freely sharing his wisdom and the student expressing gratitude not only in words but in a tangible way and in spiritual support. The truth that we cannot receive more than we give characterizes that relationship. So only those who are willing to bring their all and give that all to the relationship can receive the totality of Grace the master has to bestow.

A spiritual teacher who has attained a realized consciousness is besieged by those who seek the fruitage of that consciousness. Most of those come, not God-hungry, but wanting only the effects of an enlightened consciousness. There are some, however, who long for enlightenment for itself and not for any purpose. A few, recognizing the gift so freely given to them, seek in turn to serve. To these the master gives the most attention, placing no limits on his willingness to work with them and on the amount of time he will give to that purpose.

Because of the great number of letters exchanged, and the limitations of space, some letters have been omitted or condensed. Unidentifiable initials have been used instead of actual names in most letters referring to personalities.

To be able to journey into the inner realms of consciousness with an enlightened teacher was a sacred experience always to be cherished and treasured. Every communication I received from my teacher was carefully filed away, a treasure to be assiduously guarded. So that I would better understand Joel's response to my questions and follow his instructions to the letter, I also saved copies of letters I wrote to him, never dreaming they would ever serve any other purpose. Several years ago, however, the unmistakable and insistent instruction came from within to share these letters not only with those struggling to find their way out in the world but even more important with those who, struggling to find the Center within, might be bogged down by a realization of how high the goal of spiritual awareness is and how far they seem to be from the first rung of the ladder. I hope such persons will find new hope and rejoice, for the Kingdom is already established within, only awaiting their recognition.

My heart is filled with gratitude for the many persons who, just by being, have been a support in both spiritual and human ways. Special thanks and gratitude go to Frances Steloff for the inspiration her whole life has been and for her deep interest in this work, to Infinite Way students and beloved friends, too numerous to mention by name, whose enthusiasm to have this book available has encouraged me to complete the task, and to my teacher, Joel Goldsmith—my unceasing gratitude.   When it comes to my sister, Valborg Sinkler Crossland—who has worked side by side with me in the preparation of *A Spiritual Odyssey: The Unfoldment of a Soul*, as she has in all the other work I have done—there are no words to express the depth of my gratitude for her all-sustaining love, dedication, encouragement, and invaluable assistance.

1

Soul-Stirrings

Sitting alone in a charming Bavarian home in southern Germany in July of 1964 and looking out at the towering mountains in the distance partially shrouded with a purple haze, introspection came easily, and with it the question: Why me? Why, out of all the millions of people in the world, was it I who should be one of a very few to have had the privilege of knowing and being able to spend so many days, weeks, and months out of the past fifteen years with this great spiritual teacher? The answer to that insistent question came back quickly: "Because Joel Goldsmith was an integral part of your consciousness."

It is not surprising that such a question came at that time. Only a few weeks before, I had been in Joel Goldsmith's suite in London with his wife Emma and two other students when he made the transition, his graduation into another experience. Following that, the work of completing his class and lecture schedule in Europe had been given me as a responsibility to be fulfilled.

I then realized why, for so many years, there had been a closeness and depth of understanding between Joel and me that no storms could dissolve. I could never be separated from what is my consciousness, a universal truth applicable to every person.

Of our first meeting in Chicago, Joel later told a small group of his special students that Lorraine Sinkler found The Infinite Way on his first lecture trip there in 1949, that at that time she had a spiritual experience and from then on became ever more closely associated with the work, finally giving up her professional career as an educator to devote herself to The Infinite Way, editing the Monthly *Letter* and all Infinite Way published writings.

When I first met Joel Goldsmith I had never read a word he had written nor did I know anything about him, except that I was told that he was a teacher of spiritual wisdom. In my search, I had met many such before, so my expectations were not too great. As I shook hands with him a cursory glance was far from reassuring. Here was a short, plump, stocky, unassuming man who might well have been anything except a spiritual teacher. He had a shock of black hair peppered with a few gray strands, wore a black string tie formed into a small bow tie with ends dangling from it, which I came to think of as his trademark. His suit was that of a successful businessman.

A second glance at him found me looking into dark piercing eyes that held me. Somehow he seemed to be looking right through the outer facade to my innermost being. As we sat in total silence for what seemed like a foreverness, even though it was only for a moment, there was a recognition of a bond that was forged lifetimes ago, and I knew my search was over and I was home. We meditated and then talked animatedly for an hour about the goal of total enlightenment and the possibility of achieving that goal.

Joel was always interested in students with a Christian Science background because of his sixteen years as a Christian Science practitioner during which time he became widely known for his healing work. I had joined a branch Christian Science church in Chicago when I was twelve years old and attended its Sunday School until I was twenty. Joel laughed when I told him that I became interested in Christian Science as a child and wanted to read its textbook *Science and Health* because I liked the feel and smell of the Morocco leather binding and the thin India paper. I shared Joel's gratitude for its teachings because, for some 25 years, they had carried me through many difficult and trying periods.

Then doubts about certain aspects began to creep into my mind. I found myself agreeing with a man who told me I was much too intelligent to "fall" for any of that "religious stuff" which he considered an escape mechanism. I insisted that whatever escape I might seek from facing problems I found in music. Nevertheless, the doubts increased, and I found myself immersed in the ethical but spiritually arid world of agnosticism. However, a firm foundation had been laid and whenever what seemed like a crisis loomed before me, I found myself saying, "God is the only power," finding comfort and courage in that statement.

I poured out to Joel something of the bypaths into which my search for enlightenment had led me. We talked about Ramakrishna and Vedanta, and my particular Vedantist swami, Vishvananda, and also about Yogananda, Gurdjieff, New Thought, Theosophy and Alice Bailey and the Arcane School. Joel's comments on these teachers and teachings were honest, forthright, and direct.

I explained that I had been meditating regularly with Swami Vishvananda and studying in the Arcane School. A book, *From Intellect To Intuition* by Alice

Bailey, had had such a profound effect upon me that I wrote to their headquarters for further information and learned about the Arcane School established by Alice Bailey as an organization whose primary purpose was soul-unfoldment with meditation the keynote. This was exactly what I was seeking. Each student in the school sent regular monthly reports to a secretary relating experiences in meditation and anything else pertinent.

In my first meditation following their prescribed form, a contact with the Presence was made. There was no experience of phenomena associated with it, but a tremendous inner stillness and a sense of fullness and fulfillment from that moment on. That Something had taken over. What had been a shy, timid person became the voice for all the teachers in the district, speaking to groups of several hundreds of parents in the community in the interest of the children and teachers. There were seven fruitful years in the Arcane School, although I never had direct contact with anyone except my secretary and that only by mail. When I wrote to her resigning from the Arcane School, her response to the effect that I was indeed blessed to have found the Way for me was evidence of the broadness and depth of her consciousness. During the seven years of study in the Arcane School, meditation had become an important part of my life and a rewarding and fruitful experience. In those meditations I had followed a particular form, which included meditation on a different "seed thought" each month. When I told Joel of this, he instructed me to drop the form I was using and take for my meditation, "I and my Father are one."[1]

Joel's further instructions were to begin reading his writings, of which I had not read a single word up to that point, get some of the writings of Ramana Maharshi, the Sage of Arunchula, and after studying them to write to him.

[1] That unfoldment is described in Lorraine Sinkler's The Alchemy of Awareness (New York: Harper & Row, 1977).

That night I began avidly reading the mimeographed edition of *God The Substance Of All Form*. Before I had finished I telephoned my sister Valborg saying, excitedly, "This is it! Do you know what it says? Nothing can be added to you; nothing can be taken from you: you are eternally complete and whole."[2] It was a realization that came through with tremendous strength and clarity. To this very day I sing the song of Self-completeness in God. Three weeks elapsed after that meeting with Joel before my first letter to him was written.

Evanston, Illinois[3]
October 19, 1949

Dear Mr. Goldsmith:

Your lectures in Chicago this fall were a great inspiration to me and lifted me to an all-time high plateau spiritually. This inspiration has continued as I have studied your mimeographed lectures, especially *God, The Substance of All Form*. To have found someone who has synthesized the various systems of metaphysics into which I have delved over a period of years has meant a great deal to me. It is as if I had found what I have always been seeking— certainly I know I have found the next step along the Path.

Following your suggestion, I wrote for a copy of *Maha Yoga*[4] which I have been studying with delight. It contains some very challenging ideas, many of which require long periods of meditation before they become a part of one. As I have read, a number of questions have arisen which I submit to you. I do not expect a busy person such as you are to answer all of them, but I would like to have you aware of the direction my thinking is taking since you told me the teaching would continue even when you are not present.

2 Joel S. Goldsmith. (New York: University Books, Inc. 1962 p. 127).
3 Unless otherwise indicated, all letters up to 1959 originated in Evanston, Illinois.
4 Sri Ramana (Tiruvannalai, India: Sri Niranjamanda Swamy, 1947).

I lead off with the $64 question. If all of our experience on the physical plane is a matter of belief, where and how did the belief arise? This was always a problem to me in Christian Science. Then as I studied certain theosophical and Oriental writings and gained the concept that matter is simply Spirit at a lower rate of vibration and accepted the idea of involution and evolution, I felt I had achieved a rational interpretation of the problem of good and evil. Now once again I am completely at sea.... If the Self is one, than there is no individual consciousness, and yet you say in *God, The Substance of All Form*, "This whole teaching is based on the premise that Consciousness, being universal Consciousness, is your individual consciousness."

In the same work you state that it is not necessary to know the identity of your patient. This I interpret to mean that because all is pure Consciousness there are not two, only One. I can understand how the recognition of this heals, but why wouldn't it heal everyone who ever suffered from the claim which was to be healed?

The above questions are a few problems that have arisen to cloud my thinking. I suppose as I grow in understanding through study and meditation, any apparent inconsistencies will disappear. My attitude is one of open-mindedness. I am willing to believe until it has been proven false.

For the past five years I have meditated every morning or almost every morning for from fifteen minutes to a half hour. My meditation has followed roughly along some such line as this: I am not the physical body. I am not the astral or emotional body. I am not the mental body. I am pure Spirit, and this Spirit which I am flows into these bodies which are my vehicles for expression on the physical plane, filling the mental body with wisdom, all knowledge, etc., into my emotional body, filling it with a vibrating, magnetic, all-embracing love, which warms, blesses, and heals; into my physical body, expressing in activity and wholeness. This is the substance of my meditation.

Sometimes, in fact, usually, I take some seed thought and also dwell on that, seeking illumination. I would be very grateful for your criticism and suggestions since I believe that meditation is the method by which we achieve illumination. It is a very important and necessary part of my day. I have tried to divorce my meditation period as much as possible from any consideration of personal problems and have succeeded except when under great stress.

I cannot be grateful enough to you for the concept that all is within—the universe is embraced within our consciousness— and that consequently all flows *out from* us and not *to* us. It has effected a profound change in my thinking. I look out upon the world with a new perspective, with a vision of joy and beauty. I do not know whether or not the problem I mentioned to you exists any more. If it does, it no longer troubles me. Once again I am free and unafraid. I go forth filled with joy and gladness. My interview with you did that for me. Thank you....

I hope you will understand my writing at such length. It is because I am a seeker and I recognize how much you have to teach me. I am patient and I shall continue to study and meditate. The "I and my Father are one," leading to the "Who am I" and "Whence am I" meditation I find difficult and less satisfying than the form I referred to, but I shall follow your directions gladly. Thank you for opening up to me this marvelous vista of The Infinite Way.

Most sincerely yours,
Lorraine Sinkler

This letter was followed by a somewhat shattering reply in view of what Joel had told me at our meeting about the

degree of my readiness and where I was in consciousness,
assuring me at our first meeting on September 28, 1949
that I was one in a billion and ready for the final step of
conscious union with the Source. Up to that point I had
felt it might take many lifetimes to achieve such a state.
Joel evidently felt that I was too involved in intellectual
analysis and the doubts of a confirmed skeptic. At first
there was a surge of anger that he had responded in such
an unfeeling way to my serious attempt to communicate
honestly and sincerely with him. It was in sharp contrast
to the weekly sessions I had had in the preceding two
years of working with Vishvananda, a gentle and
understanding Vedantist swami. But my work with him
had taught me the importance of humility, at that time
easier to understand than to practice.

After several weeks of inner wrestling, I not only
came to terms with my priorities but regained the
perspective that a healthy sense of humor provides.
Instead of answering my $64 question, Joel had chided me
for asking anything so stupid. Nevertheless, the question
of how the hypnotic suggestion of the human experience
of good and evil came about kept haunting me. Years
later I was able to resolve it to my satisfaction after long
meditation.   When a sufficient depth of silence was
attained, I saw that there was no hypnotism: there was
only the One. The whole of "this world" did not exist
when that Kingdom within was achieved.   Only the
perfection of this spiritual universe remained. And that
was the reason meditation was so important—the key. It
lifted the aspirant into a new dimension where the fetters
of this world fall away.

December 31, 1949

Dear Mr. Goldsmith,

Your letter of November 11 is certainly that of a teacher—one who goes directly to the heart of a subject without embellishments in order to shift the student's approach from the basis of a human being with problems and unanswered questions to the realization that "I already am." Interestingly enough, a day or two after I had written my letter to you, all of my questions and doubts seemed to melt away. For most of them the answer was there, clear and sharp, and the others were no longer of great importance. I suppose I wanted to be sure that I was on the right track, but you are so right that one must seek and find the answer within.

I have come to realize more fully than ever before the inadequacy of words to convey deep spiritual meanings. There are many things I should like to talk over with you and perhaps that will be possible some day. Yes, I know it must come from within, but sometimes that within may translate itself into the form of a person—and I have caught enough of the East Indian teachings to believe in the value of working with a teacher, to believe that contact with an inspired individual can have a tremendous effect upon the aspirant's spiritual progress and can be a great aid in lifting one to a higher level of consciousness. That's why I hope sometime the opportunity will come to sit down and meditate with you again.

To look out upon the world and see only God appearing is sufficient to revolutionize one's world—"God appearing as." Nevertheless, giving up my old form of meditation for "I and my Father are one," as you told me to do when we talked, has left me for a time like a rudderless boat. I am following your suggestion and working along the lines indicated in your *First San Francisco Lectures,*[5] which is quite a marvelous book. Right now I am in the sponge stage, absorbing all I can from *Maha Yoga* and your writings....Certainly, they point the way

5 Joel S. Goldsmith's San Francisco Lectures were later published in book form under the title The World Is New (New York: Harper & Row, 1962).

to the path best suited to me at my present stage of unfoldment. Of that there is not the slightest doubt. It is right for me. Joy wells up within me, and I feel such deep and abiding peace. Surely no one could ask for more, and yet I will never rest until I achieve realization.

My heart is filled with immeasurable gratitude for the unfoldment that is going on within my individual consciousness. It has had its effects in the outer world, too, although I hasten to add temporal affairs have not entered into my meditation. May I share briefly one of these effects with you?

Meditation on "What is Your plan for me, Father?" and "God is revealing and disclosing Itself as my individual consciousness, and in this consciousness I am united with all life," has caused many barriers to disappear and has left a great sense of oneness with all people. Tangible results came in a completely undreamed of and unsolicited offer for me to teach an evening class at Lake Forest College beginning in February on "Teaching the Social Studies." This is, of course, in addition to my regular work in Highland Park during the day. It is a real opportunity to be of service to beginning teachers and to share with them the fruits of my own years of experience. It came through my own superintendent, where I felt a "barrier" had existed—interesting, isn't it?

Thank you for your generosity in answering my letter so fully and frankly, even bluntly. Fortunately, I was able to look at it, and myself, and chuckle just a bit—not at your letter, but at me. I am everlastingly grateful to you for pointing out the Way so clearly. Yes, God is appearing to me as the teacher I have sought so long. God does reveal whatever is necessary for one's development. Thank you.

Sincerely yours,
Lorraine Sinkler

During this interval of almost six months, I immersed myself in such of his books as were available.

July 14, 1950

My dear Teacher:

Summer vacation is always a time of taking stock for me. This past school year, in spite of a very, very full schedule of work and increasing demands upon me, has been a most wonderful year from the standpoint of my own unfoldment. So I take this first opportunity to thank you for your part in it.

It is as if a whole new world, of which I had only a small glimpse before, opened up to me after I heard and talked with you last September. In the first place my talk with you had an electrifying effect on me, the fullness of which I had approached with other teachers but never before so completely experienced....

This unfolding of consciousness, which the study of your writings and regular meditation have made possible, has not been without visible manifestation....There is much I would like to share with you, but if I do, this letter will turn into a regular testimonial, and you have cautioned us against that. Does that word of warning apply to the teacher, too; that is, between the student and teacher?

At your suggestion in your very kind letter of January 5, I have studied *The First San Francisco Lectures*[6] very carefully and have tried to apply its teaching in regard to meditation. I have not had any phenomenal experiences during meditation and I haven't looked for or expected any, but the sense of the Presence is very real and very comforting.

Right now I am working on the writings of the Maharshi—*Maha Yoga* and other writings....This year I have also dipped into Ouspensky's works, which made a very deep

6 Ibid.

impression upon me. The approach is different but I feel that the goal is the same. When I read Ouspensky, who lays such stress on the technique of self-mastery and discipline as the way, who makes it seem so difficult to achieve realization, and who also insists most of us are walking about asleep, I wonder if one can achieve the ultimate realization without going through some of the procedures he has suggested or some sort of discipline. Is it really as simple as you make it seem? Or does one go so far and then stop after he has achieved certain material satisfactions unless he resorts to "methods," "techniques," and "disciplines"?

You know I am not interested in just a healthy body or more material possessions, although I am enough a creature of the earth to enjoy having them. If I lacked a sufficiency of them I would probably be running after them like all the rest. But I am searching and seeking for that illumination few have achieved. I accept your statement that it is all within, but what is the best way of touching the within? Certainly I have only touched the fringe—the outer court—but will I reach the inner court, illumination, without the sacrifice of much more than your writings indicate, without the discipline people like Ouspensky emphasize? Did you achieve your illumination without any of the usual methods? Perhaps that's too personal, and if so, skip it.

Sincerely yours,
Lorraine Sinkler

Joel immediately put to rest any doubt about sharing one's experiences with one's teacher, emphasizing the necessity of doing just that so the student's unfoldment could be carefully watched and supported by the teacher's awareness. Joel was less than enthusiastic about

Ouspensky's work and his emphasis on techniques, feeling that none of the great spiritual masters ever reached the goal of full illumination through such methods. Instead he invited me to meditate with him and a group of ten other persons at a special hour, thereby making me the 12th person, which I felt was a signal honor and opportunity.

August 1, 1950

My dear Teacher,

I'm so grateful for your last letter which arrived a week ago last Monday and for the opportunity you have given me to share in your period of meditation.

My humanhood comes to the fore and I think of how I can ever be worthy to work with you in your hour of meditation and with those others who have achieved inner realization—and I'm not an especially humble person. Yes, I very much want to be a member of the group. I do so want to justify your having sufficient faith in me to give me this opportunity. I hope I'm far enough along the Path and not too much a hodgepodge of widely diverse philosophies and metaphysics. You know I sip a bit of most everything—only of your teaching do I take long, deep draughts.

For almost ten days now I have been meditating at the appointed time. Arranging to meditate at 11:00 P.M. Pacific time—1:00 A.M. Central time—is no mean feat....I should be able to stay up until that hour but that also has its complications. I'm still pretty much in bondage to sleep, seeming to require almost nine hours to have a real sense of well-being or else my "body starts to make a noise." That's pretty awful, isn't it? And wasn't it Patanjali who warns against sleep? I have always read that with tongue in cheek and thought, "Well, of course, but not for me—yet." And now it's for me. Nine hours or no hours, sleep or no sleep, there is this inner compulsion driving me on, and I know I must do this thing.

Since your letter arrived on Monday I have meditated at 1:00 A.M. The first evening I sat up reading *The Master Speaks*[7] for three or four hours before 1:00 o'clock. The short meditation following—about fifteen minutes—was one of the best I've had. In the stillness and quietness all about me I had a real sense of oneness. My "click" always seems to be an intense fullness in the head, and this time in the throat area, too, as if more were pouring in than I could receive. Monday, this feeling was very intense, not pleasant or unpleasant, you understand, but just an awareness.

From that first night until two days ago the struggle to be awake has somewhat nullified the effectiveness of the period. I continued the work and knew that when the new rhythm was established, the seeming difficulties would vanish. Then I would realize the *I*[8] cannot be sleepy or inactive, nor lapse into unconsciousness. The meditation on Sunday and Monday, July 30 and 31, evidenced considerable improvement—not sufficient one-pointedness it is true, but there has been a real stillness. It has seemed so clear that as God unfolds as your individual consciousness and mine, the teaching goes on regardless of bodily proximity. So I continue.

This summer I have been a member of the group Laura Perkenpine has gathered together. She is a most consecrated individual and is doing such an excellent job, giving leadership of a high caliber. It is a privilege to know her.

As I read the first chapter in *The Master Speaks* for the nth time today, I was again impressed by your emphasis on brotherhood and the universality of your approach. It was your recognition of the beauty in all teachings, whether stemming from the Orient or Occident, that struck me so forcibly when I

7 Joel S. Goldsmith, The Master Speaks (New York: The Julian Press, 1962). Originally published by the author in mimeographed form.
8 I, Me, and Mine, capitalized and italicized refer to God.

first heard you. For the few who are alienated by the broadness of your view, there must be many more who are drawn to a teaching that is an answer to bigotry and dogmatism. A teaching, which eliminates a sense of inferiority and littleness, with its wonderful vision of the limitless capacities of every individual as the fullness of God pouring through, strikes at the real basis of prejudice and discrimination.

Hourly, I thank you and bless you for your generous sharing of the vision, your kindness and understanding. I know that my real thanks will be expressed to the extent I realize that vision and make it my own, showing it forth in my daily experience as a light to the world. I'm grateful to be welcomed into the inner circle.

Sincerely yours,
Lorraine Sinkler

January 4, 1951

My Dear Teacher and Guide,

During August and September I kept the midnight vigil, meditating faithfully at the appointed time. During September, with the hay fever season in full flower, I found meditation at any hour very difficult for every effort was punctuated by intermittent sneezing. I wanted to write for help. Instead, it seemed so utterly ridiculous that I should not be able to rise above such a suggestion that I didn't write....There were moments of discouragement, not about the hay fever, but that I had made so little progress that anything like that could come to what seemed to be a very clear consciousness of truth.

Since that time it has been somewhat of a problem to reestablish the regular rhythm of midnight meditation. While I'm limping along a bit now, I want very much to continue. The stillness and quietness of the night is a beautiful and ideal time for communion. I experience no phenomena but continue to feel great peace, joy, and a very great stillness.

My meditation work is usually along the line of oneness with the Father as you have suggested. Even after this length of time I have but skimmed the surface of that vast subject and have only begun to realize the tremendous implications of that idea. I am interested in your reference to the work of the "Brotherhood." I like to think of a Brotherhood of Light, serving as a beacon to the world.

I have been thinking a great deal about time in relationship to the meditation process and the making of the contact. Meditating at the same hour, as you and a small group do, seems wise, and I welcome the opportunity to participate in the work. But if one had your understanding of time as one of the dimensions to be surmounted, a realization of all that ever was and ever will be compressed in the ever present now, would that not bring us all together regardless of when each of us meditated? Well, I'm very far from that for I don't always make the contact at a specific time. It's an interesting subject for speculation though.

School has been satisfactory, happy and harmonious... Increasing opportunities to serve are coming in the form of calls to speak on the subject of good human relations and the methods by which modern education can make the brotherhood of man a fact rather than a lofty ideal. I have several such engagements in the next few months. These I welcome as evidence of the unfoldment of consciousness—the fruit of meditation which I believe must always find expression in service.

In the area of spiritual unfoldment, I have devoted myself almost exclusively to the message of The Infinite Way this year....I know your teaching is the way for me at present. I am not yet ready to shut out these other avenues of awareness—Ouspensky, Vedanta, and Theosophy as interpreted by Alice

Bailey. With the exception of your work, these have made the most significant contributions to an awakening consciousness. Recently I have begun studying Sri Aurobindo's *The Life Divine,*[9] a truly magnificent book. It helps to clarify a number of ideas which are in the "fuzzy" stage. I seem to need the stimulation of these various approaches. Then when I need a "lift," a bit more courage or strength, I turn to your writings and with that turning comes the wonderful feeling of being at home once again.

Sincerely yours,

Lorraine

The months that followed were a time of assimilation and study, punctuated by meditation, with little of significance occurring until the latter part of May, 1951, when the study and meditation received an added impetus through one of those crises that always push a disciple further along the way.

After an especially deep meditation in which the sense of the Presence was most pronounced, I set out for school at seven o'clock in the morning, picked up the three colleagues comprising my driving group, and engaged in pleasant chit-chat with them as we drove along. We were suddenly stopped short by the head-on collision of two other cars, one of which catapulted into my new car, damaging a fender beyond repair, leaving my passengers badly shaken up and me with a severely sprained ankle.

A friend, Laura Perkinpine, immediately sent a cable to Joel in Hawaii while I was taken to a nearby hospital for emergency treatment. The prognosis of the attending physician was that I would be unable to walk for several weeks, to say nothing of the inevitable pain

9 Sri Aurobindo. The Life Divine (New York: The Greystone Press, 1949).

accompanying such a sprain. A few uncomfortable hours followed after I returned home that morning, but about five o'clock in the afternoon a significant change took place. It was as if warm, reassuring arms were enfolding me, lifting me up, and filling me with an ineffable peace. The following day I was able to return to school, with the aid of a cane walking with considerable ease.

June 15, 1951

Dear Friend and Teacher,

Every day I have been making steady gains until today I am walking about quite normally with the bandage removed and no cane. I even went for a walk this morning just for the sheer joy of walking. There seems to be pain in both legs and hips at night, but I am fine in the daytime.

The problem is to effect a fair settlement....I have a lawyer trying to arrange for a settlement with the insurance company of the man responsible for the collision. I do not want to go to court but feel it should be settled speedily and satisfactorily for all concerned....

Friday marked the close of the school year, and now I am free for three months. Problems seem to be on the increase, pulling me down to earth when all the time I want to be up in the clouds. Maybe that's good, though not too comfortable. I remember Alice Bailey once wrote to the effect that crises are the measure of one's growth. If you do not find yourself faced with one crisis after another, you are in all probability standing still. If that is true, I am well on my way.

Mother and I would very much like to attend your class in Vancouver which you so kindly said you would open to us. It is still a vague hope. Our mother, who had her eightieth birthday this year, is a remarkable person, and as Laura Perkinpine says, "She has naturally what we are all trying to achieve." If it does unfold that we go, I trust you will permit her to join the class also. Well, you can see a little of the picture. Family relationships, and very dear loving ones they are, and the settlement of my case are the uncertain quantities at the present moment. I do feel that none of us can be deprived of what is necessary for our unfoldment. That is a deep abiding conviction. Your class seems so very important to that unfoldment.

I am studying all of your material on treatment and healing as you suggested in your letter. Right now I am trying to organize the material taken from all your writings in a detailed outline which I will send you when it is completed.

Frequently, I think with gratitude and love of all the individuals through the years who have contributed to making possible that moment when I first heard you and knew instantly that this was the way for me. Since then there has never been the slightest doubt as to the rightness of that first recognition. You have that which people talk about and strive for. Maybe that is why I have a silly idea that if I could talk with you and hear you, I might "catch" some of it. It's that Grace you talk about. As it is, my debt to you is very great. The little driblets of checks I send you from time to time are only a small and insignificant symbol of a deep and lasting gratitude that is always flowing to you.

Gratefully yours,
Lorraine

A not-to-be-denied demand to know what brought forth such a seeming miracle as the quick healing of the sprained ankle led me to Joel's class in Vancouver in July of 1951. That gave me my first opportunity since that hour-long appointment almost two years earlier, to have direct personal contact with my teacher, a most significant and meaningful time for me.

Prior to the Closed Class, six lectures were given on three successive days, one in the afternoon and one in the evening. The class itself began on July 12th with each class session lasting two hours for seven consecutive evenings. Joel's earlier lectures and classes, later published under the titles *The World Is New,*[10] *Conscious Union With God,*[11] *Consciousness Unfolding,*[12] *The Master Speaks, and God The Substance Of All Form* had been taken down on a wire recorder and the records destroyed after the material was transcribed. In the 1951 Vancouver Class, however, no recorder of any kind was used. Because I wanted to be able to review the message which was coming through and having such a powerful impact on me, I took copious notes only for my benefit. In the years that followed, however, salient points were shared in some of my classes with students around the world.

In one of the first lectures, Joel spoke of birth as the beginning of death, the death of the personal sense of self. We were not born at a certain time but co-exist with God. We are as old as God. God manifested Itself infinitely right from the beginning as stated in the first chapter of Genesis: "In the beginning, God." This is not an ephemeral God, but God, the Substance of the universe, formed Itself from the beginning. We have been conscious entities since time began, evolving states and stages of consciousness, and yet always the same individual. These unfolding states are all happening to the same person. We play many parts, each involving a continuing evolution or unfoldment of individual being throughout time.

During that week of work, I had the privilege of an

10 Joel S. Goldsmith, The World is New (New York: Harper & Row, 1962).
11 Joel S. Goldsmith, Conscious Union With God (London: L.N. Fowler, Ltd., 1960; New York: The Julian Press, 1962).
12 Joel S. Goldsmith, Consciousness Unfolding (London: L.N. Fowler, Ltd., 1958; New York: The Julian Press, 1962).

hour of private work with Joel every day. My first appointment was on Friday, July 13, at 1:00 P.M. after which he asked me to return at 4:00 P.M. for more meditation with him. At that time he emphasized that the surest way to ultimate realization was through personal contact with an illumined teacher, the importance of which I had recognized long before. I was touched by his thoughtfulness at the end of the one o'clock appointment, when he sent me away with a huge pitcher full of immense bing cherries for my mother, who had accompanied me. When I returned the pitcher at my four o'clock appointment, he again filled it up for us.

In an hour-and-a-half-long appointment the next day, we meditated and talked at considerable length, especially about the nature of a truly spiritual teaching and the impossibility of mixing a mental form with the spiritual way. At another appointment, the subject of postures and exercises and their importance or unimportance came up. His only instruction was to be comfortable. He mentioned that sometimes he used a simple breathing exercise to attain an inner quietness. Physical exercise he recommended, pointing out that he swam three miles a day when he was in Hawaii. Walking was good, too he said, and food—anything to keep the body functioning normally. At one of our morning sessions, Joel emphasized that if we acknowledged God as Substance, that makes even our bodies immortal, and this we can experience by understanding that there is no such thing as Spirit *and* a physical body. The body itself is a manifestation of infinite Spirit. *It isn't the body that is resurrected or ascended, but our concept of body.* Through our realization that the body is spiritual, we will be lifted up and, as our concept of body changes, so do we ascend. Everything that exists as form is our interpretation of spiritual consciousness, unknown to material sense but revealed in all its perfection and wholeness to spiritual awareness. That is why our *sense* of body can be healed. The only change necessary must take place in our conscious awareness.

To Joel, the Bible was a story of dark and unillumined consciousness unfolding and emerging into the light of spiritual awareness. He urged me to think of myself as coming out of the orthodox religion into which I was born[13] into the gospel of John where the final revelation of *I AM* is given. If, when I read spiritual literature, I first prayed, "Father illumine these pages," I would be led to the passages needed for further enlightenment, and those passages would be illumined.

It was during one of these long appointments that I quite unabashedly astonished Joel when I said, "Before the accident, I wanted none of this healing business and no part in it."

His response was, "But that is the proof of the truth of the message." At that point, to me healing meant changing a sick body into a well body, an empty purse into a full one, or an unhappy or disturbed person into a happy one. Later I came to understand that such was only the outer effect of an enlightened awareness that enabled one to penetrate the fog of misconceptions about life and being which we all unwittingly accept. The greater awareness and clarity of vision is the enlightenment that brings soul unfoldment which is the real function of any truly spiritual teaching. Changing outer effects is but the by-product.

To have an hour or more a day with my teacher was a priceless boon, during which time many other subjects were discussed quite freely and frankly. Always there were intervals for deep meditation with him.

13 I was baptized in the Lutheran Church.

As so often happens, following a mountaintop experience, circumstances conspired to push me off the mountaintop and send me tumbling down into the valley below. But the groundwork had been well laid, and the vision from the heights of consciousness remained as a bulwark. So, after returning home, on August 4, 1951, I found myself writing to Joel:

I didn't know how much pleasure little simple things can really give one: all the carrots, celery, and parsley one wants to nibble at by just opening the refrigerator; a brisk walk along the lake, now glistening in the sunshine and again gray as clouds fill the sky; the green grass and the kind trees everywhere giving generous shelter from the steadily shining sun.

Now there is no rest in me. Outwardly, yes. I smile and beam—but inside there is a strange hitherto unknown sadness, a tugging away that will not let me rest. You have brought me to the gates of the Kingdom, and there is no peace for me until I enter it. Sometimes I find myself trying to take it by storm, but whether by storm or a quiet slipping in, inside I must get.

And on August 16, this:

Strangely enough, I find myself wanting to and actually spending more time meditating than reading. Light is most frequently the theme of my meditation, but I feel there is so much more involved in the concept than I have yet glimpsed. It has come to me that as the light within grows, that is, as I become a better transparency for the light within and it shines forth, it is not unlike the headlights on an automobile and the reflectors one finds along the road. As the light comes within range of the reflectors, it is reflected back. As we let the light shine forth, the light in those with whom we come in contact is kindled and reflected back to us, but it is still the one light. Perhaps that's not too good an analogy, but it makes sense to me. Also, light dispels darkness effortlessly, just by being, but darkness can never dispel light. This light is the activity of truth within consciousness.

2

Beginning Steps on the Path of Service

It soon became apparent to me that no one is called to a spiritual activity for himself or herself alone. Whatever light is given a person must be shared with those who seek that light. So slowly, gradually, and gently, over a period of several years, I was led into increasingly active participation in Infinite Way work, the beginning phase of which culminated in the establishment in Chicago in August, 1954, of the first Infinite Way Study Center in the world.

A few months after meeting Joel, I became a part of a group that met once a week to read his available writings. Later, when Laura Perkinpine the group leader moved away, we met in our apartment once a week. This proved to be the first step toward an activity that subsequently absorbed every waking hour and cut deeply into my hours for sleep. That absorption came so slowly and gradually that I was unaware of the extent to which it was taking over my life. If I had known that, I probably would have called a halt then and there, because my primary purpose was my own spiritual attainment. I did not want to become involved in anything that would usurp the precious time devoted to that purpose or deflect me from it.

My thoughts in regard to group leadership I shared with Joel in a letter of August 24, 1951:

I have thought a great deal about this whole question of leadership, especially in a group where there are several sincere students traveling along the Path. In other situations I have always believed that leadership was an evolving and revolving function, expressing first as one individual and then as another. In our Reading Group we have felt there was no *the* leader, at least I have. It has come to me very forcibly, however, that we do have a leader, and that leader is the Christ—the activity of Truth in individual consciousness. I like to think that as Truth becomes active within consciousness, it bubbles over into expression as some individual, and at another moment it might be someone else, yet always the Christ of individual being is the leader. Do you follow me? I'm trying to apply the concept of group dynamics to a spiritual activity and get away from the personal sense of leadership which is so often the cause of dissension and disruption.

And now I have a wonderful story for you. Wednesday morning I received a letter from my lawyer to the effect that the insurance company has offered a satisfactory financial settlement of my case regarding the collision of last May. That in itself is not so wonderful. But listen to the miracle! Do you remember the effect the healing of my sprained ankle had upon me? I knew I had to learn how to do that same thing myself. I was fired with such a burning desire for this truth that it led me more than half way across the continent to Vancouver. Every obstacle was surmounted.

When I went to Vancouver, I had sufficient money for our trip by drawing upon so-called permanent savings, so I did not think for a moment about the cost in dollars. Money just didn't enter into the calculations at all and I considered it no obstacle; it was to be used. What settlement I would receive from the insurance company, if any, was not a consideration. Now, amazingly enough, the settlement the insurance company has offered will take care of all the expenses arising out of the accident—car repairs, lawyer, insurance, and the insurance doctor—and just leave about enough to pay for our trip to Vancouver! Isn't that a kind of miracle? The accident, such a dark picture at the moment and seemingly so uncalled for, was the incident that led me to the class and the beautiful unfoldment that followed and in the final analysis provided the money for it. I'm very grateful. Few people in the world have as much of good flow out into their experience as do I.

And I am meditating, regularly, faithfully, and one pointedly. Again, there's a terrific sense of urgency within me, a driving force that doesn't even give me much sleep, a new experience for me.

Monday I return to school. The first week beginning August 27 is a week of pre-school conferences and meetings. That will be my testing time—to be in the world but not of it.

With grateful thanks,
Lorraine

October 17, 1951

Dear Joel,

The little group continues to meet in our apartment although sometimes there are as few as three of us. Yet I feel the work must continue. The opportunity should be there for people who want to come, so I wait and meditate. As I meditate it comes to me that we must go a step beyond just reading together. People reaching out for this message need lectures explaining The Infinite Way and these held in a public place accessible to anyone interested....I know the teaching that "takes" must be God revealing Itself with the teacher a clear transparency. To do such work one must see clearly and be able to transcend human appearances. Illumination is the word, isn't it? Do you suppose I shall ever achieve that high goal? But of course, "that which I am seeking, I am." Wonderful words, those! I guess the human me just craves a little reassurance.

The human me feels very much alone these days. There's a strange kind of detachment that has settled upon me. I seem so far away from people. There's a great gulf between them and me that I can't bridge. I'm sure they don't feel it, but I do and so many times I think, "What am I doing here?" I know—I'm here to bless and that's where the sadness comes in. People don't want the blessing, do they? It's as if I were on another planet or in another world and no one guessed it....

Gratefully yours,

Lorraine

November 4, 1951

Dear Joel,

I can't express how grateful I am to you for your last letter. I carry it with me and read it over and over again, always finding comfort and serenity in it. It was exactly what I needed at this particular stage.

It is well for you to say "turn back—if you can," for I think you already know that this I cannot do. It is too late for that. The path may be steep and the ascent arduous, but the summit beckons one on, even if doubt as to one's ability to reach it does creep in. I know what it means...yes, the price is dear; yet I have this hope, that treading the path of The Infinite Way I shall have more with which to meet these trials.

I suppose we are all tempted by the illusion of material happiness, but it isn't too great a hurdle. Loneliness, that feeling of being so far away from people, that I have known always—it is just that it is greatly accentuated now. As for betrayals, long ago I learned to look for the best in people but to expect nothing of them, least of all loyalty. I needed to have you remind me, though, that far from decreasing, such experiences will grow as one proceeds along the way. You see your message is written for the man on the street as well as for the aspirant seeking liberation. The man in the world finds happiness and the increased goods of the world to be pretty much the end product. Sometimes the aspirant forgets to see clearly and is temporarily led astray by the same temptation Jesus faced in turning the stones into bread. That's why we have teachers to help us see life clearly and see it whole.

Most of all I needed reassurance that I am on the Path, that the Way is opening. Sometimes I feel I have not taken even the first step, and the goal seems so unattainable that doubt as to my ever reaching it creeps in. If one were sure! That's where faith comes in, isn't it?

Until this summer, I was quite comfortable living with my very real and abiding desire for liberation or illumination. I thought of its achievement as a long range process, quite remote from the present and probably not to be realized in this incarnation. You made me feel it was a present possibility and that the resultant stirrings within are not that delightful sweet placidity that remoteness sometimes induces. Now every moment counts, and great waves of doubt sweep over me as I think, "What if I don't realize this present possibility?"...

I am so happy to hear about the Tape Recordings. They sound like the solution to doing this work. I am sure I shall find a way to use them although the way is not clear to me at this moment....There should be a way of reaching a wider group....I haven't forgotten that what one knows in consciousness must inevitably be known to the world. That I have to prove....

I have a desire to make use of this new material and experiment with new techniques of teaching truth, using these recordings as the basis, and thus be about my Father's business. If only you are right that it is to be my privilege "to introduce a new world of spiritual teaching in Chicago," I should feel I was beginning to realize my reason for having been born, fulfilling my part in the great Plan. I have no concern about my capacity to teach, only my readiness spiritually to go forward. The one thing I don't want to do is to move faster than I am inwardly ready to move. All I want is to be a light, to serve, to help reveal the kingdom of God. If waiting will do it, then I will gladly wait with what patience I can muster; but if by sharing what I already know, little as it is, will reveal more, then I would proceed at once. St. Francis said it for me: "Make me an instrument of Thy peace"; and you, when you said we should be "the willing vessel to let that flow through which will fulfill whatever we were brought here to do."

I wish I could find a way to say "Thank you." Shall I say, "Thank you for making me see the undreamed of possibilities of this present moment?" Yes, a big thank you for that.

Gratefully yours,
Lorraine

In so many of my letters to Joel over the years I shared with him a tremendous sense of inadequacy as to my readiness for spiritual attainment and my feeling that the vision of living out from the mystical consciousness of oneness, instead of becoming closer, seemed to recede. Such an attitude, Joel often told me, was essential. It would keep the ego from surfacing and keep me earnestly seeking greater awareness. Despite that sense of inadequacy, occasionally a person here and another one there called seeking healing.

December 17, 1951

Dear Joel,

....Today when a call came from Q, a mentally disturbed person, I immediately sat down to meditate seeking light on the truth. Such certainty and assurance as I experienced! And then came the miracle! I knew—but exactly what the impartation was I don't remember—only the certainty of one Consciousness unfolding as individual consciousness remained clear as crystal....

My whole approach seems different now. When a call comes for help, I no longer wonder what I can do about it but just sit down and turn within. Perhaps I'm beginning to learn how to meet problems your way. Certainly I don't use any hackneyed statements. I don't even remember exactly what comes to me during meditation, but sometimes I feel as if I'm about to be lifted right out of my chair—a sort of soaring sensation.

Lately the Presence has been so real to me that even my desire for some kind of a sign such as a blazing light or a lotus has abated. I don't know whether that's good or not. I have felt that if all that the Father has is mine and the Father knows what things I have need of, then that light is already mine and will be revealed to me at the instant I need it. What do you think? Is this a step forward or am I lulling myself to sleep? In the meantime I continue steady in the conscious awareness of the Presence.

This Christmas I can truly say, "Joy to the world" for the Christ is born in my consciousness. You have shown me the

Way and have opened my consciousness so that a tiny bit of light is peeking through....For the gift of gifts, I thank you.

Gratefully yours,
Lorraine

Joel assured me that it was not necessary to see lights or a lotus or anything that might seem to be an evidence of greater awareness. Instead attention should be centered on Consciousness, not on effects.

January 20, 1952

Dear Joel,

My first letter to you in 1952—another year, another moment in eternity. Certainly 1951 was a good "moment." I remember taking my early morning walk on New Year's Day a year ago and with it taking stock: "Where was I in terms of the preceding year?"... Once again I find myself taking stock but this time with such joy. It's as if I weren't even the same person, so great is the difference. I know something has happened to me. The Spirit has really taken over, and I have put my foot on the first rung of the ladder that leads to a full and complete realization of oneness with God. Even to have begun the climb makes the whole world new. Small wonder the full realization is incomprehensible to human thought....

I love my public school teaching and it must be my work at the present moment or I wouldn't be doing it, but I feel that it is only a preparation for the real work. Until a month ago I had counted the long years ahead until I should be eligible for a pension so that then I would be free to devote all of my time to the work. During the holidays it came to me so forcibly how I was outlining and limiting my unfoldment—that the how or the when was not in my hands but in the Father's. So I continue, secure in the realization that nothing can keep me from fulfilling my purpose in being born. I am a beholder, watching God unfold the work for me as you have taught....In the vacation weeks I climbed high up on the mountain so that I feel the Presence with me every minute of the day. My daily meditation is just an intensification of that.

Gratefully yours,
Lorraine

February 13, 1952

Dear Joel,

Thank you for your wonderfully helpful letter reminding me that I do not travel the Way alone. That you are always standing by to encourage, to admonish, and to inspire is something for which I am grateful every moment. It is a special kind of gratitude, too, that goes beyond the common meaning of the word. There ought to be another word for this indescribable feeling of thanksgiving that wells up within me as I think about this wonderful gift that has come to me.

It was in 1942 that I first realized there was such a thing as a Way and the importance of a teacher to help reveal the Way. Then came an insatiable desire to find such a teacher— my teacher. Sometimes I couldn't sleep for thinking about it. As I came to accept the dictum, "When the pupil is ready, the teacher appears," I turned within to do all I could to prepare myself. Doubt used to creep in—was I good enough? Perhaps I was one of Ouspensky's "dead alive" people, a million "perhapses." It was then I began meditating regularly. I had my reward for the teacher did appear on September 28, 1949— just seven years after I began the search in earnest. I dare not think what it must have been like for you to search alone or should I say without visible human aid? Even with a teacher, there are difficult moments.

...I haven't forgotten about the Tape Recordings. I am working on that aspect of our group work for I know it will be of the greatest value. In my last letter I wrote about the spiritual awareness growing in our Reading Group. They seem to like the fact that we do comparatively little talking, spending most of the time reading—and "Goldsmith" at that—and finishing with a meditation period. They like the impersonal aspect of the group. Although there is much love for one another, it is not on a human level but that wonderful kind of love that expresses itself in concrete form and yet is impersonal, never binding but always freeing the individual. I think, too, that they recognize that no one sets herself up as a leader but we all strive to follow the leadership of the Christ.

I remember your saying we must set everyone free every day—no ties, no one obligated to anyone. We are proving that the Kingdom of God does not come with words but in the quietness and stillness of one's inner being. Our group work of the past month has created that atmosphere of quietness. I see more than ever that the real teaching is in the Silence....I said to Mother and Valborg in regard to this, "Laura sowed better than she dreamed of, for even though some students dropped away temporarily, they have come back. The seed she planted is bearing fruit, only it needed a little time to germinate."

Two weeks ago Sunday, Mother celebrated her eighty-first birthday, and one part of it I must share with you because you will love it. When I reminded Mother that you had said, "Remember you are all ageless. You are from the beginning—right out of Genisis," Mother said, "Yes, and I'm going on to Revelation!" and a little later, "I'm not even to Isaiah yet, only to Exodus."...

Sincerely and gratefully yours,
Lorraine

March 2, 1952

Dear Joel,

Welcome back to the Mainland! It's nice here, too! We have a few snow flurries in the air today but in spite of that, spring is here. Even a blizzard will not make me believe otherwise. Geese are flying northward, and the courageous Iris is poking its head above the ground. Doesn't it sound tempting to you?

A couple of weeks ago I had an interesting session with a new book by Kenneth Walker, *Venture with Ideas*, a further exposition of Ouspensky's and Gurdjief's teaching....It is not my way even though momentarily it produced its impact....I'm beginning to suspect that the Way is straight and narrow....I need to hew pretty close to the line using my precious moments to absorb The Infinite Way with as few distracting philosophies as possible....

That you are working in the field of labor-management relations is a sign of the times and is indeed the "greater works."... The news that you are back here is good, for it makes your coming to Chicago seem less remote. I know you will come when it will mean the most to all of us. My own feeling is that I must not dwell upon a natural desire to see you but only prepare myself inwardly so that I shall be ready to receive.

Gratefully yours,

Lorraine

It was becoming increasingly clear how straight and narrow the way was and the importance of adhering closely to the basic principles of The Infinite Way. To mix them with other conflicting ideas, rather than shortening the journey for a young student, could only lengthen it or wholly divert one from the Way. Glimpsing this truth made the desire to work closely with my teacher even more imperative. It looked, however, as if Joel's coming to Chicago for classes was remote. But Joel urged patience.

April 4, 1952

Dear Joel,

It's comforting to hear you say again how you have learned to sit and wait until you receive your orders from within. It is a great and wonderful thing to be able to do that and never intrude the little "me" into any of our work or actions. I hope that's what's made me so slow to take any step forward.

Ever since Vancouver I have had a feeling I should teach The Infinite Way but such a feeling and the inner signal to go ahead are two different things. I knew I must be free of any personal sense in regard to the work and that healing must be an important part of the work. So I have waited....

My deepest desire is to travel the Path, but I see more and more that one cannot go very far alone—one must carry others along, that is, stretch forth a helping hand, a cup of cold water. I know I must walk alone, but the Light within must cast its glow upon others reaching out for Truth....

I thought again of your great love and kindness and understanding and your always standing by to give us those little boosts that give us renewed zest to continue on our spiritual adventure—"the shock" to send us up the next note on the octave, only such a loving "shock" quite different from Gurdjieff's harsh "shocks."...

I've had a valuable lesson in the last few weeks. It was one of those things to which I had given intellectual assent but that's not the same as having it a conscious realization. I refer to your point on the healing consciousness and how it must be free from love, hate, or fear of error—how we must be up on that high level of consciousness where we look on every person and situation seeing only the Christ.

Well, I let myself personalize error and get churned up over some unfortunate thing that was happening at school. While down on that level, the doorbell rang. It was a student unable to make it up the stairs who wanted help. She turned to me and said she had come because she knew if anyone could help I could with my "uplifted" consciousness—not so uplifted at that moment. She could scarcely move through some hip strain or dislocation, was in great pain and greatly disturbed because she and her husband were planning to leave early Friday morning for Louisiana. I reassured her—but it takes more than that. Words are pretty empty things. Here was a call, and I was helpless for the time being. I turned within but couldn't reach It. I knew she was not being helped without her calling and telling me so. She had a bad 24 hours. The following day she told me her trip had been postponed and her husband was insisting on hospitalization for her. And then after a day and night of struggling, that beautiful stillness, quietness, and confidence engulfed me. She slept perfectly Thursday night and left on her trip Friday noon almost as originally planned. A card a few days later told that she was getting along beautifully. She's back now from a beautiful trip and so grateful. She said something happened to her—not just a healing but an actual lifting of consciousness. She looks different. Bless her dear heart. She said, "Lorraine, you went out there to Vancouver and caught fire, and now it's spreading to us." Can you know how grateful I am?

I go into all of this detail because it was such an impressive learning experience for me and I know you are interested in what helps me grow in spiritual stature. The healing could have been instantaneous if I had been on the beam. It brought me up with a sudden stop in the realization,

"Choose ye this day whom ye will serve." If I wish to be a light, I have to keep it burning 24 hours a day, seven days a week.

Thank you for your always priceless letters and for letting me work with you.

Gratefully yours,
Lorraine

July 30, 1952

Dear Joel,

....September seems the right time to begin the activity of playing the Tape Recordings. There is always our apartment, but I lean toward a rented space in a hotel.

A couple of weeks ago on Monday I had luncheon with A.B.... She will be writing to you about a new opportunity to carry into operation her desire for a haven for those who need it, an idea which has been presented to her. I encouraged her to write to you. By now you have probably heard from her. She leaves no resource untapped and opens all doors....

I sit back, a beholder of the wonder of the Spirit unfolding in infinite form and variety.

Sincerely yours,
Lorraine

Joel's response to the idea of "havens" for students was anything but positive. To him, a place could never be a "haven." A resting in consciousness was the only true haven.

While the idea of an expansion of Infinite Way activity was taking form, certain outer difficult situations had arisen. The spiritual support and words of encouragement of my teacher were invaluable at this time and are an indication of the irrevocable bond inherent in such a spiritual relationship.

August 15, 1952

Dear Joel,

....I have read and reread your letter with all its helpful suggestions. This month has surely carried its trials and challenges for me....

If I am to show forth a healing consciousness, there can be no room in that consciousness for doubt or fear or resentment. I think my biggest problem was the deep question that arose as to wherein I had failed, for you specifically say that we go on to new experiences from *success to success*. This conflict with the school administration doesn't look like success to me. My concern was that I was not showing forth the Spirit or this wouldn't have come. Then your comforting letter says that we achieve the ascension only after the crucifixion and resurrection. Is a complete negation of the little self with its demand for recognition part of that crucifixion? If it is that, I accept it gladly.

This much I know, until a year ago I was completely tied emotionally to my work at school. I should have been most unhappy at the thought of ever giving it up. Now I am completely detached from it and if I should be lifted out of it tomorrow, there would not be a single regret. My heart and my treasure are no longer there. Perhaps that is freedom, real progress, and a different kind of success.

The reward for mastering resentment and fear was quick and speedy. Calls came for help, and I was ready. I did not have to rise to the mountain top for I was already there and could look out from its heights with new vision....

Lovingly yours,
Lorrain

August 27, 1952

Dear Joel,

....I'm so grateful for your last letter. Ah, yes, I know we can't go forward while we cling to the old, so I release it and "go forward" to "where wings will carry" me. It is always forward, and every step prepares us to be more effective instruments to show forth the glory of God. I think I've always known from the first words you spoke to me that you would lead me to the "Throne." Your faith in my eventual realization means much. Sometimes when I strive so hard and reach out with such intense desire, I hear within, "How silly you are. Why do you seek a sign when all the time I AM here. When you know that, what more do you need?" It's sort of a fine line, isn't it, between the attitude of watching "for the bridegroom cometh," and yet not being so overly anxious one doesn't hear His approach?...

I know the Recordings will be a glorious experience for all those in whom this message finds response. I only pray that I am ready to be the instrument for this work. My work is to lift consciousness through meditation, and to the degree that I rise in consciousness through meditation, the listeners will rise, too. The work is so big, and I am so little. But it isn't the little "I" is it? I know you will be with me and that this is not my activity but only God's. Maybe I am outgrowing the cocoon stage, and wings will carry me forward, but I shall go to it, not from failure, but from success to success.

Lovingly yours,
Lorraine

The advent of the tape recorder and the Tape Recordings heralded a new form of teaching spiritual wisdom. This enabled the listener not only to hear the voice of the teacher but to experience his consciousness. Up to that time there appeared to be no possible way of presenting the work unless a group of trained teachers—who were not only steeped in the principles of the message but had the consciousness of them—could be raised up. It brought a shift in emphasis from reading the Writings or having unenlightened teachers present the message to hearing it as it came directly through the revelator. Those involved in the work who were hesitant about their ability to speak to a group could go ahead and make the message available because using the Tape Recordings obviated the necessity of having to present lectures to a group. To Joel the Tape Recordings were "the great link," so that if students were sincere, they could not miss.

Although the recordings proved to be an important step forward in presenting the message of The Infinite Way, working out the technical aspects of the new activity was fraught with many difficulties, enough to make a less courageous soul give up. The whole recording industry was in its infancy, and much of the equipment available was untried and in the experimental stage. Technically, the tapes were of a very poor quality because the duplication of them was at first very amateurish. Later, with experience, this factor improved.

Using these Tape Recordings in a public meeting also posed problems. Because of the poor quality, the words often were muffled. Eventually, we were able to work out all these bothersome details with the use of a speaker and amplifier, so that at least the sound was more audible.

Our first public meeting was at the Palmer House and in a letter to Joel, I wrote as follows:

September 26, 1952

Dear Joel,

Valborg and I arrived over an hour before the appointed time, laden down with books and a recorder which is no small thing to carry. Some better method of handling that must come and will, I'm sure. It would be very difficult without Valborg, but with her help we managed to transport it. She drove me to the door while I waited for her to park, and together we went up to the third floor. There we found that no room had been set up, but Valborg rustled up the floor captain and the room was quickly made ready,... a beautiful place, the walls partially covered with an interesting Dutch tile, comfortable chairs, restful and peaceful, a quiet dignity pervading all.

The recorder was placed on the table in the front of the room; your writings were displayed at a table at the rear at which Valborg sat while I took my place in the front row, also facing the recorder.

As people came in, they quickly sensed the spirit, for there was complete silence preceding the opening of the meeting which began with meditation. I opened with a few words about receptivity to truth followed by a period of silence. Then came a very short welcome and introduction, much briefer than I had planned because I sensed that it was unnecessary. I could feel the devotion and consecration before I rose to face the group. The attention during the playing of the recording was deep. At the end of the recording, a few announcements were made and a short statement about meditation given. For our meditation we took the question, "What is God?" I led off at the beginning with what came to me as I meditated and from that went into a silent meditation—a beautiful one.

How does one evaluate such an evening? Of course it can only be in the fruitage that comes forth from the inner unfoldment that occurs. How great that was must prove itself. It seemed to be very real, but succeeding weeks will be the test of that. I have steadfastly refused to measure the success of this work in terms of numbers. If only one person goes away uplifted with a truer, purer vision, it is worthwhile. Last night there were eighteen of us, a small number to be sure, but that is unimportant. Only two were from our Evanston group. It was a group ready for your message, familiar with your writings, spiritually alive, alert, and dedicated. I would rather begin slowly and build on a firm foundation of genuinely sincere and earnest students such as are ready for this work than to have a crowd of those to whom it is meaningless...

Lovingly yours,
Lorraine

How did I feel that this moment had finally come? Complete self-surrender. In that moment it seemed that all the aspirations of a lifetime were brought into view. All this time the seed had been growing within me. To let it grow freely, unhampered by the weeds of desire, has been the dominating motive of my life and has filled its every moment. Joel assured me that the meetings would continue to be successful because I had been "called." They would not be an ego-trip but Spirit flowing forth.

October 12, 1952

Dear Joel,

Thank you for your letter.... I know that the secret of spiritual living and the fruitage is in the word "let." In quietness and confidence, God's activity maintains and supports Itself. In this, I rest.

We are moving along. Here and there another seeker

finds our meetings.... Last week I borrowed a dolly from school to use in transporting the Webcor, [*a cumbersome tape recorder*] which helped considerably. As we approached the Loop, Valborg said, "Do you really think we can use this when we go into the hotel?" But that was what I had borrowed it for and so we did to the amusement of a number of spectators. I felt a little like my great aunt in Norway, who, when chided for her lack of concern about her clothes, said, "Those who know me know I'm Fru Sollie, and those who don't, don't matter." And those who knew me knew I was about God's business, and those who didn't, didn't matter....

We have just received a letter indicating that the Palmer House has no time available during November and December.... I am dwelling in the "secret place" and letting the outer take care of itself. It is a way of great inner peace, and in that peace I remain.

Lovingly yours,
Lorraine

When the Palmer House was no longer able to provide space for our meetings on a permanent weekly basis, we moved to the Central YMCA. The experience there I described in a letter to Joel:

November 22, 1952

Dear Joel,

....We worked for some time rearranging the chairs until we were completely satisfied with the set up and then plugged in the Webcor so that all would be in readiness. I turned on the switch only to be met by complete and absolute silence. I looked unbelievingly again and yet again and then began turning knobs. Despite all my efforts no light went on, nothing moved, the machine was completely dead. It was then about 7:30 and we were baffled that our machine which worked perfectly at home would not respond to my repeated turning on and off of the switch. At this hour no technician was available but we learned from a cafeteria assistant that it had something to do with DC and AC current and that connecting an AC machine to DC current had probably blown a fuse if it had not burned out the condenser. By this time it was close to eight o'clock and people were beginning to arrive. What to do?

I sat down in that ten minutes and did the only thing there was to do—meditated. I knew that I would have to conduct the meeting even though I had nothing planned, nothing organized, no lecture prepared. All I knew was that it was up to God to take over and I was able to sit there and realize that, instead of wringing my hands and wondering what I should say. At the appointed hour after our opening meditation I began to talk, easily and naturally, quite unperturbed. That was the miracle! I talked for twenty-five or thirty minutes and I haven't the remotest idea of what I said although undoubtedly I based my talk on the recording we were to have heard. How satisfactory it was I must let someone else decide. I was only filled with deep gratitude that I could talk with such ease and without any specific preparation. God had appeared as this group and God would fulfill Itself. Such an audience! The love that radiated from them is something I shall not soon forget.

Following my remarks I asked for questions because this was one occasion when that seemed appropriate. A pause and then one earnest student who, to all appearances had a speech block, asked the first question. I could easily have answered it but I gave the group an opportunity to respond, which they did. One question led to another. Almost everyone participated and in such a beautiful spirit—no attempt to show how much anyone knew, no spirit of controversy, only one Mind operating and expressing as a desire to share from the one vast and illimitable storehouse.

I do not think I am rationalizing when I say I believe it was a worthwhile experience for all. Of course it wasn't like having your inspired teaching but perhaps it was what we needed at the moment. I have to believe that, because I can't believe that the hours of spiritual preparation I put into these meetings, that feeling of the Presence with me always, could fail to bring forth fruit after its kind. Our experience seemed to weld us into a group whereas before we had been unidentifiable individuals; now we felt more of a common tie binding us together in true brotherhood.

School is wonderful these days. The children are something out of this world, an inspiration and a tonic. I work very hard with them but the reward of seeing a child look out upon life with new insight, greater understanding, is very great and makes even the longest and most strenuous day a joy.

All of this difficulty we've had with our meeting place and the converter problem has added up to moments of discouragement, but what forward step hasn't had those moments? I keep remembering you and your trials in making those recordings and this message available to us and then I am patient and trust. Occasionally some beautiful evidence of the value and importance of this work comes along like a touching note I received last week from a faithful student, doubly precious because of the effort it cost this dear unlettered person to write it. When it means so much to even a few I am grateful to be the channel for bringing this message to them— the instrument. I've thought a lot about the word instrument recently. An instrument must be pounded into shape, ground and tempered to be the most effective kind of tool. Maybe that's the way it is with us who accept the role of "instrument." We, too have to have all personal sense pounded and ground out of us, be fired in the crucible until we are tempered steel.

After two such disconcerting experiences, we secured a small room used as a private dining room in the Fine Arts Building on Michigan Avenue for five dollars each evening we used it.

December 31, 1952

Dear Joel,

We are all overjoyed that you are going to be here even for as short a time as two days. It's wonderful news, the news that I've expected for some time....

Valborg and I gave up all engagements for Tuesday and went downtown to make suitable arrangements. At the Congress Hotel we found just the place—simply ideal. As the enclosed notice indicates, we are to have the Pine Room overlooking the Drive and Grant Park. It's a beautiful room, paneled in pine, restful and inviting, seating from 75 to 125 people comfortably and it's cheaper than the other rooms we looked at, although far more attractive—$20 per night. The Congress is easily accessible and has been revamped and redecorated.

We thought that since we were meeting there, you would perhaps like to make that your headquarters, so we reserved a large room for you there overlooking the lake. Valborg is so wonderful at talking to people, and she explained that you would be seeing a great many people so it is important for you to have an attractive room. The price is from $10 to $12.50 per day and we have engaged it for the morning of the 5th through the morning of the 7th.

Well, you can see that at least you are going to have a place to put your head at night. We want you to be comfortable, satisfied, and pleased with everything so that you will soon be back with us—and that for a much longer period of time....

> Lovingly yours,
> Lorraine

January 11, 1953

Dear Joel,

Thank you for your letter, so kind, so generous. Of course you must know that I [*not you*] am the one that blesses the day I came to know you, the one who is blessed and who never ceases being grateful for God's goodness to me.

Thank you for your memorandum asking me to take up work for L.B. I know you had a definite purpose in mind, and I have faithfully followed your instructions. What has meditation brought me in regard to this? Only one Consciousness individualized as L.B. and as me and nothing but that One. We are one in the infinite Consciousness which is forever flowing forth into expression as perfect body, harmonious relationships, abundance, guidance, infinite wisdom and intelligence, and a peace that passes understanding. There is no lapse into unconsciousness or failure of this One to function or take the form of whatever is necessary for Its full and complete expression. It is the law to individual experience, the cause of every effect. "That they may be one, even as we are one. I in thee and thou in me." Nothing to change, nothing to be healed, only God operating, God acting. Also there has been the feeling that all I ever need to know is revealed to me, Truth in Its fullness and completeness and entirety, the Truth that makes us free. Am I on the right track?...

I had a beautiful experience yesterday when I talked before the Association of Childhood Education.... For two weeks I tried in vain to find time to work on the talk I was to give and I just could not drive myself to it. This work in The Infinite Way, my real work, was so much more important to do. Yet as the time approached, there were none of those butterflies in the stomach or any other indication of nervousness, despite the fact that I was talking to a highly selective audience. When the time came, it was effortless, no consciousness of myself at all. The words just flowed simply and naturally and I put my notes aside.... God really does live our life when we just let it. I could see how working with this Recording Group has freed me from that sense of personal effort which makes doing anything like this so difficult. It's wonderful being a beholder and watching the wonders unfold.

These days I have felt very close to you. It's as if you were right here and I were smiling at you. No, no psychic manifestation for that side of me just doesn't seem to be developed. Maybe it's more real than that kind of experience, more like dipping into the one Consciousness and finding you in it. I don't visualize you particularly nor feel that you're talking to me, but just that you're here. I find it very comforting. Perhaps I'm moving toward the great experience. Maybe like in the *Story of the Other Wise Man*, I shall find it in this service to others, or it will come all unawares when I least expect it.

Again, let me tell you how happy we are that you are coming and always my thanks to you.

Lovingly yours,
Lorraine

January 31, 1953

Dear Joel,

I'm enclosing the schedule of interviews with you which I have arranged and which I hope meets with your approval....

How well I understand your need for a little time to rest in the Spirit. I'm sure that the people who want to do something for you are only moved by a great desire to show you their love and appreciation and to welcome you most warmly so that you will come again. You do know that, don't you? We all appreciate and marvel at the amount of work you do and everyone wants to smooth the way and make it as harmonious and as easy for you as our poor little efforts could make it.

Naturally, I have a great desire for a little time with you alone, but I do think of myself in the capacity of a server. All these other people must come first that they too may have the rich blessing that you gave to me long ago. What an experience they have ahead of them! I am wondering if you will feel that I have grown since you last saw me. It's quite a while, you know, and something should have happened in that time. There are a few things about the work that I would like to talk to you about privately, but I'm sure there will be a time for that....

Valborg will be down at the Congress to be of what assistance she can in getting your appointments in and out. I imagine she will plan to go down about 10:30 unless you have any other idea on the subject.

Please give my love to Nadea [*his wife*] and tell her I will write soon and am sorry that she will not be here.

Lovingly yours,
Lorraine

Joel was delighted with the reception he received in Chicago. When we had dinner together, Joel expressed his satisfaction with the spiritual work that he felt had brought forth such a response and stressed the importance of the work that should be done in preparation for such a meeting. I found myself asking

Joel wherein I had fallen short in having the problem we had at the central YMCA. Wouldn't I have been led directly to the right meeting place if I had been more on the beam? He smiled, "Lorraine, don't you know that every mystic encounters challenges? And for what purpose? Only to force him to take another step higher."

At dinner I told him that one of the students in our Reading Group always waxed enthusiastic about "Grace" as the most beautiful word in the English language. Up to that time, it was a word that had been meaningless to me except as denoting a physical kind of movement such as being graceful. With that, Joel went into an equally enthusiastic dissertation on the subject. He spoke of Grace as a freedom from taking thought so that we no longer have to plan but indicated that such a state of Grace is not brought about in a hurry. It takes patience to achieve it. When we have a realization of that I within us, then we are living that Grace. There is no need then to earn a living, but there is a need to work. That is because work is God's way of expressing through us and as us, but if we do it for a living, we lose our heritage. God does not require that we work for a living but only that we work since some talent is in everyone of us and must be expressed. We are expressing our individuality through work. The living will come and that more abundantly.

February 8, 1953

Dear Joel,

Your words, during those three days you were here for work, recall to me the Tibetan's teaching that the masters are

completely uninterested in individuals, but that when the little
spark of light within each grows to sufficient proportions
through service, it attracts a master's attention. Then he
draws that individual into his circle to prepare him for further
service, not because of the individual or for the individual, but
because that individual can further the divine Plan through his
work. Many things you said recall that to me forcibly. In those
three days you were able to reverse the point of emphasis for
me.   Up to this point I was thinking of realization and
illumination, and for what? For me. Now I realize that it can't
be for me, for my pleasure or joy, or even ecstasy, but
illumination can come only when I lose all desire for it because
of the joy it will give me, and desire it only that it may make of
me a more perfect instrument for the work I have been given to
do.

I'm always a little disturbed by my own feeling of
inadequacy and slowness of speech when I see you and it's
unusual because I don't feel it in other situations. In those I
am always master of the situation and in full command. Ah,
that's the secret right there, isn't it? With you, I am the
student and you the master. Anything I might say to you
would be so pointless and useless and so I wait for you to speak.
It's the way it must be, I guess, but it does make me feel like a
tongue-tied school girl and inadequate. I didn't even have the
grace to thank you for luncheon and dinner! Just in a complete
fog about the niceties of life!

And you, how generously you gave of yourself to everyone
and especially to me! I shall treasure always the beauty of the
paper you read to me and am humbly grateful to you for
sharing it with me. You sense my need for the mystical
approach and always give it to me, lifting me to a clearer
understanding of what is to be, what must be, and even if I
wanted to I couldn't prevent it. You say I have been chosen and
the work is given me to do—not my work, but the Father's.

Then there isn't anything for me to do but let it flow, in all its beauty, its pain, its joy. If the Father has chosen me, then the Father will provide for each step of the work, and I relax and keep the little "I" out of the way so that the universal *I* can pour Itself forth.

That's a pretty wonderful outcome of three days' work— even three years. Yes, I go forward with greater confidence, greater assurance, because I don't have anything to do with it....

Lovingly yours,
Lorraine

March 8, 1953

Dear Joel,

The Infinite Way is surely active hereabouts. If I were asked to prove that statement, I might be hard put to it to do so, for our groups remain about the same as far as numbers go, but there is a Spirit abroad. Something is stirring. I feel it so keenly and deeply that there is no rest for me in one sense of the word. On the other hand, there is that wonderful peace that comes with a sense of fulfillment. The calls for help have increased and some fine things have come out of them and others yet to come. I'm grateful for your recording on "Spiritual Healing" from *The 1952 Honolulu Closed Class* which I felt inspired me the least of any we have had. However, it has been very practical and has helped me to see that one continues to work in the face of unfavorable appearances. I think I told you that I just expected any problem to yield at once and was perfectly satisfied to stop work at once if it did not. I'm learning persistence and patience—to begin all over again when a second call on the same problem comes.

A week ago last Wednesday a woman who has been a

student a long time, but who has only come to the recordings since your lectures, asked for spiritual help in writing a children's book. She has just had one published but the second one wasn't coming through. The first couple of times I sat down to take up work, all kinds of ideas came about infinite Intelligence expressing, but I didn't *feel* it. There wasn't that click. Then after quite a bit of that sort of thing the *realization* came that every idea of whatever nature is already complete and finished in divine Consciousness. It is already done. This woman arrived the next night at the Recording Group, beaming and saying that she sat up until 3:00 A.M. and put the book in the mail this morning, and she had never done anything with such ease nor felt so refreshed about it. All the words in the world are of no avail until that certainty comes, that assurance dawns, and then that is all. Pretty wonderful!....

I'm sorry that when you were here you didn't see our contraption for transporting the Webcor which two of the youngsters at school made for me. It is quite a help and quite clever. Laura gave it a name at once. She dubbed it "Little Joely," so every week "Little Joely" comes out for a promenade down Michigan Avenue and through the Fine Arts Building. I think it is a very appropriate name....

Lovingly yours,
Lorraine

March 23, 1953

Dear Joel,

Happy Spring to you, or is it perpetual summer in Hawaii? I think I would miss the change in seasons, especially when the change is as mild and as gentle as it has been here this year. Soon I shall be removing the bucket of ashes, the shovel, and Christmas tree boughs from the trunk of the car, which I carry all through the winter months to help extricate me from ice or one of our mid-western snowdrifts. Not once have I had to use them this winter....

In "Fulfillment," *The 1952 Honolulu Closed Class*, you speak of our reaching a point in our experience where the Finger touches us, and the implication is that we have nothing to do with that. That sounds completely mechanistic. I'm trying to read between the lines and I would interpret it to mean that we reach a state of receptivity in which we open consciousness to the Truth and then we find it was with us always. Evolution is the only way I can explain why that receptivity is present in some and not in others. Ouspensky implies it is a matter of chance, of accident, and if one is fortunate, he meets *someone who knows*, who has *real knowledge*. I don't accept that for there is a lack of justice in it....

There is always the question, "Am I doing all that is necessary for my unfoldment?" Can you understand? Please don't be impatient with me for being impatient with myself.

Lovingly yours,
Lorraine

May 14, 1953

Dear Joel,

You must think of me as the prodigal because it is such a long time since you have heard from me. Busy and difficult days lie behind me, ahead, too, I suppose....I stand fast and devote my time and attention to the first business at hand, meditating, studying, listening, and striving to maintain a conscious awareness of God, a healing consciousness, grateful for the opportunity given me to let the light shine....

I've encountered my first "stubborn" case. I continued to

work with no perceptible results for Mrs. A....I take you seriously when you say the responsibility rests with the practitioner, always knowing where the practitioner must place the responsibility.   In some way, I must have missed the realization, and yet I felt I had it. I don't see how It can fail, and since I don't do it, I can't fail either.

Lovingly yours,
Lorraine

It troubled me deeply whenever a person who called me for help did not have a healing. In all of Joel's writings he stated that the primary responsibility rested with the practitioner. So I felt that in some way I had failed. I wrestled with that problem for many years. I could not find comfort or take refuge in the oft repeated cliche "lack of receptivity." If God expressed and manifested Itself as individual being, how could there be any unreceptive person?

In those early days I was thinking of healing as a change in the outer appearance. It took me years to realize that the real healing was awakening the student to his true identity as one with the Source of all that is. Spiritual healing is revealing. If a person were awakened to the perfection and wholeness of being, the healing should be evident in proportion to the degree of the awakening. If that were the purpose of the work, then what seemed like a slow healing might be the greatest blessing. It would lead to a greater unfoldment and deepening awareness.

3

"And the Winds Blew"

Touching a way of life that brought such a sense of purpose—and with it the zest to achieve that purpose—could easily have led to a complacency that might well have ended all spiritual progress. But instead of experiencing any self-satisfaction, the tender little sprouts of awakening consciousness were to be strengthened by standing against the winds of adversity which reached gale proportions in the form of both family and professional problems. Worst of all was the feeling that I had failed my spiritual teacher, even though through this trying time he gave me every possible encouragement and spiritual support.

It all added up to a minor Gethsemane, albeit necessary to developing that spiritual stamina vital to attaining the spiritual goal.

June 11, 1953

Dear Joel,

Yes, your letter to me on June 3 was indeed heartening, for I'm unhappy only if I feel I have lost the Way and am somehow not living up to my highest understanding at all. I found myself wondering if all these things in my personal life crumbling around me were an evidence of a lack of spiritual realization which would truly be cause for concern. That you think such may not be the case gives me courage to go forward....I know that all experience is only that we may grow in Grace, be strong, courageous, and unafraid.

Lovingly yours,
Lorraine

Dear Joel,

Thank you so much for your reassuring cable and letter. It came when the picture was very dark and confused and though we knew you were with us, it was so good to have the added assurance of the cable. It was a very thoughtful thing to do.

Valborg has not yet been released from the severe pain which has persisted with a strange fierceness....She can see this as a turning point, a time to take a step forward, and every day she grows stronger in the Spirit. However, you can see that she still needs help....

I received a friendly letter[1] from the President of the Board of Education thanking me for my patience and stating that the Board had unanimously voted to continue the additional compensation the three assistant principals have received in the past even though the position no longer exists, this compensation to be gradually absorbed and equalized as additional increments to the salary schedule are made. Therefore, there will be no cut in salary, nor will there be any increase, but neither will there be additional duties.

For me that is really a very satisfactory solution. With my whole heart and soul in The Infinite Way activities, I could ill afford to assume additional school responsibilities. I trust

1 A conflict had arisen over the failure of the Board of Education and the Superintendent of Schools to keep a promise to give me the principalship of the school in which I had served for some twenty years as teacher and assistant principal, the resolution of which conflict is indicated in this letter.

this incident will be a source of strength to those who feared that the whole school setup under a new administration was utterly hopeless and that it was foolish and dangerous to lift one's voice in protest. A cleansing process is at work, a leavening influence, the nature of which they do not know but the effects of which will show forth. To me it was wonderful proof of the fact that one must never act from fear. Fear would have said, "Do nothing. It is hopeless." But how can one be afraid if one's whole desire is to live in God-consciousness? Impossible! No, God gives one courage beyond human knowledge. Thank you for your help and support throughout this experience.

Our summer Recording Groups are wonderful experiences. Even after almost record breaking temperatures in the day, the evening cools (Infinite Way weather, you would say). The attendance is good, averaging about eighteen and the attention perfect. One really feels that the place is holy ground and it is a blessing to all who participate in these meetings. I can see how right it was to continue during the summer for we have added a few new people to the group who had never attended before.

Lovingly yours,
Lorraine

August 3, 1953

Dear Joel,

Yes, to realize the principle is my only concern—that and to get it to operate through and as me. It's wonderful how that principle becomes one's guide, direction, and sustainer in any and every situation.

I am looking forward to our Infinite Way fall activities with great enthusiasm....I have been asked to conduct an

Infinite Way class in addition to the Recordings, but I don't feel quite that urgency about doing this that I had about beginning the Recording Group last year. That makes me feel it is wise to wait—there is no hurry about it....

You said the time would come when I would teach The Infinite Way, and I am sure it will, but just how that will unfold is not clear to me now. It must be the Spirit fulfilling Itself, and then It will pour forth in a most wonderful way. I begin to catch a glimpse of what it means to have no life of one's own, but to let it always be an instrument of the Plan. It leaves little opportunity for personal desires. Well, so be it....

August 27, 1953

Dear Joel,

....This week marks the end of my vacation, if such it can be called. Monday I'm back at school, again face to face with the new situation and its problems. Right now I feel strangely indifferent to it all, which is probably good. It's been a strange summer, not at all what I had anticipated. There has been little opportunity to indulge in those moments of exaltation and exhilaration which I long for and which come only as a result of sustained periods of quiet and aloneness. Instead there was always someone to whom I must minister and a host of practical things to be done to help this one and that until I reached the point where I really was "weary in well-doing." I felt like a "do-gooder" and began to wonder if I were not wasting valuable effort in trying to bring about human good and perhaps I would be wiser to concentrate on the spiritual. It's a fine line.

I realize love, even impersonal love, must be expressed in a practical way, but last week I found myself saying to Valborg that I felt like Susan at the end of the second act of *Susan and*

God when she said, "Sometimes I wish I'd never heard of God."
Well, sometimes I wish I'd never heard of being kind and
generous and outgoing. Am I at a low ebb or just achieving a
new sense of values?

Last Saturday and Sunday, though, were two perfect
days—absolute quiet, a gentle calm pervading all and
unlimited time to be with just myself. Then there was
exaltation, exhilaration, and renewal, yes, a real touching of
the Spirit.

Lovingly yours,
Lorraine

September 26, 1953

Dear Joel,

....This week is a very special week for me. Two of the
most important events that could happen to anyone came at
this time of year. Four years ago from today I had never read a
word you had written, and you were only a name I had heard
casually mentioned. On September 28, four years ago, I met
you and had that wonderful session with you which made the
whole world new. It's never been quite the same since then.
Two years later to the *very day*, we began group meetings
downtown to enable people to hear the Recordings—two years
ago this Tuesday. So you can see why I look upon this week as
so very special....

We have proceeded slowly and in an unspectacular way,
but there has been no forcing of the way, no possessiveness of
anyone, no exclusiveness, no struggling to draw people to the
group, just a confident realization that those who are receptive
come, drawn on the invisible plane by the Christ of their own
consciousness. That removes all sense of striving. I've tried to
follow your original instruction to me that my meditation be to

lift the consciousness of those present....

At first, four years ago, my only thought was my own unfoldment, my own realization. I never dreamed of being actively engaged in the work. With clearer vision came the compelling desire to make this truth available to receptive consciousness. I remember wrestling with myself over that and thinking how stupid it was of me to desire any opportunity to be in the work when all I had to do was look around me and there was plenty to be done: there were plenty of people on whom I could shed this light I long to share. When I began to act on that realization, things really began to happen, and the first thing I knew we had begun meeting downtown. It surely is true that right where we are is holy ground as you have so often told us. Lately I have felt that I was on the threshold of some new and great expansion of activity. The idea of an office in the Loop has been pounding away at me, but as long as I am working at school every day, it does not seem possible. When the time comes, I'll surely know it, and the way will be open.

Lovingly yours,
Lorraine

Joel answered my letter of gratitude with one expressing his gratitude for the work coming through me. Because this work and all true Infinite Way work is an impersonal activity of the Christ, it will infiltrate human consciousness and be the catalyst to dissolve it.

October 2, 1953

Dear Joel,

....Sometimes I wonder why the whole world doesn't

embrace The Infinite Way, but already at the same moment I know how far from ready most are to accept its teachings. With all its beauty, love, and joy, it is an austere teaching, requiring singleness of purpose and the brushing aside of all attachments to the things of this world. It's difficult for me to know my degree of nonattachment while still enjoying a sufficiency of things. I've thought about that a great deal. I comfort myself with the remembrance that there is no thing that I really desire, but then why should I, since I have everything I need? I guess it's an academic question, for how could any sincere student of The Infinite Way ever lack anything needful or set store by *effect?*...

Lovingly yours,
Lorraine

October 15, 1953

Dear Joel,

Bless you for your two dear letters. They brought tears to my eyes. Silly, isn't it, and yet at that moment I was engulfed in such a surge of understanding and a yearning to cover you with blessings—as if you weren't already—that I was weeping with you....

This past week I've really been hitting on all cylinders. There has been a quick and sure response to every problem that has come to me for my recognition which means that my meditations have been quite "super." Scarcely any time is spent in getting into the meditation. Almost instantly I'm in "the secret place," and it comes to me as an ecstatic fullness in the head—it's the only way I can describe it—and that is my "click," my signal that all is well. The "resting" in that is really something! Still no phenomenal experience but such a welling up of love and thanksgiving that my breathing almost stops.

There must have been a definite rise in consciousness almost like the occultist's initiation. I can't account for it—I suppose one never can—except that I have been very literally following the instruction about praying for one's so-called enemies. Up to this point there was simply a passive ignoring of them, a kind of detachment so far as they were concerned, but this week I was impelled to take up definite work for them. Perhaps that's part of it.

Yes, you have made the narrow way that you have trodden with such great effort a wide, smooth, highway for those who follow after. The blessing of all these people will be with you always and carry you along and lift you to greater and greater heights. Those who have felt that will always stand by you.

Lovingly yours,
Lorraine

Joel gave two Closed Classes and two Practitioners' Classes in New York during November. This was clearly a leading of the Spirit because it was at these lectures in New York that he first met Frances Steloff, owner of The Gotham Book Mart, a person who has had a profound impact on the literary fortunes of so many promising young writers. She had gone to the lecture only that she might take with her a frustrated and unhappy woman, who she hoped would find some solace there. Instead, she herself was touched by the message and played a significant role in interesting a major and well-established publishing firm in Joel's writings.

It was Joel's custom to mingle with the audience after the lecture, cordially greeting those who crowded around him and answering their questions. When he was told that the owner of The Gotham Book Mart was there, he immediately turned from those around him and went over to speak to her. In less than a minute he had made arrangements to be at her shop at nine o'clock the following morning.

Just as she opened the door of the shop the next morning, he arrived, bringing with him several mimeographed copies of classes he had given on The Infinite Way. With her orthodox Jewish background she had reservations about carrying books, the major theme of which was the Christ. She told him that when she carried the writings of any person, she really promoted them in every way possible. It was agreed that he leave the books with her and that he would stop to see her and have her decision on his return to New York after work in England and on the Continent.

On November 1, I wrote to Joel about the classes he was to give in New York:

"There is a remote possibility, still very remote, that I may get away for part of the Thanksgiving Week and go to New York for some part of the class work."

The remote possibility came to pass, and I found myself in New York the week of Thanksgiving—ostensibly for the purpose of visiting suburban schools. In the intervals between Joel's morning and evening classes, I sandwiched in visitations to schools, as well as the only matinee of a Broadway play that time permitted, so that I would have something of a fun nature to talk about with my colleagues at school. Unfortunately, that matinee was on the same day I was scheduled to conduct the group meditation prior to the class itself. After rushing from the theater, there was only a short time before the meditation began, a most inadequate kind of preparation for lifting the consciousness of a group.

When Joel mounted the platform at the end of the meditation, he spoke sharply about the lack of preparation and oneness in the room, quite obviously an incisive public criticism of the work I had done. If I could have vanished into nothingness at that moment, I would have been grateful—certainly a part of me did. Furthermore, since Joel was preoccupied with a critical personal problem concerning his relationship with his wife, Nadea, in that week he had only twenty minutes for a brief appointment with me. This was in marked contrast to the one to two hour appointments in Vancouver.

Leave Your Nets[2] was released at this time. When I commented to Joel, in my brief interview, on the depth and beauty of the book, he became pensive and spoke as if his very soul were in every word he uttered and with an intense sadness, "Lorraine, every page of that book has taken its toll of my butterfly wings, my own struggle to leave the 'nets' of this sleeping world."

Just as my first class with Joel in Vancouver had been a landmark in my spiritual involvement and evolution, so I had expected great things from this second class in New York. The experience in Vancouver had been gentle and comforting, leaving me with the promise of increasing spiritual fulfillment. Instead, New York left me with a strange ache inside, and the sense of being a total failure, as the following letter indicates.

2 Joel S. Goldsmith, *Leave Your Nets* (New York: The Julian Press, 1964). First published in abbreviated form in London by L.N. Fowler, Ltd., 1953.

December 4, 1953

Dear Joel,

Last week was a wonderful week for me, and I'm so grateful to you. I see you steadily climbing the ladder of Spirit and reaching undreamed of heights. It was inspiring to be a witness to it. I have always loved your interpretation of the Christ,[3] which has been a purely academic and theological term to me until I knew about The Infinite Way. This latest revelation takes us forward to a much deeper understanding of the meaning of the Christ. I marvel that the whole earth didn't melt as it came forth—maybe it did a little for some of us.

Tuesday night when you stopped midway in the class so filled with the Spirit that you could not continue was the holiest night of all. In my bag I found this little note I wrote to you in the early hours of the morning and never sent:

Thank you for last night. In that hour I was so carried away by what you communicated in word and Spirit that all sense of person disappeared. You talked to a whole class, but it was as if you were talking only to me. It was for me—my message—given with such tenderness, such compassion, such love, I forgot there was anyone there. I soared with you and long before you stopped my eyes were wet with the wonder and the beauty of it. Truly the Spirit was upon you. All night long those words have pursued me and their corollary for me, "I, the Lord, have called thee."

The Spirit is upon you and whether or not you want to, you cannot stop. The activity must and will go on and for you there is no rest. You are the servant of the Most High.

Why didn't I send this to you then? I don't know, but I want you to have it now....

Thank you for the lesson on meditation the evening of my opportunity. For a few minutes I was stricken for having failed so completely. There was a stoppage of activity that must have been a little like death—the shock that sends us up the next

3 See the Tape Recordings, *1953 Second New York Practitioners' Class.*

note on the octave—and then a quick inward prayer, "Father, let me not miss the lesson in this through any sense of self. Help me to be a better transparency for the Light so that the Christ which knows no failure may shine through." It was a hard lesson, but the harder the lesson the greater the growth. Perhaps it was a deep desire to teach us, and me in particular, that brought forth another session akin to the *Deep Silence of My Peace.*

We have to go through these periods, don't we, and reach the human depths that we may in due time touch the heights of spiritual vision? It's a long, weary, heart-rending road, filled with loneliness, the inability to communicate one's deepest feelings, and an inexpressible sadness at failing to measure up to the Truth one has glimpsed. Now that I have come this far I wonder why I have been so driven all these years and why I didn't leave well enough alone and just live a nice, pleasant, human life, but I guess that was not for me. There is no turning back now. Within me I carry my particular burden—a bundle of contradictions: deep humility and a willingness to be obedient and at the same time a terrific inner rebellion at all restraint and discipline. Even so I know that some day every vestige of that will disappear in the fullness of light....

For so long it was only my own unfoldment, my own realization I cared about. I think that working with these blessed people here in Chicago is what did it. Their sincerity, their earnestness, their devotion to Truth is so great I wanted only to help them on the Way even if it meant a sacrifice of the preoccupation with my own spiritual progress. I do not know if this is good or bad, a step forward or backward, or if it be the great temptation. I only know it is something I must do. In the doing God has become so near, so dear, so close to me that the sweetness and the gentleness of It is a constant benediction.

Lovingly yours,
Lorraine

After the New York classes were completed, Joel remained in New York for about a week and then took off for London and the Continent. Before Joel returned from his first trip abroad since the advent of The Infinite Way, he sent a cablegram dated January 22, 1954: "Am coming to Chicago to share with you." On his way he stopped off in New York primarily to see Frances Steloff, a most fruitful visit. At this time Frances assured him that she would be happy to carry his writings. Furthermore, she contacted the Religious Editor at Harper & Row who agreed to print an American edition of *Living The Infinite Way* which had already been published in England by George Allen & Unwin.

Joel arrived early Tuesday morning, and during the day I had several hours of instruction and meditation with him. Although I never complained about the problems that arose to confront me as I went forward on the Path, the sense of inadequacy I felt at my own unfoldment was quite obvious. This he understood and explained that few who embark on this Way realize that it meant supplanting not only the bad of human experience with spiritual unfoldment and fulfillment, but also the good. For the student unprepared for this drastic and sometimes cataclysmic change, it could be a shattering experience. There were some in whom the awareness of spiritual identity came as a gentle cool and refreshing tradewind. He felt much of my unfoldment had been of that latter kind, but warned me that there could be cataclysmic occurrences. He indicated that in making the transition to the mystical consciousness a certain inner struggle is inevitable. The intensity of that turmoil will vary according to one's degree of lifetimes of preparation. That inner strife, however, is essential to spiritual unfoldment.

After our work together, Joel came to our apartment for dinner and a visit with Mother, Valborg, and me, and as a special bonus, to celebrate Mother's 83rd birthday. At this very special time Joel shared many of his experiences on his trip abroad. Mother gently told him how busy I was, to which Joel quite unconsolingly replied, "She doesn't know what it is to be busy yet. Just wait!" How true that proved to be!

Just ten days later, Mother had a heart attack and was taken to the Evanston Hospital, where she lingered for thirty-three days, bedfast but lucid. Although private duty nurses around the clock ministered to Mother's physical needs, Valborg and I took twelve-hour shifts around the clock to be at her bedside where we could hold her hand.

From the very beginning of this problem, I was in close touch with Joel, telephoning him in Hawaii every day as to the progress or lack of progress. His support was invaluable, and although I wrote few letters to him during those traumatic days, his letters of reassurance and instruction came every few days. He emphasized the importance of not being satisfied with good appearances. Every experience, good or bad, required reinterpretation as he had pointed out so clearly in *Metaphysical Notes*[4]. My work must always be to disregard all appearances, good or bad—even life or death.

March 13, 1954

Dear Joel,

I've tried to write to you during these difficult, difficult days, but there have been people around every single minute. We have felt your love and help but even so it has been hard.

4 Later published as *Conscious Union with God*.

Never once did we accept the possibility of Mother's going on, and perhaps that made it more difficult. Then there was the deep personal attachment and a great unselfish love which seems to leave a void and an inexpressible sadness—yet I know it shouldn't. That it does, disturbs me, too, for I see how far ahead the Way is. We have to free ourselves from everything that holds us and I guess the Father has a way of doing that for us.

On Monday afternoon before Mother went on I had a very clear realization, one of the few during all this time, that "the Father knoweth what things ye have need of" and if it were an adjustment here or a new experience, it would be forthcoming. In that sense I released her, and a few hours later she had gone. In the hospital she had said, "Lorraine, let me go. I'll always be with you wherever you are and look after you." Once when Valborg was there it was, "God, my work is finished now." Yes, there was a kind of completeness to this sad, difficult life. She had had so much sorrow and had lived above it so gloriously.

Mother loved me so dearly and so unselfishly that I knew she would even give up her human sense of life for me. It worried me that perhaps she thought I would be freer without her which hardly seems possible since I had such complete freedom and understanding with her. It was a sacrifice I could not accept.

So, Joel, you can see I'm struggling. I'd like to be able to tell you I've risen far above such earthly feelings, but I have to be honest with you. I miss her physical presence.

We are so grateful to you for your faithful work for all of us. As I look back, Joel, I think Mother had a sense of eternality and timelessness throughout the weeks she was so ill. Everything she said pointed to it. Never once did she speak of anyone except with the utmost love and kindness. Every hurt seemed to have been forgotten and everything was in terms of "forever and ever." I have wondered if that first night when she had the attack and apparently was gone in my arms if she did not for a moment touch Reality—Eternity—and could not come back to remain, but only that we in those thirty-two days might learn a few more priceless lessons. Mother spent much of her time praying and never once did we detect the slightest fear of making the transition. She seemed to know that all was well even in the midst of intense suffering. And yet that last day she wanted your help so much. I know she had it and that it helped to make it easier for her. We are grateful for it, so very grateful.

Perhaps part of Valborg's and my struggling comes from a sense of great fatigue. For thirty-two days one of us and sometimes both of us were at her side so that she never reached out her hand that we weren't there with loving reassurance that all was well. Now we seem depleted and exhausted— another appearance. Tomorrow I return to school after five weeks' absence.

The Way lies before us: to work and to serve. Help me follow it. Instead of feeling stronger, I feel so far away, so little, and as if it were only imagination and wishful thinking that I can ever achieve spiritual light. Thank you always.

Lovingly yours,
Lorraine

March 21, 1954

Dear Joel,

Yes, I do know the depth the heart can ache! I never before knew deep sorrow or grief, but now I know. By this time it should have left me, but it hasn't. There is still a dull ache and an unutterable sadness. Is that the price of a truly beautiful relationship or do you say it is the price of attachment? Yet, surely one cannot go down into such great depths without rising the higher for having touched them. Almost everything else that I have ever experienced I've been able to shut out quickly, but not so this time. It must have a purpose, so I do not chafe at it but accept it as a deepening and enriching experience. I have never asked for happiness, just that "peace that passeth understanding."...

Soon there will be no distractions, nothing at all to keep me from a completely one-pointed life. The last few weeks, dear loving friends have been stifling me with consideration and kindness. They do not know my need to be alone and so have filled my every waking moment, but soon that will cease, and then I must settle down to the only purpose I have in life. Perhaps in this quietness and deep silence which can now be mine, I shall experience the ultimate Reality. Please tell me what to do and help me on the Way.

Lovingly yours,
Lorraine

April 6, 1954

Dear Joel,

....It is comforting to learn that "harmony in human affairs often is a lack of spiritual awakening." I can see that crises are necessary to force one forward, but I've always been a little apologetic about them, due to my early training that a lack of harmony was evidence of a lack of understanding. When everything goes along peacefully, we *believe* we are living a life of detachment and living in the Spirit. Then bingo! Along comes a pressing problem and one sees how much this peace is just plain ease and comfort and how easy it is to let situations rob us of our peace. So I can see that crises of one kind or another are the shocks we need to free us forever from any concern about human experience, and we never know how much concern we have until we face some difficult situation.

You have said as we progress we will have fewer problems of our own, but they will come to us in the form of our relatives, friends, and patients. Sometimes I think that's even a greater hurdle than having the problems oneself—at least until one has reached the fullness of *impersonal* love. Don't you think that even Jesus felt that when he said, "Oh, Jerusalem, Jerusalem?"

Thank you for the second paper on "The Wisdoms." The two received thus far seem to be meant just for me. Certain intellectual perceptions are now approaching the realm of realized truth for me. I find myself constantly turning to "God is not in the human scene" and am beginning to see why that is true—that God, the changeless, could never be in the fleeting, temporal scene. This scene we behold is only the concept, the illusion, the appearance, always fluctuating between the pairs of opposites, whereas God just is—unqualified.

Out of this has come a clearer interpretation of what this last experience was. In spite of all my good teaching, I have been accepting what my eyes behold. Now I can see and really feel that all that was appearance, that all there was of Mother is God being, and that never changes, never is any less or any more. We, too, Valborg and I, are that Being, and none of the pain and sorrow happened to us. There are moments when time and space seem to be transcended.

Lovingly yours,
Lorraine

4

An Infinite Way Ministry

On March 14 came the news for which students in Chicago had waited so long—Joel's first Chicago Class. Two lectures, open to the public, would be given on August 21 and 22, and from August 23 through 28 there would be a Practitioners' Class in the morning and a Closed Class in the evening.[1] During the ensuing months, many letters passed between us regarding the forthcoming classes. Although August was a busy month for hotels in convention-ridden Chicago, we were able to make arrangements for the meetings at the Sherman Hotel, centrally located in the Loop and reasonably priced.

While preparations were going forward for the classes, another idea, which I shared with Joel in the following letter, was beginning to take form in consciousness, an idea that was to lead to a further expansion of Infinite Way activity in the Midwest.

May 12, 1954

Dear Joel,

Thank you for your very good letter and card and clipping... The May *Letter*[2] is surely filled with inspiration and

1 A Closed Class was a class open only to students who were able to attend all sessions and who paid a minimal tuition.

food for thought. It's strange how some ideas hit one with tremendous force at certain times even though one may have heard of them or "known" about them before. In this *Letter*, the statement "Could many statements of Truth be greater than one statement of Truth?... You have the infinity of truth in any statement that you know" was like a sharp sword. That's a wonderful point and certainly removes all strain, enabling one to relax and let the light pour forth....

I've taken up *The Wisdoms* sentence by sentence, sometimes spending several meditation periods on a single point to make it my own and savor its full meaning. What comes hasn't been particularly original as yet, but even if it is an "old" truth, it comes alive for me in these moments.

So, for example, it came that the reason we can resolve all appearances by getting back inside ourselves is that in that state we recognize and know our true identity, that is, we are aware of our oneness with the only Consciousness there is. This Consciousness is the creative force and in our oneness with It, we see what we call creation, the forms as which Consciousness appears, in all its perfection, glory, and completeness. Inside ourselves, our vision is undimmed by suggestion, hypnotism, or "sleep." We behold that which IS. All these veils that mask true identity are wiped out. The center within is like a great pool of light which simply pours forth, completely unaware of the darkness of the world of human beliefs.

I know that in The Infinite Way we do not take the name of the patient or the problem into the treatment. Am I interpreting this correctly when I say that in treatment from the standpoint of "is," we do look at whatever is presented to us, not denying it, but simply recognizing that all that is, is God, and waiting for the Father to reveal the true identity of that which appears? Nevertheless, in that sense, the problem is taken into the treatment. In other words, we see that here is

2 Letters had always played an important part in Joel's work. In his years as a Christian Science practitioner, Joel sent out a monthly letter to patients and students who turned to him. This practice he continued as The Infinite Way ministry unfolded. At first it consisted of a single article in *The Infinite*

something that is, but our treatment is to see *what* it is.

Our room in the Fine Arts Building is not as good in the warm weather as during the winter, since we are disturbed by all the aspiring artists who seem to be trying to reach high "C" while we are trying to listen with undivided attention to a recording. For a long time, I have felt that we must have a place of our own in the Loop and I think that time is now. I don't believe I can resist the call to do this any longer. I see so many reasons for this next step. Even though it were a small space, it would be possible for much more activity to emanate from it....

It would serve as an office for me on Saturday and perhaps some evenings. I know, too, that the day must not be too far distant when all my time will be devoted to this work. Perhaps this is a step in that direction. So now for it to be revealed!...

Only four more weeks after this one until summer vacation! Happy thought! It will be a quiet summer devoted entirely to Infinite Way work. I want to eat, drink, and sleep it. The more activity in my consciousness, the more on the outer plane and the greater the fruitage. Thank you.

Lovingly yours,
Lorraine

Joel's guidance in regard to establishing a public Infinite Way activity in Chicago proved to be invaluable, setting forth and emphasizing a basic principle of The Infinite Way: The Infinite Way is never to be organized. It is to remain forever a movement in Consciousness, a movement destined to permeate human consciousness unhampered by the limitations of any form of organization or proselytism of any kind. This would in no

Way Messenger, a monthly publication sent out by Harry Royal Stender. When the two men came to the parting of the ways, *The Joel S. Goldsmith Letter* was begun in January, 1954, and continued as Joel's link with his students.

way obscure or obstruct the activity, for Consciousness draws unto Itself Its own. Truth can never be organized. Only complete freedom from organization can assure its continued unfoldment.

Years later when the Illinois Legislature instituted a sales tax on books, Valborg and I went to the State Department of Revenue to inquire about paying this tax and what forms were to be filled out. When the man in charge was told that this was an unorganized religious activity, he quickly asked "Who is the head of it here?" To this I replied "I am."

"What do they call you?"

"Call me?"

"Yes, Reverend?"

"No, I am not a legally ordained minister."

"Do they call you 'Doctor'?"

"No, I hold no doctorate degree of any kind."

"What about, 'Mother'?"

With that I said, "They just call me Lorraine."

Then he asked why we didn't avoid all of this and simply file as a tax-free religious organization. When we explained that this was contrary to our principles, his response was, "That sounds like Jesus."

May 24, 1954

Dear Joel,

Thank you very much for everything—your very helpful letter and The Wisdoms...

We are looking for a room for our meetings...I feel that a permanent location would make possible a greater expansion of activity, or shall we say that our concern about finding such a place is an evidence that we are at the beginning of a new birth of activity which we do not yet see in visible manifestation.

You say so many times that The Infinite Way can never have a "Center." Certainly what we contemplate would in a way be a "Center" for it would be a place where people could come for help, to read, to hear recordings, and to meditate, in addition to serving as an office. Do you approve of that?...

Lovingly yours,

Lorraine

Joel approved of what we envisioned as a room for our meetings centrally located in downtown Chicago. He pointed out that it would be an individual activity with no government from some central headquarters and would succeed or fail according to the degree of conscious awareness of the individual who headed the activity.

June 18, 1954

Dear Joel,

We are still in the process of negotiating for a permanent location and tomorrow should perhaps bring a decision...It is at 30 West Washington in a beautiful building, and if you remember Chicago, you know that for a location, that is the best there is...Right now there is no visible means of meeting the expenses incurred except out of my pocket, but I know that if this is God's activity, it must support itself.

I feel our place should have a name. Do you object to having simply The Infinite Way on the door? Should my name appear as practitioner and teacher or what? We felt it should be called The Infinite Way because that is what it is—a place where people interested in The Infinite Way come together, and

I think that in no wise implies any kind of organization. Another name we have thought a good deal about is Metaphysical Workshop....

I am not going any place this summer but expect to be here and get our downtown room in working order and get ready for your coming...I think the group for your class as it is shaping up will be an inspiration to you, too, and I know how much your class will mean to them.

Lovingly yours,
Lorraine

June 19 did bring a tentative agreement to lease a small suite at 30 West Washington Street, consisting of a room about 30' by 40' with four large windows. Connected to it was a small foyer or entrance room. This was double the amount of space my sister and I felt we could handle financially. Heretofore we had contemplated about half that amount of space but this space and building seemed so desirable that we felt it must be Grace pushing us to negotiate for it.

In the course of our discussion with the manager, when we told him that it was for an office for The Infinite Way and for small group meetings, he inquired what The Infinite Way was. How could one explain to a hardheaded business man that this was a mystical movement in consciousness? Instead of going into that I somewhat hesitatingly responded, "It is a kind of metaphysical teaching."

"Oh," he said, "Connected with a hospital?"

"Well, not exactly." And that was all that was said about it. He could not immediately assure us of possession of these quarters. A group of 30 women were at the moment renting them and their plans for vacating the rooms had not yet been finalized.

Joel was heartily in agreement about using The Infinite Way as the name on the door of our new meeting place in the Loop but wanted me to have my name also listed although without any specific title such as "Teacher' or "Practitioner." No one could make one a teacher or practitioner for that was a matter of the degree of conscious awareness attained and an ordination to carry on such a ministry came not from man but from on High. Consciousness would draw unto itself its own. It came to me to keep the entire activity as impersonal as possible and for that reason the only words placed on the door were The Infinite Way with no name attached.

July 18, 1954

Dear Joel,

It's been a long time since I've written, and you must have wondered what has happened. The days have flown by as on wings and have been even busier than during school days. It hardly seems possible that in a month you will be here.

Most of the summer has been spent in working out the place for our meetings, and that is now settled. Last week I signed the lease and will have possession August 15.... We are on the 11th floor at 30 West Washington, just a wonderful location in the heart of the Loop and in a very good building.... We are happy and grateful for it and are working out the furnishings so that it will breathe beauty, peace, and harmony. Isn't it nice it will be open for people to use during the classes? It's so close it will be very convenient, only about two blocks from the Sherman Hotel where out meetings are to be held. I don't know why I'm taking all this on except that I have to do it.... Interestingly enough, it seems that before anyone knew of our new place, as soon as the step had been taken, there was an automatic increase in activity and corresponding flow of Grace with which to carry it on....

Lovingly yours,
Lorraine

This first Infinite Way Study Center in all the world was a charming haven of peace and love set down in the midst of the hustle and bustle of the Chicago Loop. It was the "upper room" prepared with love and furnished with pieces from my apartment and Valborg's attic, at no financial expense except for some twelve very comfortable folding chairs. Truly it was an experience of *I*-haveness, Consciousness unfolding *as*.

The draperies on the windows were left-overs from a larger apartment; a long Seraband Oriental runner with a deep blue background provided a touch of elegance and homeyness. Lounge chairs, end tables and lamps from my apartment and Valborg's attic plus a used davenport given by a friend made it look like an inviting and attractive living room which was open to those who found this haven of peace and rest several days a week for study, meditation, and to hear Joel's recorded classwork.

At the beginning there were five meetings a week at which time I took out the folding chairs stacked away in a closet and afterward put them away. At first, and for a long time, there were no volunteers to help with any of these chores. All the preparatory work on this room was done in a couple of days before Joel arrived for class. Valborg and I surveyed our work with considerable pride. Joel smiled approvingly when he saw it but his comment was somewhat deflating. "Lorraine, this is just peanuts. Wait."

Joel's plane landed at Midway Airport about two o'clock Friday morning, August 20, for his first classwork in Chicago. At about 8 A.M., after what I thought should have been adequate time for him to rest, I telephoned him to welcome him to Chicago, only to be greeted brusquely by an indignant voice, "Get me out of here at once. The plaster is falling down, the room was not made up when I arrived, and there are empty liquor bottles strewn all over. Get me out of here."

Overwhelmed by the diatribe that followed, I telephoned Valborg and asked her to go with me down to the Loop to see what we could do to pacify Joel. Moving him to another room was well-nigh impossible, because every room at the hotel had been fully booked by the annual convention of the Loyal Order of Moose. But Joel insisted on another room, so for an hour Valborg and I begged and pleaded with the manager to find more suitable accommodations. Finally, the manager offered us a small suite for him. When Joel heard of these arrangements he assumed his normal peaceful attitude of nonreaction.

Despite this inauspicious beginning, the evening Closed Class and the morning Practitioners' Class were deep spiritual experiences. As far as numbers were concerned, these Classes far exceeded our expectations. We had anticipated a possible maximum of thirty-five, but there were well over one hundred people at each class. A special moment for me came on a rainy Wednesday morning during the Practitioners' Class. Near the end of the session Joel boomed out, "There is no externalized illusion." I had read these words before but the irrefutable conviction in his voice illumined those simple words and I found myself inwardly saying, "Of course, of course! An illusion is a mental misperception and could not be out here." With that realization came a conviction that I did not have to change anything out here but be freed only of a misperception of the omnipresent divine perfection. Out of that came some real fruitage.

During the time Joel was in Chicago for the class, there was the opportunity for some illuminating private sessions with him in which he again pointed up many of the principles he had set forth in some of his letters. One of the things we talked about was Mother's transition which he used to point up the difference between human health and spiritual wholeness. Again, he emphasized that I was fairly quick to reinterpret discordant human appearances, but tended to accept the harmonious human appearance without reinterpretation, not recognizing that both were part of the dream of human existence. When we stop clinging to the human concept of life which begins at a certain date and ultimately terminates through disease, accident, or age in death, we are close to that life of which Jesus spoke when he said, "Destroy this temple and in three days, I will raise it up."[3] That can be a possibility only as we are willing to let go of our human sense of life, recognizing that life is not dependent upon a body and bodily functions. Appearances—good or bad—can never testify to truth.

On Wednesday evening, when I went to the Jade Room to check on the arrangements, after having had dinner with Joel, I found Valborg and her assistants in despair. They had received word that hundreds of Moose would be having a cocktail party across the hall. At that late date there was no possible way of moving our meeting to another room. I wondered what fireworks would burst forth over this incident, remembering how in the midst of

3 John 2:19.

a Class in New York when there was noise outside the classroom, he had bellowed forth, "This will not do, Mrs. C. We will have to have another room." This time, however, Joel was calm, collected, and understanding, giving one of the very best lessons of the entire week of classwork. In fact, he remained unperturbed even when a kitchen band began banging away outside the door. At that precise moment he said, "Some people appear to be good, some people bad, and some intolerable."

For me, the climax of the whole week came on Sunday evening when the class was finished. Valborg, R., and I had dinner with Joel at the Palmer House. It was then that he told me that he would have time at Christmas to give me the special work and experience I so longed for, even though he would be in Hawaii and I in Evanston. Subsequent events recounted in my letters proved that he kept his promise.

August 31, 1954

Dear Joel,

I'm still up in the clouds. If only I could have had just one week alone to dwell on the wonder and the beauty of it all...But Monday it was back to school, meetings all this week, all day long. On all sides the question comes, "What did you do this summer?" And when I said that I was home most of this summer, there was always the quick response, "Oh, I didn't do anything exciting either." The idea that one could be right at home, not go anywhere, and still have an adventure, exciting beyond human capacity to envision, would be completely unintelligible to them. I smiled and responded in kind to the chatter of these friends who were my colleagues, but it was a forced, frozen smile. Inside was an ache such as I had never felt quite so deeply before. I am not the same. An impassable barrier which never again could be surmounted rises up between them and me. Yet even in the midst of that there was an almost fierce joy that I could not be experiencing this if I were not drawing closer to the ineffable experience for which I wait.

I love the beautiful pieces of ceramics you gave me. Both the salad bowl and relish tray are lovely, distinctive in shape and design. There is a quiet and gentle beauty about them— and signed pieces—I like that, too. I thought you said you didn't have good taste? How could you lie so? They are especially precious for themselves and most of all because they are a gift from you.

The last dinner with you, Sunday evening, was beyond words. I could sit and listen forever as one story after another unwinds. You're a marvelous teller of tales, each story with deep meaning. I'd like to be one of those fortunate ones to sit for five hours without speaking. There might not be speech but there would be communication. Thank you for sharing so much, such deep treasures with me.

I hardly dare believe your promise to me. I was beginning to lose hope that I should ever earn the right to be directly taught by you—but no, we don't ever earn it, do we? It is only the gift of Grace that brings anyone so great a promise. I had the feeling all the time you were here that this was a test such as all disciples must undergo. I wasn't sure just at what moment it would come and I don't even know now just what it was but I knew that if I passed it, I should be permitted to go on, but if I failed, I would be among the countless who *almost* made it, but didn't quite and thus were left behind. I value all the hours you gave me to talk with you, which I surely did not expect with your full schedule—it was one of those added things so much more prized because not anticipated.

Every class I've ever had with you has been a soul-stirring

experience, but in this one, strange as it may be, in the midst of the responsibility of the class, there was the greatest peace I have ever experienced. It is paradoxical that I should be so keyed up, rushing around at breakneck speed, so vitally alive and awake, and yet so quietly peaceful. Right now I think it would be perfect to just go off somewhere and forever after rest in that peace and quietness and forget all the world's problems. I don't feel a bit like doing anything for the world. I would just like to forget it and its problems. It is not given us to do that, is it?

This whole summer—the weeks of preparation, the frustrations, and the final glorious climax... *all* are woven together into a tapestry of rare beauty. It cannot always be all sweetness and light. There must be dark threads in the tapestry to accentuate the light; the bitter makes the sweet all the sweeter; the valley experiences only help to make the summit of the mountain higher and the view more magnificent. It's been a glorious time.

What you have done for me is so great, so deep, so far-reaching that you could growl at me and terrify me as you did with your displeasure (really I was scared) and I could gladly bear it only hoping to be given some little opportunity to be of service....

I know there will be times when I shall not measure up— only be patient with me. No, I don't even ask you to be patient, just don't give up on me. Thank you always.

Lovingly yours,
Lorraine

September 10, 1954

Dear Joel,

...I laughed at your gentle hint about the peace and quiet

of the New Thought Temple in Cincinnati for it had all the earmarks of a dirty dig. Will you ever let me live down the Moose? Every time I see a picture of a real moose, I shudder and have visions of the kitchen band with which we were serenaded the night of their cocktail party, when I would have been so grateful to have the floor open and swallow me up....

Well, I'm down out of the clouds, just tumbling down and landing with a resounding thud. Wouldn't it be nice if there were something more substantial than a cloud where one could rest? Heavens, what am I saying? "He hangeth the earth on nothing." That's it. Resting even on a cloud or on any *form* brings change, a shifting of positions, a going up or a coming down. The past couple of weeks have been a period of adjustment, and not all easy. There have been many ripples to mar the peace and calm of the surface. Is that to be expected, or what?...

Maybe these experiences with persons are the first stage in my transition from an innate desire to please people and see them happy to a complete resting in God, a losing of concern for people. Well, I'm working at it, even though I'm far from arriving. I'm still awfully soft inside where people are concerned. I think you sensed this in me as one of my hurdles when you read me such a lecture on not doing human good but instead giving spiritual help which is the real gift.... I suppose all these experiences are a part of my own unfoldment and learning, my own attainment of a degree of wisdom in this work and a more complete reliance on God.

You are so right about the importance of the healing work. Our work here will stand or fall on that. You gave us much to work on when you were here. If we don't do good healing work with all the help and instruction you give, whoever could?...

The idea in "The Wisdoms" of true nonresistance is very helpful. How else is it possible to achieve an attitude of genuine nonresistance? This makes sense to me. As long as we believe there is something to change, we're bound to resist it. No, there is nothing to fight, nothing to overcome, nothing to battle....

Lorraine

September 28, 1954

Dear Joel,

Thank you so much for your letter. And so you are off to wonderful new experiences, and the whole world is to be the richer....

Did you say something about being busy? Quite suddenly there isn't even time to eat, let alone sleep! Yes, people are actually becoming concerned that I'm not eating enough or properly.... There have been moments when I wondered how I could ever get through the year, but these are only moments and I quickly turn from that suggestion, realizing there is only *this* moment and no other....

One of the students in your classes is a little concerned about one statement made in one of the closing sessions in regard to the time factor in making adjustments in the body after the healing has taken place. His question is how can that be if there is nothing to change except a false concept? Shouldn't the destruction of the concept reveal instantly the already-existing perfection? Why should a "new liver" have to be created since there is only one? Can you clarify that point further?

Lovingly yours,
Lorraine

Later it came to me that any spiritual healing is an evidence of momentarily transcending time and space and can come only through spiritual awareness. We are still living in the two worlds of human consciousness and spiritual consciousness, and probably most of the time in human consciousness which is the world of time and space. Truth is here for all to receive but how many have *realized* it? The realization of it is an imperative. Conditioned as most persons are to everything occurring in time and space, it is difficult to realize that a seemingly hard physical condition can disappear instantaneously. As spiritual discernment increases the time factor enters in less and less.

October 17, 1954

Dear Joel,

Thank you for your letter, telegram, and cards...C. and E. came in from out of town a couple of weeks ago for one of the recordings. We had a most interesting visit afterwards. They seem to be quite advanced students. Why, they don't even want to do any healing work! When they asked me if I didn't feel the same way, I had to confess most apologetically that I loved the healing aspect of the work, but felt like a nitwit in admitting it. They seemed to have had remarkable mystical experiences....

Again, I found myself wondering why these never have been my lot, and the cold, hard answer comes back to me, "You're just not far enough along. That is all." Yes, all manner of doubts assail me. Most of all doubts as to my readiness and fitness to do this work. Perhaps I don't have the consciousness for it. Joel, I will work, make very effort, make every sacrifice, and have infinite patience, but what if this is all just wishful thinking and because I love it so much I imagine I'm called when I really am not? What a mess!

I've come up against some tough healing problems, tough in the sense of being slow to yield. What do I do in such situations—just keep on, or what?...

Lovingly yours,

Lorraine

Joel was quick to respond to this urgent cry for greater light, emphasizing an oft-repeated principle that we cannot judge by appearances whether these appearances come through the ear or the eye. He also gave me a quotation from scripture which has carried me through many different situations: "Let the heathen rage." It is personalizing a problem that makes it difficult to yield.

There was a word of caution too, when he pointed out the importance of not being influenced by the attitude of students or their response to the work, but to hew straight to the line. My own integrity must be the determining factor in the work I was doing. Above all the goal must be attaining my own conscious oneness. If I cater to the whims of students, I could easily become a doormat and the students might break my heart.

5

The Old Ends and the New Begins

To every aspirant on the spiritual path come spiritual crises that mark a transition in consciousness. These crises may be triggered by some fairly insignificant outer event, serving to point up the next step and to highlight the goal yet to be attained. The immeasurable distance which seems to separate the aspirant from approaching that lofty goal may lead to an inner turmoil as the little "I" makes a valiant effort to prevent that extinction which must be the final outcome. This is initiation, a sacred experience of the soul unfolding; an experience that can never be shared except with one's guru or teacher, nor can it be described. It is an experience in consciousness, the validity of which is made evident to the disciple by its fruitage.

During this transitional period, the spiritual support Joel gave me was immeasurable, one letter following another. Always I was reminded that dissatisfaction with the progress which I was making was essential to any real progress. In giving this encouragement he indicated that he spoke of his own frequent struggles which tore him apart. It is through the inner struggles, the warfare between the shadowy self and the Self that the goal is attained. Every temptation of this material sense of world raises its head to be seen through. Then the old fades away to make way for the new consciousness.

To this disciple, one such experience brought with it a transition in consciousness that transformed her whole life, and with it came increased activity and work.

December 22, 1954

Dear Joel,

A joyous Christmas be yours today and every day. I wish I might have had some choice little piece to delight your heart. You must have found many such on your travels, so won't you please think of one very modest little thing you might want as my gift to you, purchased with this check and given with love and deepest appreciation?...

Thank you for your last letter, beautiful and very wise. Your last words were, "Be wise," and straightaway I go forth and act the fool. Wisdom is hard to come by. Yes, I needed the admonition and heeded it not. Still that silly, foolish, stupid desire to please people haunts me, and I let it use me. After it is done, the senselessness of it hits me, and the stupidity. Maybe with much pain the lesson is being learned and becoming part of the fabric of my being that there is no pleasing people, that henceforth the whole criteria for any action must be, "Does it please God?" Then one would not fall by the wayside. I see it now so clearly as a form of egotism, though it appears in reverse, wanting to be thought well of, a subtle well-hidden desire for the praise of men. You could not be harder on me than I have been on myself unless you should decide as I did that I might as well give up trying. That's where yesterday found me.

Then, today, the entire day was spent in our room downtown and there were three perfect hours all alone when I felt enveloped once again in the deep peace. It was all-embracing, warm, and comforting. Again, I felt God's hand in mine and knew the road would never end for the Way is infinite and there is no turning back or stopping midway, and all things for the journey are provided. Above all a guide would be there, patient and understanding, ahead of me, but always close enough to light the way and to help me over the roughest places. If the guide upbraided me, it was only to lift my limited vision above undue concern with the self to the wider vistas ahead....

I know all the answers: Truth is within me, and nothing except my own blindness can hide from me that light which is already there, steadily shining, awaiting only my recognition. Maybe it's the Oriental idea of obedience, too, trust and faith in one's teacher. True, God is the Teacher, but I am one of the fortunate ones, after years of waiting and praying, whose teacher appeared as form. Maybe it's waiting so long, then the joy of finding the teacher and teaching that makes me look on it as such a priceless treasure.

Thank you for your great, great gift to me.

December 28, 1954

Dear Joel,

How long does the torment go on? You speak of a night of it, but there have been days and nights and nights and days. There is no sleep. There is no peace. There is the paradox of a numbness and deadness in the midst of intense pain. Such aloneness. In this aloneness I seek refuge in "The Wisdoms": "All conflicts must be settled within your consciousness." That only makes it harder and more acute. The conflict is plain: "I" is "dying." Can it be accomplished? It is deeply imbedded within me, so many years, so many times has it been bruised, and it still persists....You know, or do you? You had more truth with which to meet it! Does that make it easier or harder?

Now for the first time it is clear why esotericism insists on such a long and rigid discipline. One couldn't go on, knowing how high the price is, unless bit by bit, the vehicle had become tempered steel, cold, immovable. What happens if the dark night comes before the iron has been forged into steel? Does one just sink into the depths and exchange oblivion for the scorching pain? One could endure the pain, even ask for it, if only there were some hope, but tonight it seems that even you in your love and understanding could not open the soul to any light. There has been such a deep longing to be a fit instrument.... Is all the love, devotion, and striving for naught?

Lovingly yours,

Lorraine

This was indeed initiation - an inner experience in Consciousness. No words can describe the experience.

December 31, 1954

Dear Joel,

Bless you for your letter of December 27, which just arrived. How deep is your understanding! You ought to be awfully happy about me, for I'm not unhappy about myself nine-tenths of the time, just ninety-nine one hundredths.

How often does one go through these harrowing experiences? It was strange because it had no relationship to anyone in the outer world. Instead it was a struggle between the Self and the self, all taking place within. By the end of the day a sort of ecstacy overtook me and "there was no more night." It seemed like death and birth all rolled into one.

We reach this higher state and then again the world overtakes us. How does one keep the treasure safe and untarnished?

Lovingly yours,
Lorraine

January 6, 1955

Dear Joel,

Your wonderful cable brings hope even in the wilderness. I knew you were with me but I longed to talk with you. Your message was a kind hand placed in mine, a sadly needed assurance, and a call to go forward.

Is it possible that this marks the end of the old and opens the new as you said in your cable? It seems so far off as the struggle continues. It subsides and then seizes me again with renewed force.... I accept all as God, God purging me in cleansing fires to make of me a fit instrument.

I used to think the Way would be all joy. I loved God so much that to be unhappy in Its closeness was unthinkable. Now I catch a glimpse of the heartbreak and the complete aloneness as one proceeds, unable to share the experience, only its fruits. Knowing that, I still love the work as it is shown forth here. Perhaps I love it too much. This week I had to get to the point where I said, "God, fulfill Thyself as The Infinite Way, even if that means leaving me out. I love it enough to sacrifice my part in it. Maybe it will grow faster and better without me." Those were hard words to say and to mean about something one loves more than anything in the world.

Yesterday I threw myself into the work with the children at school with complete abandon, but for the *first* time in all the years it brought no release. Never before had their healing influence failed me. Is that another sign pointing out that the end of a whole way of life has been reached and a new one opened up? Am I to leave *all*—my nets, my way of earning a living, and rest in faith and trust on the Infinite Invisible?

Such action would seem like utter folly since I am still drawing slightly on my income from teaching to help maintain the room downtown. Yes, the activity of the past couple of weeks would testify to its folly. Perhaps this act of supreme faith is what is required. I search myself, and it seems the only thing that holds me is the question, "Am I ready?" I believe that if I am ready, if there is the spiritual preparation and flowering, all human problems would be taken care of. The reason they aren't is because too many times people leave everything as an escape or from personal desire instead of being called. Am I the only one who will know when this moment comes or will you—did you—as my teacher see it?...

Last night, I sat meditating quite late and early in the morning too. Over and over the words came, "The Lord shall be to thee an everlasting light and thy God, thy glory." And again the words from Revelation, "Now is come salvation...."

No words can thank you , but gratitude pours from the heart.

P.S. 6:00 P.M. Tonight the answer seems crystal clear. There is no choice. I must finish out the teaching year until June since I am under contract, close the door on that part of my life forever, and launch forth into the deep waters of Spirit, letting God live my every moment.

January 9, 1955

Dear Joel,

A degree of equilibrium has been reached. It was Thursday when the decision came. It seems strange now that it was so hard to decide and took so long. I know what it means, but it's all right.

There is a difference. The old is at an end. Now I feel it. There is no sadness and there is no joy, no elation, no satisfaction, no dissatisfaction, just a steady purpose. It's as if a part of me no longer felt. Do you remember Celia in T.S. Eliot's *Cocktail Party*? Celia who chose the way and was devoured by cannibals? Shall I be able to say of them as I did of a snake, "What difference if they are cannibals?" Yes, as they devour the personality and feed on all that is left of self-love, self-justification, self-glorification, *I* remain, looking on, indifferent, immovable, impenetrable. I see a hundred ways every day in which human personality crops out. It's far from dead in me. A long uphill road ahead!

I know the struggles will come and go, each time more severe, shaking me loose from my moorings, but only that I may swim out beyond the surface waves into deep, calm waters. There is a new certainty, a quiet but deep determination, a release, a gentle fearlessness.... I want to pour out page after page. You are the *only* one with whom I can share these struggles. All my faults, weaknesses, and stupidities lie open before you—even those I don't see, you see. Yet there is complete trust and understanding. I feel safe even when you're laughing at me or scolding me. Oh, Joel, work seriously with me that I may go forward. Please help me achieve God.

January 11, 1955

Dear Joel,

I do rejoice, rejoice that I have been called; rejoice so much that I find no satisfaction in reaching a plateau where I can rest even for a short time. The ascent must continue regardless of the cost. Perhaps this little breathing space is necessary, but the upward surge is very strong. I have been awakening in the middle of the night at 4:00 A.M. and last night at 3:00, the call to get up and listen was imperative and could not be ignored. I sat until 5:30.

Over and over, "The Lord shall be to thee an everlasting light and thy God, thy glory...The light shineth in darkness...The glory of the Lord is risen round about thee...I have put my Spirit upon you," as a light. And if the Lord is my everlasting light, the light shines even though the darkness comprehends it not. "The sun shall be no more thy light by day"—not even a visible sign of the light is necessary, for the Lord is my light....

I feel your work. I know you are doing everything it is possible to do and the rest is up to me. I'm in the midst of something that is so close I cannot let it go without a fuller experience of it. To come so far and then stop—nothing would be so hard as that.

Jesus' ministry did not really begin until after the three temptations had been faced, until he had proved himself free of all desire to demonstrate anything or even prove anything, but could just rest in his realized oneness with the Father—a lesson for me....

Am I relying on you too much? Am I indulging in too much introspection? And is that, too, a form of self-love, sweetly disguised? Should I remain silent even to you and keep all this within? It is so hard to be patient and wait, wait, and wait. I want to take the Kingdom of Heaven by storm, and it can't be done.

Lovingly yours,
Lorraine

January 16, 1955

Dear Joel,

Thank you, thank you for the beautiful letter from your student which I return with deep appreciation for your generosity in sharing it with me. Thank you, too, for your last letter which arrived on Friday. How much you have poured out on me in the last week! Honestly, you must be sick unto death of hearing me sing the same old song. Each of us follows a pattern and how dull it must be to the person who listens to the ceaseless repetition.

Yes, Joel, of course I shall go on until June, putting my loving best into the work of each day at school and remaining silent. Please don't think the feeling I must stop teaching was made in the height of an emotional binge. It has long been under consideration, and now the call is so strong I don't see how I can resist it any longer.

You have taught me well, each lesson taught has been thoroughly learned. The first was that nothing could be added to me or anything taken from me, that my good is not dependent on any person or any place, that my self-sufficiency is of God. And the second was that the activity of Truth in consciousness is shouted from the housetops as demonstration: what is known on the Invisible Plane does become visible. Now those two lessons are a kind of staff to lean upon and also to push me forward. In their light it seems right to take next year and devote it solely to this work that Truth may flow out from consciousness in a flood tide. If nothing flows out, well, then I'll know.

Certainly to carry a full time job—and a heavy one—and to try to carry on Infinite Way work with the devotion it requires and one loves to give is difficult. Even though every waking moment I am not in school—and even some of that time is devoted to it—it is not enough. I recognize the wisdom of not rushing into anything and have not done this. True, the inner experience of the past few weeks has been powerful, and this feeling of the necessity of devoting myself entirely to the work undoubtedly crystallized during that time. However, no outward steps have to be taken at this time, so I shall wait. You may not feel the readiness or the necessary preparation in me. In that event there is, of course, only one answer.

Yes, you are right. Some come to the meetings only to get, but even that is but a stage along the way, and how will they learn to give unless they witness the eternal givingness of God in action? In time they learn that wonderful lesson, "Begin to pour," and catch the vision. There are others, though, who do bring devotion and love to the work here that rewards every effort to make it available to them. They are the ones who sanctify the hours we meet together. The others come and go, and even if they leave, a sadness is quickly healed, but those of our household are finding their self-completeness in God. You can understand how I love to serve them and know my reason for being. We have something very beautiful here and very precious. It is still only a bud, but if it is well watered, a perfect flower will unfold. True, I may not be the one to wield the sprinkling can, but the opportunity is here. Most of those who come give freely and lovingly and their dedication is unmistakable.

Sometimes it seems there could not be such a beautiful group of people gathered together anywhere else in the world. The love and devotion that flow out at our meetings is so great it almost stops my breathing. The Christ is there expressing as every one of them. Occasionally one not of this household finds his way here, and we can only offer a blessing and let him go his way. Sometimes there is a recognition that there must have been something present in my consciousness to attract what appears as a disturbing element and that means there must be greater purity flowing out from me. The students who come do support this activity lovingly but they are few in number, great in spirit but not in numbers. The ones one might expect to do more don't come through at all, but that is neither here nor there. These first few months it has been necessary to draw on my own income to meet expenses at the Center, not much, but a little. That doesn't disturb me at all. I feel perfectly at peace about the whole thing and have an inner sense of rightness about it.

"There is a rest unto the children of God." That rest has come in the hours and hours of meditation given to me every day. Even with school there have been five to eight hours a day of sitting quietly, listening, and waiting, taking deep draughts of the Spirit. A stability comes with it and a wonderful quietness after the storm. Once in a while, there will come a little lightning and thunder and rumbling of an impending storm, but mostly there is a quietness and assurance. And such a burst of activity outwardly has come forth this week—very beautiful and so clearly the effect of those hours and hours of meditation—an increased use of our facilities downtown and a noticeable increase in the healing work. How good God is to let me go through the cleansing fires! The pain is as naught for the assurance of God's grace which fills me with something deep and satisfying for which there is no word. So much love has flowed these last few days. It surely is from the Christ to the Christ.

Over and over come the words, "You cannot succeed and you cannot fail." Thank you for that. The song of gratitude in my heart thunders in the silence.

Lovingly yours,
Lorraine.

January 17, 1955

Dear Joel,

Yes, yes, that's it—no convictions, nothing but to be an empty vessel that God may rush in and fill one. To know nothing but to let God reveal all things through us! Does that only come in those long, dark hours, dark because we struggle to hold on to an identity separate from God, and then losing that separate selfhood brings the agonizing moment of being cast adrift, lost, anchorless? It must only be a moment, though it seems everlasting, before God rushes in to minister to us. If one could always hold on to that glorious vision of God taking over! Wouldn't it be easier if one were isolated from the world? Would the same old suggestions come back to drag one down over and over again? The world holds me so little—always that's been true and always there has been that desire for God from a child. You'd think it would make it easier, but it seems to work in reverse and slow up the process. It's been a steady movement forward but interminably slow....

I really had to laugh at Valborg who knew of three incidents this last week where I had tried to be humanly helpful that had boomeranged. She said, "Well, Lorraine, three times this week you've cast your bread on the water, and each time it has come back as stones around your neck." That's what comes of human good. It certainly is just another guise of evil, so interchangeable are the two. Valborg doesn't know how nearly I came to drowning with those stones. Yet if they brought me to such depths to gain deeper spiritual insight, I should bless them and be grateful to the people who hung them around my neck—only they didn't do it, just my own stupidity.

Another aspect of this business of "pleasing" people and being "nice" to them struck me. In school, in my dealings with children, parents, and co-workers, I am as fearless, firm, forthright, and confident an individual as it is possible to imagine. There, I feel completely adequate and secure. I know exactly what I'm doing. On the contrary, in this new field...there has not been sufficient depth of inner experience to give me that same certainty and assurance in working with people in this area. That's the growth that has to take place and a tiny, tiny beginning already is working a transformation. There is a certain firmness just beginning to show forth, an independence, a certainty, and it all came about this week.

I wonder how much longer I will be trying to divide myself between two jobs, but I'm just waiting until there is no possible doubt as to what to do. There, too, is a conflict. On the one hand it seems unwise to make any change until my part in the Infinite Way activity here is established beyond doubt. If I did only that work, wouldn't it grow by leaps and bounds because I know it comes forth from the Invisible Plane? Am I relying too much on my salary instead of God? Would I be freer, or would I be plagued with the problem of supply and become so concerned about that that I enter another kind of bondage? How full of contradictions am I! I'd like to hide them from you but you know anyway.

Lovingly,
Lorraine

January 29, 1955

Dear Joel,

Thank you very much for your last two letters which were waiting for me when I returned home on Saturday from downtown—always an answer and a call to awaken.

Yes, you are right. Our goodness must be sacrificed too. Human goodness and badness are so closely allied that it is hard to determine where one begins and the other ends, both purely relative and both sin in the sense of setting up a separation or acknowledging something other than God. There is no big or little in that.

It is plain to me that my goodness was a subtle form of self-love and self-satisfaction which in that searching light became evil and had to be rooted out. Always looking away from the self insofar as the grace of God makes that possible and constantly dwelling in God, resolutely turning from both good and bad appearances, has brought a temporary abatement of the intense struggle. Perhaps a new plateau has been reached. It seems impossible to go back to the former state.

The quiet hour at three in the morning brings a flood of warmth in the cold stillness of a bleak Chicago night, and a holy hush, no words, just assurance and certainty. How wonderful to have found it! It is the most perfect hour in the whole twenty-four, cherished above all others.

In the midst of so much activity, the contemplative life lived away from the world looms as a beautiful snare. You make me realize it is just that, a snare! The call to work and to serve is too strong and so with each day's work comes an opportunity to see in everyone and everything the one Actor, Be-er, Do-er. I was finally able to secure *The Cloud of Unknowing*, so now have settled down to that. It looks promising.

February 3, 1955

Dear Joel,

The soul's journey back to being one with God comes to each as an individual and a unique experience, and yet how universal it is! "The Wisdoms" are the modern *Cloud of Unknowing*.

These inner struggles are really the second exercise given for contemplative prayer, feeling one's self overcome forever, the true meekness. How beautifully he describes it when he says that with that meekness God descends "to take you up tenderly—to dry your spiritual eyes." It was like that when the storm subsided.

Perfect and imperfect meekness! Imperfect meekness "to struggle and sweat"—such an accurate description—"to get a true knowing and feeling of yourself," but the perfect meekness is "pure contemplation on the greatness of God rather than on your own wretchedness." Pg. 100. And "a perfect apprentice asked neither for release from pain nor for an increase of reward, nor for anything other than for God Himself." Page 101. He feels that "strong and deep spiritual sorrow," page 106, "but only according to his ableness to endure it." Page 109. There is such hope, too, "yet He does not give us grace nor this desire to any soul that is unable to receive it. He who feels called to the work is able to work therein." Pages 61, 62. It is that one-pointed love that pierces the darkness because "He may be fully loved who cannot be defined at all. By the affection, he may be secured and kept," page 36. "God Himself will work with your soul...Then you will know what joy is to let Him have His will with you" page 54—the joy of self-surrender.

Praying for one's enemies has been a task taken very seriously recently. Is it not true that as soon as all sense of an individual's being an enemy is removed and no feeling, or only one of great kindliness much akin to love, remains is he no longer one's enemy even though the seeming enemy may still hate and feel revengeful? Would the enemy's attitude be completely transformed through this prayer, and until this is evident should the praying continue? I've been thinking about this in connection with my own affairs. Such compete detachment has come that it is easy for me to look at certain persons with a most kindly feeling and to look through the appearance to their true identity. A great feeling of warmth comes over me then, even my smile is warm, sincere, and friendly. Insofar as it is within my power they are free from any bondage. Yet, that they are not free within themselves is obvious. Must one continue praying for the enemy until the enemy himself is free?

Lovingly yours,
Lorraine

Joel never answered that last query, perhaps because he knew I would find the answer within as happened so many times. And I did. The work is never on or *for* a person. The work *is* always to contemplate what is, dropping the person and realizing spiritual identity. Then when the person no longer brings forth any reaction in us and drops completely out of thought, our work is complete. It may not bring forth any noticeable change in the person for whom we are praying, but we are free of a false concept of that person which is all we were ever dealing with. The person is always that divine Consciousness individualized.

February 8, 1955

Dear Joel,

Thank you so much for your letter, encouragement, and help.

The conviction that this work is "it" for me and must claim my every moment persists and grows in strength and certainty. You have said, "Wait," and so it is, but the urge is insistent.... I am not eligible for any kind of a pension for many years to come since I have not reached the minimum retirement age. Then a small pension would come to me. Certainly none of that should enter into the picture. If this is the next step forward, all that is necessary will be provided. I've known such very"lean years" that even that possibility means little to me. Instead it would be an opportunity. It is all a question of readiness and inner preparation. I keep my own counsel and wait—no hasty, irrevocable action—but pass on to you these steps as they come to me.

The healing work is coming along. It has been beautiful and seems to date from one night about two weeks ago. Over and over the passage from Revelation kept coming back to me, the passage that was given me on that very important night, "Now is come salvation and strength and the kingdom of our God and the power of his Christ." A couple of weeks ago, "the power of his Christ" were the particular words that held me and suddenly came, "Why, of course, the power of true identity. Christ is the identity, and the recognition of that is the Word with power." Strange, I've read and heard these very words for years in your writings and on the tapes. Nothing original about my hearing them, but in those early morning hours they lived for me as if the words were heard for the first time. After that came a freedom, a relaxing in the healing work never experienced before. It all seemed so simple, so easy, and there were healings and so effortlessly.

Lovingly yours,
Lorraine

It was becoming more and more clear to me that to undertake an Infinite Way ministry, a healing consciousness was an absolute prerequisite. True healing work is lifting the student to Soul-awareness, and when that happens, gratitude pours forth from the awakened awareness of the Soul-center. That gratitude would provide the supply to carry on the work, but the practitioner must never ask for it. The practitioner's work was to sing the song of spiritual identity, the song of the Soul.

It was at this time that the *1954 Infinite Way Letters*[1] were published in book form, and Joel was ecstatic about it and felt it would do much to increase the awareness in a student seriously engaged in Infinite Way work. In a subsequent letter, Joel explained that he was so inundated with the demands of the work that he might sometimes be slow in answering my letters. For that reason he was glad I was self-sufficient.

March 6, 1955

Dear Joel,

Don't you think I realize and appreciate the vastness of your work and marvel at the work accomplished?... The promptness with which you take care of the mail is a marvel. The amount of work involved sounds colossal but how wonderful it is that the work is spreading far and wide. I wish I might help, but one small way is to stand on my own two feet.

Between friends there must be perfect faith, and so it is between teacher and student, a relationship of absolute trust with no explanations ever needed. No doubt can mar it. It is seeing truly and not through rose-colored glasses, not placing one on a high pinnacle from which he must inevitably fall. No, I have been through that too many times to fall into that snare. It is different—just perfect trust. Maybe it's a little like the feeling one has for a beloved parent: great faith, understanding, security, and trust, and yet recognizing how much the world is still with all of us and all its frailties. Heavens, even your politics used to disturb me no end, and an unspoken prayer went up that you wouldn't mention politics while you were in

1 Joel S. Goldsmith. (Los Angeles, Calif.: Grover Jones Press, 1961, 2nd Printing).

Chicago. But it isn't important.

The thought of my being a "merry little bluebird" is so far from my temperament I can't help laughing at the picture it conjures up. Nothing birdlike about me, and not much merriment, but let's hope sufficient anchorage in God to maintain a fairly even keel most of the time.

...The idea of telescoping time into this moment demands rising to a very high dimension where the consummation of all possibilities becomes a reality this moment. Time is no more and eternity becomes a fact. It would be worth a high price and sacrifice to achieve that realization. There is a sense of urgency about understanding this thing which is recognized intellectually as of the utmost importance. Ouspensky and Nicholl grappled with time and the idea of eternal recurrence but that phase of it is a dismal concept, a hopeless, continuous reliving of human errors. Whereas, "since before Abraham was, I am with you" is a message of hope and comfort—the perfection of being now.

Many people are asking when you will be here for another class. Now that you are experiencing the joys of housekeeping does one dare to suggest such a thing? [*Joel had bought a two bedroom house in Kailua at 22 Kailua Road.*] We would have a fine class here if you came—might even try for a quiet hotel— no Moose, no Lions, no Elks, or any of the rest of the zoo. What do we do? Keep on asking? We want you very much.

March 19, 1955

Dear Joel,

...I have been playing and replaying *The Easter of Our Lives*. It is beautiful. Perhaps it is the sense of perspective it gives that is most helpful. That sense of being deserted and betrayed, how many times must we feel it only to discover that there is no such thing as desertion or betrayal?   The quiet power in your voice reveals how deeply you have experienced just such desertion and betrayal, but how much higher you have gone each time, so far beyond those to whom you poured out your all and who then turned on you.   How many must have been renewed and strengthened by this message but tonight it is just for me and I'm saturated with it, cleansed and full of peace.

P.S. Sunday evening, March 20.   Did I say "full of peace"? Well, an acquaintance whom I have not seen more than twice but who knows of my work and who is Curriculum Coordinator in Park Ridge, a suburb due west of Evanston, called to tell me that there will be a principalship open there next year.   She would like to have me consider it, feeling that I'm just what they need and so on.   I know it is the Christ drawing her and the Christ will know the answer.   She has asked me to talk with the superintendent who is very much interested in having me come there.

How strange the world is!   The goal for which I struggled so many years within my grasp, the opportunity most desired now dumped into my lap completely unsought, but at the very moment when I am about to end that whole chapter.   What does it mean?   Is it the answer or the great temptation?   My first reaction was of Jesus being shown all the kingdoms of the world and the devil saying, "All these things will I give thee, if thou wilt fall down and worship me."

The prestige and all that goes with it are as nothing to me.   There is no feeling of elation, perhaps considerable sadness that this decision has come to me to make, but I shouldn't even feel that.   There is only one possible goal for me—to do the Father's work in whatever form it is given me to do.   Yes, it has its interesting aspects—to take over a school—it may be a brand new one now in process of building—and operate it on spiritual principles, always seeing the One as teachers and pupils. While I would have more responsibility, I would also have much more freedom. If I am to teach next year, this would be the better thing to do. You have said, "Wait," but now a decision must come. You know what fills my life, what is my life. The decision had seemed so clear and so simple—a final bowing out and now this comes. Surely God could not bring me thus far and let anything turn me aside and tempt me into some seductive by-path. Is this God's way of telling me I am not ready yet and so suffer it to be so a little longer or is that first reaction the correct one, that of the great temptation? That sense of God living my life is very strong, and so it cannot be my decision but God's, and the way must be made unmistakably clear. So I listen...

Please be with me in this moment of decision.

Lovingly yours,
Lorraine

April 1, 1955

Dear Joel,

...Your beautiful long letter of March 28, so full of wisdom and understanding, came yesterday. I have read and reread it many times and see the lesson in it. My desire to leave worldly pursuits is not permitted—no desires, only that God fulfill Itself. That is true surrender. Your letter brought a new insight into "leave your nets," that one could go on in the same pattern and still have left one's nets. It is letting the Father work in one, with no sense of self working, at whatever the Father gives one to do but without attachment, with no concern for the fruits. Then I knew it didn't matter what came. It would not be my work but God's if I could be pliable, soft, and malleable as the water in Lake Michigan I sat and watched today—one day a mirror of the sky, all quietness and peace, and then again showing forth its power and strength in roaring waves. It is not easy....

It seems people far away appreciate what we have here more than those who have it right in their midst, and perhaps that's part of the function of the Center. I spent most of this week of vacation downtown. On Wednesday a stranger walked in, and after much aimless chatter and meaningless "metaphysigese" fell silent and then said the most beautiful thing of all, "It is difficult for me to leave this room now that I am here—there is eternity here." Her eyes filled and there was a long silence....

Today was the first day I felt vacation, a letting go and a doing of what I wanted to do. That doing took me for a walk down to the lake and the little park at the end of the street, where I sat for a couple of hours. It was high noon with the warm sun pouring into me, reaching my very heart. There was stillness and an overpowering silence. If there were the sound of cars in the distance, I did not hear it, only the birds and the gentle lapping of the water. They did not break the silence; they merged in it. I sat and sat, no words, no thoughts, just an ineffable peace. I closed my eyes, not wanting even to see, just to feel. I was starved, sad, alone, and here was a table in the wilderness.

A joyous Easter to you....
Lovingly yours,
Lorraine

April 3, 1955

Dear Joel,

Friday, a table in the wilderness; and today, Sunday, my cup runs over. This morning we picked up the Chicago tape[2] at the post office and I have just finished listening to it for the

2 The First 1954 Chicago Closed Class, Reel 3.

second time. Like it? That isn't the word. I don't know what word to use. "Live the life of a contemplative even while in the world—no desires—God's wondrous love for us"—it's all there. Even before I heard the tape its message was working in me as you can tell from my last letter.

Again the last time I saw you, it was crystal clear when you said sometime—sometime you would work with me for a fuller realization, open the soul for illumination to pour forth. Ever since then I have felt that work in me....

Lovingly yours,
Lorraine

During these days of decision, it was a source of strength and courage for me to realize that God fulfills Itself at every level of consciousness. The direction that fulfillment was to take was immaterial. God's fulfillment of Itself might come as a principal of a school or as a spiritual practitioner and teacher. Whatever the activity, it must be the Christ revealing harmony in human affairs by lifting these affairs above a human activity into the spiritual.

April 10, 1955

Dear Joel,

...In my last letter amidst all the thank you's, I neglected to thank you for the excellent story, the clipping about the effect of the silence of the Quakers on the Nazis in Germany. That is a gem. There is no greater lesson than that lesson of silence—and one of the most difficult to learn.

It reminded me of my own experience with silence and

nonresistance many, many years ago when I was an undergraduate in college. The college operated on the quarter system—twelve weeks to the quarter. I was absent seven out of the twelve weeks with pneumonia and returned looking a shadow of my robust self. I was told that the only thing I could do was to drop out for the remainder of the quarter and forfeit the credits. It seemed essential to me at that time to finish school as rapidly as possible so I could begin working and relieve Valborg who carried the entire responsibility of supporting mother and me and sending me to school.

I appealed to the president of the college who explained why it would be impossible for me to make up the work since they were all lecture courses. I didn't argue with him, I just sat, and sat, and sat in spite of repeated suggestions that the interview was terminated. He was too polite to throw me out and so he continued repeating his explanation while I sat and said nothing, but prayed all the time. I knew God, who had brought me through pneumonia and thus far, would not forsake me now, so I waited expectantly.

At the end of an hour and a half in a final desperate effort to be rid of me, he gave me permission to try to make up the work but added pessimistically that it couldn't be done. Interestingly enough, the make-up work done for one course was subsequently used for their correspondence course in that subject. That was one outcome, and the other came several years later in the depths of the depression when teachers were a dime a dozen. That same president wrote to me out of the blue and invited me to join the college staff as an instructor, which offer I declined. So even though my use of silence was purely intuitive with no knowledge of the spiritual law underlying it, it had far-reaching repercussions and was most effective.

No decision has been reached in regard to the principalship....The more I dwell on the possibility of going there, the more foolish and impossible it seems....

You say so beautifully, "Let the Master Itself increase The Infinite Way work for you, in you, and through you." But how much more increase can there be and still continue in the present situation? As it is, there is neither time to sleep nor to eat, Joel. Even to myself I have not magnified, nor even given a second thought to the really terrific schedule under which I have operated this year, a heavy school schedule plus meetings downtown in the Loop thirty miles away, five times a week! I merely accepted it all as the work given me to do and am so grateful it has been possible. But it has been difficult, oh, so difficult. I wouldn't know what more than fifteen minutes for any meal or four or five hours of sleep out of the twenty-four would be like. Sometimes such a great weariness, even a physical ache, overtakes me, it seems impossible to go on, but one does because there is no stopping, no turning back.

This has been the severest kind of discipline and perhaps the most valuable. It was not self-imposed by an act of my will, but forced on me almost without choice and that is its value. I'm grateful for it. The other kind of discipline would surely bolster the ego and make one think she had achieved something. This puts the self in its proper place. I do not ask for an easy way, just that nothing keep me from following the Way. Surely you must know by now that *nothing* else is important to me. Of course, if this is the work for me to do, I know all else will be taken care of. It is as if I had come to the parting of the ways and the turn is not clear. It seems clear to me that it must not be on the basis of human reasoning or thinking....

Lovingly yours,
Lorraine

Immediately upon receiving my letter of April 10, Joel wrote announcing he would be in Chicago for work with me. He said he would also give three talks
to ten students, only ten, to be chosen by me. The opportunity to have several days of work with Joel was another example of the guru's watchful care of his disciple at this most critical time in her spiritual ongoing.

April 18, 1955

Dear Joel,

If I believed life to be dependent on the heart, I don't think I'd be here, for when your letter came this afternoon, it seemed my heart stopped *completely*. This is the surprise of surprises—the most wonderful news anyone could possibly hear. It's so wonderful that I had to read it fifteen times before its full import percolated.

Your reservation is already made at the Palmer House. I shall meet you at the airport. I've never been there, but suppose there will be no difficulty in locating it. I imagine it's the main airport way out southwest.

Also, may I extend the number of invited students for Tuesday evening and Wednesday to 15 instead of 10? It seems that those who have demonstrated their desire for this message by their faithfulness and sacrifice of time and money should be included, and there are that many who have not missed a single meeting at least twice a week and some three times since September. No one will be invited anyway until next Monday because so few people can keep their mouths shut that I don't want to put too great a strain on their silence. I shall arrange for a substitute at school so that I can be free to spend as much time with you as you have available. How much is for you to decide.

This is surely an example of Grace for there is not anything I could have done to deserve this great opportunity.

Ten minutes later: We've just had a terrific wind, hail, electric storm, and all the lights went out. Even the elements are excited!

Lovingly yours,
Lorraine

Shortly after Joel arrived in mid-morning and was settled in at the Palmer House he handed me a transcript of "The Easter of Our Lives." This tape had meant so much to me a few months before when I had been going through that inner crisis which triggered a new level of awareness. He asked me if Valborg and I could edit this for a pamphlet. That marked the beginning of the work on which we labored indefatigably until September 1981.

One of my first questions to Joel was "What should I do about the principalship in Park Ridge?"

"I'll tell you what to do. I'll be here several days. In those five days, don't talk about it and don't think about it!"

Amazingly enough, even though I spent hour after hour with Joel, there was never a mention or even a thought about this important pending decision. It had been dropped into that vast reservoir of the Infinite Invisible and there Omniscience revealed the answer to me, the wisdom of which I have never doubted. Yes, that April trip of Joel's to Chicago was a turning point for me in which it was clear to me which fork of the road to take.

May 2, 1955

Dear Joel,

It's Monday evening, just after our meeting, and this is my first opportunity to write to thank you for some of the most beautiful days I've ever known. The drive out into the country, when I could just listen to you talk or sit in the silence as we sped along the highway was something to be remembered always. Yes, every moment of those four days was perfect, even to the last final part at the airport. Your contagious enthusiasm in showing off those big "birds" was just the right culmination to it all. It gave me wings, and I haven't stopped soaring....

Do you have any idea how much you gave us in those three sessions?[3] The response here was wonderful. There is such deep gratitude....We had never heard anything like it before, and one senses the spirit of dedication and consecration your talks aroused. Wednesday afternoon was the zenith for me. That lovely dinner afterward with M.A. was difficult. To sit and smile and try to talk when one was stirred by a mighty Force which came through during that Wednesday session was hard. I wanted to live with what I had heard, dwell on every word, and, like Jacob, wrestle with it
until I had its blessing. It seems I could have gone the whole distance then and there if only I had been alone....

Lovingly yours,
Lorraine

May 14, 1955

Dear Joel,

Well, this is it! We have worked very hard on this manuscript[4] going over and over it, changing a word or sentence here, leaving out something else there and

3 The 1955 Chicago Private Class.
4 Joel S. Goldsmith, *The Easter of Our Lives.* (London: L.N. Fowler, Ltd., 1955).

occasionally adding a phrase. We have tried to make it flow, make it easy reading, and make a smooth transition from one idea to another.

One thing is certain—Joel shines through every sentence. We have made every effort to keep it that way and therefore have made a minimum of changes. It is so clearly you speaking in every phrase. That was one reason we worked so hard. We didn't want to take away any of the Joelisms and yet there needed to be provision for greater clarity.

You will notice that we have eliminated the use of "caps" and underlinings. This you may not like, but we believe the writing should be sufficiently clear to create its own emphasis. Of course, if you insist, go ahead and underline—but it will be better if you don't.

Look it over carefully, and if you want further changes, ship it back. After all, this is our first experience editing someone else's work. We've done plenty of it on our own papers, but that's a different story. At this moment, this is our best, but there is always a next moment. Each time we have gone over it, we have made changes so that could go on forever. We thought we'd better ship it on as it is to see what you think about it. If and when it goes to the printers, we would like a galley proof on it to check carefully for errors.

One of the most interesting things about this was the way the one Consciousness functioned. Many times independently of each other, Valborg and I made the same changes, using the very same words. When we worked together, we found ourselves saying the same thing simultaneously. When one bogged down, the other came up with what seemed to be just the right word or sentence....

We both loved doing this job. It's more interesting than anything I've done in many a day—I guess since I spent a summer working for Row Peterson revising a history textbook. We hope you like it but would be so happy to do further work on it.

And now, what next? With love from both of us,

Lorraine

May 23, 1955

Dear Joel,

Yesterday I wrote a long letter to you which I decided against sending. It was one of those letters which make you laugh, not that I object to your having a good laugh at my expense, but it seemed such a waste of your time to have to read it. After writing it and tucking it away in the envelope, everything was all right.

God has seemed about five billion miles away from something called "me," and "me" was in the ascendency. Meditation brought *I* back....

I guess I'll go down this Saturday and book passage for Hawaii to arrive June 25, if possible.

Lovingly yours,
Lorraine

Because of the editorial work Joel had given us to do, I did not go to Hawaii at this time. From then on my contact with Joel included reports, not only on my spiritual unfoldment, but also on the new project of preparing Joel's work for publication, an activity which became so time-consuming that my first concern seemed to sink into the background. Yet that really was not true, for there was no separation between the outer editorial activity and the inner spiritual striving. They were tied together in one unified whole.

June 4, 1955

Dear Joel:

Thank you for your very wonderful letter, the contents of which made me happy and grateful. There is nothing I should like to do better than what you propose [*a companion volume* to

Spiritual Interpretation of Scripture]—no hesitancy about this. It is a very real opportunity and a beautiful kind of fulfillment.

You will be interested to know that last year Valborg and I began to compile Bible passages which would illustrate various aspects of The Infinite Way with the idea of publishing them with illuminating comments somewhat like the old *Runner's Bible*.[5] So many things intruded that little progress was made. To do what you propose is a further expansion of that original idea, even though different, and will be very thrilling to work on. Your interpretations will be a major portion of the book. It will be a wonderful addition to Infinite Way literature and can embody principles which I would love to see pointed up clearly and concisely in a book or a portion of a book.

I shall begin at once to read and make notes. What about the recordings? Do you have transcriptions of them for us to work on? Am I to understand that it is all right to use things you have already published—probably excluding the cloth bound books? A great deal can be accomplished this summer and of course Valborg will work right along with me....

Thank you so much for giving me this opportunity. You know it will have my love and devotion and whatever can be accomplished by that will be accomplished.

> The idea of a companion volume to *Spiritual Interpretation of Scripture*[6] to be compiled from the work he had already given was later abandoned after two chapters were completed, one of which was subsequently incorporated into a revised *Living The Infinite Way*.[7] Joel's vision, however, did come to fruition in the material Valborg and I prepared from the Tape Recordings to be used for the *1971 Infinite Way Letters* on which we were working and which was to have been published under the title of *Living by the Word*. On September 11, 1981,

5 Nora Holm, *The Runner's Bible* (New York, N.Y.: Houghton Mifflin Co., 1913). An anthology of scriptural passages with brief commentaries.
6 Joel S. Goldsmith, *Spiritual Interpretation of Scripture* (San Gabriel, California: Willing Publishing Co., 1947).

however, after asking Emma Goldsmith for permission to use Joel's letters to me in this book, permission was refused, and I was dismissed as editor of The Infinite Way Writings, and its publication was abandoned.

June 26, 1955

Dear Joel,

...I'm really working....You thoughtfully said speed was not important, yet here I am, driven as never before—an inner impulsion that will not let me rest. Something pushes me, and I just go through the motions but with constantly increased momentum, or so it seems. There is no burden but just an indescribable sense of urgency that keeps me working constantly now that school is out. It's becoming a sort of round the clock thing with five or six hours out for sleep, a couple of hours of work, a half hour or so of relaxation in the form of a walk to the lake, listening to part of a Recording, or a bite to eat, then a couple more hours of work and so on with only an occasional telephone call to interrupt, except for the hours in our room downtown. When the typing stage is reached, more reasonable hours will have to be followed on account of the neighbors who do not appreciate the noise that my little typewriter makes, but there will be plenty of scribbling that can be done at odd hours.... The healing work ought to be good because my mind certainly is "stayed on God" doing this work— it doesn't get off that subject for five seconds. That's really the best part of it. Yes, everything seems to point in one direction.

Did you ever see anyone who moved forward out of her old groove leaving her professional career to do Infinite Way work with such deliberation and slowness? Sometimes it seems to take forever for me to take another step because I wait for the "push." The only saving part is that usually a step, when

7 Joel S. Goldsmith, *Living The Infinite Way* (New York, N.Y., Harper & Row, 1961).

taken, is forward and does not have to be retraced. So things are happening. There's a movement going on inside. No need to talk of it, but when it finally leads to action, you will know.

If you have a minute, let me share with you one of these simple pleasant experiences that is an evidence of Grace. We've had our Webcor tape recorder almost three years and while it has been reasonably satisfactory, it has always been "tubby" and has had far too much bass in playing right to left. Recently it has seemed to be on its last legs so much so that we've had to have the Revere on hand just in case it decided to puff its last. It finally did puff its last. Yesterday was our first opportunity to take it to the factory way over on the West Side, and we were there bright and early.... The repairman who remembered me took it and said, "Well, if you had brought this next Monday, you would have had to turn around and go right back, and with your machine, too. You're just in time. We're closing this noon for a two weeks' vacation, but if you'll wait now, I'll see what I can do."

He worked on it for an hour and a half, brought it out from the shop and said, "Now, let's see what your grief is going to be in the way of cost. I put two new heads on and two new tables (or whatever they call them). That's about $30 but wait and I'll find out." He talked to the manager, came back, and began writing a ticket while I stood there just rejoicing at how good it sounded and that he had finally repaired it satisfactorily. I began to reach for my checkbook when he said, "Here, give this slip to the watchman when you go out. There is no charge." Now can you imagine that? Wasn't the whole thing, just a simple incident, a beautiful reminder of "Thy Grace?" No thought, no planning, but everything perfect and perfectly timed. And is the machine good now! Just wonderful—much better than when brand new.

Lovingly yours,
Lorraine

July 4, 1955

Dear Joel,

Well, the die is cast, and here I am launching out onto the waters of the Infinite Invisible....With this final action is a feeling of release—not freedom from anything but only the freedom to do the work I cannot keep from doing. It isn't that I expect to be less busy or have more time, but now there will no longer be a division—every hour can be given to the practice of The Infinite Way. It was after Christmas that I knew this was coming and that I would resign [my position in Highland Park] but it has taken all this time for it to crystalize into action. There's been no jumping hastily into the thing but plenty of time to consider all aspects of it, and each time they add up to doing just this.

The end of the school year was the strangest one I have ever known. For the first time in 25 years I packed up all my personal belongings at school and took them over to Valborg's attic. Heretofore everything has always been left so that it would be ready for the next year. Now ten minutes at school will clear up any remaining business such as giving my good friends special materials I've collected for which I have no further use.

Class day, the last day of school, has always brought a lump to my throat, but this year for the first time I watched it all without one single emotion and all the time a song running through my head, "I'll never see this again"—no sadness, no joy, just a feeling that the end of the chapter has been reached. So today the final step has been taken, a chapter closes, and a new one begins. Now there is just a continuous dedication and a very humble prayer to be a good instrument so that this will not be in vain.

Tuesday, July 5, 1955

...Meditation is one of the greatest contributions of The Infinite Way to spiritual unfoldment, if not the greatest. To me it is the Way. That is what first drew me to The Infinite Way. It is surely right that a textbook on meditation should be an important part of Infinite Way literature. [*Joel had indicated that he was beginning to work on such a project.*] Nothing would be of more value to students. I remember so well, as if it were this moment, when I first met you. I had been meditating about seven years using a form, a rather beautiful form. You said, "Drop all that now and take this one idea, 'I and my Father are one.'" That was really the beginning of this wonderful experience. So if, through a book, you can give that to others, how marvelous it will be.

...*The 1955 Seattle Private Class* Tapes are out of this world and leave me speechless. One incident in connection with them interested me very much. I preface this by reminding you that I never was conscious of receiving "messages" or "getting" what you are teaching in some other place as so many people are. Well, as I listened to the recording of the class you must have given on Thursday in Seattle, I sat bolt upright. You were saying practically the same thing that had popped out of my mouth when I talked with Ray, (the principal of Ravinia School): "No one can do anything to us. We do it to ourselves." It was the same day (I have a note on it because it impressed me) and probably the same hour. So that's one time it must have come through consciously. Do you suppose I'm looking for that sort of thing more than I was?

Please do arrange to stop over here and be assured that if you do not wish to see anyone, nothing will be said about your being here. We'd love to have you give even one talk—you know—but whatever way you want it, let it be that way....

Lovingly yours,

Lorraine

Joel recognized that the decision to leave my professional
"nets" was entirely a spiritual one to be nurtured and
protected in the Silence and by living as a beholder of God
in action . In his letter came the welcome information
that he would stop off in Chicago August 8, not for any
group work, but solely to work with me.

July 20, 1955

Dear Joel,
     Thank you so very much for your letters. Yes, it was
quite a decision in one way; and in another, none at all. When I
picked up the telephone to call Chuck (my superintendent)
there was a complete vacuum for a second, and the same thing
happened when I mailed the official letter of resignation. It
was the natural culmination of not only five and a half years,
but of a lifetime. When I was a little girl and life was so very
difficult, I held almost continuously to "Eye hath not seen nor
ear heard the things that God hath prepared for them that love
Him," and eye hadn't seen. That's for sure.
                         Lovingly yours,
                         Lorraine

Well do I remember walking to the corner mailbox that
July 4th, pausing for a few moments, and then opening
the flap and thrusting my letter of resignation into it.
There was no awareness of time, no thought, just the no
thing-ness of a total inner silence at the momentousness

of that action. Years later, in a bit of reminiscing with Joel when I spoke of the total vacuum, he responded, "That was the healing—that vacuum."

That action was a complete surrender to and resting in the Infinite Invisible. No longer would there be a monthly salary check on which I could rely—there would just be God. Just God? What more secure reliance could there be? From that day on there was always a sufficiency and later "the twelve baskets" left over to share.

July 22, 1955

Dear Joel,

...You remember it was on July 4th that I gave up my position in Highland Park? Well, three days later the telephone rang and it was the superintendent of a suburb adjoining and just west of Evanston. He is a total stranger, never heard his name before. He wanted to talk to me about the principalship of a school in Glenview. When I told him I was not available and was doing some part-time editorial work, he still wanted to see me. So I went out and spent an hour with him in which he did all the talking, telling me how attractive the position was—more money than Park Ridge, nothing but supervision, a full time secretary, and I could arrange most meetings for the day so that I would not have to be out at night. I never said a single word about myself, just that it was all in my papers on file at Northwestern University. Well, today he called again and hoped I would come and sandwich in the editorial work because he thought I could "make a unique contribution" to Glenview.

I told him it was out of the question for this year, that he wouldn't want someone whose loyalty and attention were divided, and I wouldn't want to accept a job into which I could not throw my whole heart and soul. But don't you think it's interesting?

It's important to me for three reasons. First and least important, it was fulfillment just to know the job was mine without question. Then it proved that the solution of the Park Ridge situation was a spiritual demonstration, for this time there was none of this "Should I?" or "Shouldn't I?" business. The answer was clear and simple, no hesitancy, and best of all no feeling of having given up anything—perfect freedom. Most important was the proving of several principles of The Infinite Way—that when one has God, the whole world comes to lay its treasures at one's feet, only then we don't want them.

Early in 1955 I began praying for those who to all intents and purposes were my enemies. I didn't pray for them so that something would come to me but only that there might be no barrier between me and my realization of God, and then I found myself really wanting to benefit them. Desirelessness entered in, too. Only one thing counted and look what came unsought! Don't you think it is beautiful? It helps me in my work with others to have seen the principle operating so unmistakably....

Speaking of reaction—I'm not living up to that aspect of the teaching very well for I'm reacting with great joy about your impending visit. If I don't settle down, you'll probably come along and send me into a tailspin. I'm so grateful for everything it is even worth a tailspin.

Lovingly yours,
Lorraine

August 8, 9, and 10, 1955, on his way to New York, London, Europe, South Africa, and on around the world, Joel stopped in Chicago to discuss projected books and the wider aspects of Infinite Way Activity. He brought with him transcripts of *The 1955 Chicago Private Class* and

The 1955 Kailua Study Group, Reel 17[8] asking me if I could use these as the basis for a book to be published by L.N. Fowler Ltd. in London. I was to have it ready in the next few months for him to take to this publisher while he was still in England. I gladly agreed to undertake the work, grateful that he would entrust me with such an important job. Almost immediately, he produced another set of papers, some unorganized bits of material on meditation his secretary had lifted out of some of his already published writings. As he showed these to me, he said somewhat plaintively, "I'm supposed to do a book on meditation for Harpers and this is all I have." Undaunted, my quick response was "Would you like to have me do it... gather together all pertinent materials from your tapes and some of your mimeographed material?" This offer met with a quick affirmative response in Joel.

These few days of Joel's sojourn in Chicago that August left me committed to the job of preparing two books of Joel's work for publication. Thus was launched the gruelling but rewarding work that consumed a great many of my working hours and encroached on time would normally have been given over to sleep.

Joel also agreed to talk to the students in Chicago. Interestingly enough, the time chosen for that meeting happened to be the first anniversary of the opening of the Infinite Way Study Center. This memorable talk was later incorporated in *The 1974 Infinite Way Letter* under the title "Peeling off the Onion Skins."

On the final days of his visit, we drove out into the country for luncheon at Honey Bear Farm, at which time I shocked him with a philosophy that has carried me over many rough places: "Expect the best but be prepared for the worst."

8 The above mentioned transcripts were to be used as the core of a book for the London publisher, L.N. Fowler which was finally entitled *Practicing the Presence*, (London: L.N. Fowler, 1956; an enlarged edition in New York: Harper & Row, 1958).

The long drive gave me an opportunity to tell Joel more about my early years, how much bickering and quarreling went on in our home between our mother and father. Finally, shortly before my eleventh birthday our mother abruptly announced that she was leaving our father and taking us with her to Chicago. Early the next year divorce proceedings were begun. For a few years our father paid alimony and then stopped, insisting on a settlement.

For years we struggled, living from hand to mouth, because my father had no sense of responsibility about providing for his children and seemed not to care what happened to them. The story of Jesus taking the tribute money out of the fish's mouth much impressed me. I believed it totally, feeling certain that it could be the experience of anyone who truly accepted such a possibility. I was in a quandary, however, because we never had fish. My mother had spent two years in her late teens in Norway, her father's country. She had so much fish that she would never have it in the house after that experience. As mother pounded the round steak to make it tender, this 12 year old stood watching, fully expecting that the money we needed would somehow appear out of it. Such was the faith of a child and although there was no tangible miracle, perhaps the miracle was that we survived.

When I casually spoke about my father's never even mentioning his three daughters in his will and leaving them without a penny, adding, "It would have made a big difference then, but it doesn't matter now," Joel responded thoughtfully with, "No, not to you, but it does to him."

August 13, 1955

Dear Joel,

I'm still purring about the wonderful three days you were here. Thank you so much for all of it—the deep quiet hours, the hours of instruction, and for the hours when you were just you. Everyone was so grateful for your talk—and it is a honey. You're very good to me. Still say I'm the most fortunate person in the world. My consciouness can't be that good—it must be that good practitioner I have. He really knows his stuff.

Well, it's full steam ahead in high gear for me....I've been typing so fast and furiously that it would appear the Spirit is upon me—whole new words unknown even to Webster appear occasionally—but I'm afraid all that's happening is that my little finger gets anchored on the wrong key. That surely does things to one's spelling....What I would like to do is to go over the collected material with you when it has been organized ever so slightly so we can know what's going into the first chapter and so on....

If you don't think it's necessary or don't have the time, it's all right and I'll struggle along. Otherwise, if I can possibly get it assembled by August 25, I'll be in New York.

One hot summer morning in late August, Joel telephoned me from New York to tell me that a ticket was being held for me that very day at Midway Airport for an afternoon flight to New York on a huge Constellation plane.

Hurrying and scurrying around to make arrangements on such short notice for someone to take over the Study Center, to gather together manuscript materials, and to pack a small bag for the trip left no extra time to indulge in fear or concern about my first flight. But as I boarded the plane, this reassurance came to me: "He hangeth the earth on nothing."

At the hotel in New York, Joel's first words to me

were, "I have stolen your first chapter for the book on the Scriptures to use as the introduction to the American edition of *Living the Infinite Way*[9]. During those few days in New York, most of my time was spent doing the chapter "Meditation" for the same book. Of course, at lunchion and dinner, there were opportunities to talk and for instruction in the deeper aspects of the work. On one occasion, Joel became very quiet as he warned me, "There are three temptations every aspirant must face: money, sex, and death." My quick response was, "The first two pose no temptation to me, but I have never really come face to face with death, so I don't know how great a temptation that would be."

August 30, 1955

Dear Joel,

The return trip was beautiful, too, and already I feel like a seasoned air traveler. Proof? Instead of watching the clouds and land below—it was a bit hazy, so visiblity was not too good—I dug out the manuscripts and began studying them quite oblivious of the fact that I was in mid-air. But it is a thrilling experience—my first, and one I shall never forget.

All of it was thrilling—and that no one could possibly understand. To spend most of one's time in a hotel room struggling with a typewriter, and I mean struggling, and call that thrilling would surely earn for me the title of crackpot— but it was. It was the joy and satisfaction of fulfillment, of working on that which gives meaning to life. What more could one ask?

But there was more. I never cease to marvel at what a direct contact with you does for me. I should be used to it by now but it is one of those things that is always new. I don't feel

9 Joel S. Goldsmith, *Living The Infinite Way* (New York: Harper & Row, 1961).

it at the time so much as afterwards. In fact, at the moment I don't feel. I come full of questions, most of which are never asked. Nothing is said about the funny little things that trouble me. I long for moments of greater awareness, but those moments seem to recede and be more remote than ever. The few moments of meditation with you made me feel even more how empty I was; I think I hated for you to see it but knew you did. Then what happens? I return home; there are no more questions but in their place is awareness and renewed dedication.

Lovingly yours,
Lorraine

September 13, 1955

Dear Joel,

I rejoice with you in the good news in your letter. You have waited a long time and now comes the fruition. It must be a little like the lifting of the sword of Damocles and now there must be a greater sense of freedom—although I could never think of you as anything but free. Now to greater things—and may your joy be full.

Your card from London was a gentle reminder to hurry but be assured the work is going forward steadily. I haven't even taken time to write to you because of that. Every minute has gone into it, and sometimes under adverse circumstances as at present...

You said we'd need 100 typed pages for this enterprise. Right now it doesn't look as if it could be more than 75. If I had the other transcripts it would help, but so far none has come. To find the right tapes and then to take them off is so time consuming that it takes far more time than I should devote to that aspect of this particular project if you are to have it before you leave England. I have taken off some but do not have enough material... Is there anything I can do to get them? If it is not possible for me to have them, of course, I shall go along as I have been doing but you will have to understand why production is slowed down.

I heard your Sunday School tape for the first time the other day and was completely charmed. That is simply delightful, one of the sweetest things I have ever heard—great possibilities in it. I loved every word of it and heartily approved of your approach with children. From an old time school teacher that is high praise: delightful and charming!

I could not wish you anything better than that a little of the joy you have shed on others should be yours for then your cup will be truly running over. So be it. Always my loving thanks to you and my deep gratitude.

Lovingly yours,
Lorraine

September 24, 1955

Dear Joel,

...It is six years ago on September 28 that I first heard you talk and at five o'clock I had that never-to-be-forgotten interview with you which changed the whole course of my life....

September 28, 1949 is as clear and fresh as if it were this very moment—maybe it is, for it was a bit of eternity and that is for always—and the joy of it is with me. The joy has remained through even the darkest days. When I felt utterly forsaken, there was some little area of consciousness that kept me going forward. Many times it was pretty deeply hidden by the thick mass of self, nevertheless it was there, a kind of anchor, the joy that "no man taketh from you." Today for some reason or other the words with which my morning meditation always began for the five years preceding our meeting have come back to me with tremendous force:

I play my part with stern resolve, with earnest aspiration; I look above, I help below; I dream not, nor do I rest; I toil; I serve; I reap; I pray; I am the Cross; I am the Way; I tread upon the work I do; I mount upon my slain self; I kill desire; and strive, forgetting all reward. I forego peace; I forfeit rest, and in the stress of pain I lose myself and find my Self and enter into peace.[10]

I think it's happening. Strange that it must always be in the "stress of pain" that we lose ourselves and find the Self. My heart is always singing even though the notes are not always gay and light—underneath there is always a harmony, no matter how sad the strains may be.

Lovingly yours,
Lorraine

At 5:45 P.M. on October 10, Valborg and I completed the final proofing of the manuscript at the Infinite Way Center. We wrapped it for mailing, and I literally ran to the main post office in the Loop to reach there before it closed at 6:00 P.M. When I returned slightly out of breath, I heaved a big sigh of relief. A man who had been listening to one of the recordings said somewhat sanctimoniously, "It shouldn't be that way. Everything should move effortlessly and unhurriedly, all according to schedule."

The next time I saw Joel, when I told him about this rebuke from one of the students, his comment was, "Pay no attention. People like that have no idea of the demands made on those of us who give ourselves to the

10 From a Study Course provided by Alice Bailey's Arcane School.

world." Some people mistakenly believe that no work is
involved, that you wave a wand and "presto" it is finished.

                                        October 10, 1955

Dear Joel,

Well, here it[11] is: We shall be interested to know what you
think of it. While it has involved no "blood and no tears," there
has been sweat a plenty!!....

This letter would not be complete without my telling you
of what tremendous, immeasurable help Valborg has been in
going over the manuscripts with me, word by word, period by
period, and always making invaluable suggestions. She has
worked steadily day in and day out.

Thursday will see me taking a sun bath and just sitting!
Back to work on Friday. I've tried to convince Valborg that we
should drive down to White Pines State Park for a day, but she
says her back yard is just as pretty and lots easier to reach—so
I guess the back yard wins.

Valborg and I are fairly bulging with "principle."
Whenever anything comes up, we look at each other and say,
"What is the principle?" And it is always one found in the
manuscript. Being thoroughly grounded in these principles
does make it easier to apply them instantly to whatever
situation arises. The manuscript really should be called "The
Principles of The Infinite Way."

                          Lovingly yours,
                          Lorraine

                                        October 22, 1955

Dear Joel,

Thank you very much for your cable and letters....Yes, it
was hard work, very hard and continuous, and many times I
was weary, but there was a wonderful joy always with me....I'm

11 This refers to the completed manuscript of Joel's *Practicing the Presence*,
taken from the transcripts of *The 1955 Chicago Private Class* and *The 1955
Kailua Study Group, Reel 17*, ibid.

so grateful to be able to save you a little work and thus free you for the larger work....You may expect a great deal from those who work for you—although I have never felt that you were driving me; it was only myself and the work that were driving me. Strangely enough, working for you doesn't frighten me at all; it's only when I go off the beam and fail dismally in the spiritual way that I'm really scared. How well you know! Well, anyway, you may expect a great deal but you are most generous in your appreciation....

Yes, we've had a bit of a holiday. Where? Valborg's back yard won, and we had all of one lovely sunny day out in it.

Lovingly yours,
Lorraine

6

The Spiritual Bond: A Unique Relationship

The relationship between a spiritual teacher and an aspirant on the Path is always a special one. It is warm, tender, and loving, yet withal impersonal. It involves complete trust on the part of the aspirant and an unimpeachable integrity in the teacher. The whole relationship has but one object: the opening of the student to an awareness of that I within that is the real master. The teacher is the guide on that journey, pointing the way and sharing his light to reveal the Light within. A little of that closeness can be glimpsed in some of these letters.

November 1, 1955

Dear Joel,

Thank you for your letter and all the good news in it....
Thank you, too, for sending the woman asking for help to me. Immediately a warm, friendly note was sent to her but I have not heard from her yet. It reminded me of my own experience with an occult group and of the man who really started me on the Path thirteen years ago. When he suggested a certain physical discipline and I demurred because I doubted my ability

to fulfill the requirement, being just a cream puff at heart and having no will power, he said, "Don't tell me that. Anyone who could resist what you have resisted has a will of iron." He didn't know it wasn't will at all, just a conscious resting in God's love that made me impervious to all attempts to manipulate my mind. Only once was I awakened in the night with the distinct feeling of being "worked on." I immediately laughed out loud at the idea of being touched by any such superstitious belief that human thought could touch me for good or evil.

How strange the world is! The educational world won't let me alone. Today a letter from a professor of education at the University of Illinois—never heard of him before—inviting me to participate in a critical analysis of a projected publication, an encyclopedic anthology designed for young people. Isn't it interesting the way these forms of recognition and opportunities for service persist in coming to me now that they are of no importance?

I can't end this hodge-podgey letter without telling you how glad I am that you are going to hold forth in Steinway Hall [in New York]. Would love to be there and it may be possible. Never a day passes that I do not pause in gratitude for the great freedom God has given me so that whatever the call might be, it would only be my own stupidity, stubbornness, or lack of perception that would make me fail to answer it. It is very wonderful to be without ties. My only tie is the deep love and devotion between Valborg and me, but in it is a perfect freedom to come and go and only the desire that each find fulfillment in her own way or rather in God's way. Surely this gift of spiritual freedom is Grace made manifest. Never a day passes, and many times during the day, that a deep hymn of praise and gratitude does not well up within me for it. Few people are so deeply blessed as to have that rare combination of love, understanding, and freedom. Best of all I know its Source.

Do you know what helped me most in realizing that freedom? The last chapter in *The Third San Francisco Lectures*[1]. But with every gift comes a responsibility and with this one it is the responsibility to use it wisely to fulfill Its purpose in me. That is my prayer: to follow where it leads....

Lovingly yours,

Lorraine

The recurrent inner strivings boiled over in a number of letters to Joel, typical of which is part of the one of November 17, 1955....

Yesterday we thought of you in spring-kissed South Africa...It recalled to me last spring when the trees here were bowed down with a profusion of blossoms and our beautiful drive into Michigan.... Your work in far away South Africa is a glorious triumphant journey. There must be moments though when you have longed for your little house by the side of the ocean and all that it symbolizes. It all has a fairy-book quality about it. That is not too strange a way to put it since back of every fairy story there are the deepest truths.

The work on the Harper book [*The Art of Meditation*] has been moving slowly, but moving. It seemed so hard for it to take any kind of shape but things are beginning to cook now....Yesterday a most wonderful vision of the last chapter came from a study of Kailua #3[2]. Don't you think it would be beautiful to end with a chapter on meditation as a band of Christ-consciousness around the world?... There is a meditation on "God so Loved the World"[3] that is very moving and Soul-stirring. That is the time indelibly engraved on my

1 Together with The First and Second San Francisco Lectures it was published under the title *The World Is New* (New York: Harper & Row, 1962).
2 The 1955 Kailua Study Group, Reel 3.
3 The 1953 Second New York Closed Class, Reel 2.

memory—two years ago this Thanksgiving—when you really put me in my place and annihilated all there was of Lorraine except for some roots that die but slowly. That was the toughest lesson I have ever had to take, except for those silent struggles one has all alone....The road had been pretty rocky these days—outwardly very satisfactory but an inner strife precipitated by apparently unimportant incidents.

You speak often of Jesus having Judas with him right up to the Crucifixion, and for a long time that was a great comfort, but no longer. If everything is taking place within our own consciousness, then Judas must have been a part of the consciousness of Jesus. So, if I am having Judas-experiences, then there must be Judas in my consciousness. I can't blame the Judases, not any of them. That is a very hard saying, and long searching has not revealed to me just what within me is externalizing in that form. Of course, we never do see ourselves with clear perspective, although I try so hard to look at myself clearly and relentlessly and do not try to spare myself. Is the secret to recognize Judas as a universal belief and see through that to the Christ-identity which *must* be the reality of Judas as well as of Jesus?

A week from today it is Thanksgiving. No matter how difficult the way, the vision is beautiful beyond all words, and I am blessed even to have glimpsed it. The storms may come and go but now there is an anchor inside that holds me securely to my moorings even though I may be battered no end by the buffetings of the angry sea. So to you now, as always, my love and most grateful thanks for making every day Thanksgiving Day.

And in another letter of November 24, 1955:

This business of the self is so subtle that it creeps in all unaware, and we find ourselves thinking, "I can do something or be something," and then one reaps the whirlwind. Guess we should be glad for that if it brings us back on the beam....

The toughest part is that there are no scapegoats, no one to blame but oneself. When the thought of forgiveness came, there was no one to forgive—not even the satisfaction left that I could be good and holy about forgiving someone, no enemy to pray for save only one—"I," yes "I" was the enemy....Once again you are probably in stitches, laughing at me and not taking it a bit seriously—after all you've already learned this lesson and it must be as funny as marveling at first graders struggling with one plus one are two when we already know the multiplication table.

The thing that set me on the downward road this time was a feeling that what was most needed was a greater revelation of God and with this intense desire the sense, "Why, Lorraine, you haven't the remotest idea of what this is all about. You've been working all this time and not only have you not set your foot upon the first rung of the ladder, but you haven't even seen the ladder." That was followed by an inner probing and Soul-searching which proved disturbing because of what was revealed....Thank you for understanding all my foolish struggling.

December 4, 1955

Dear Joel,

One thing is certain, and that is if you just continue this gallivanting around the world, we'll all be educated on the postal rates to any place at all. Still don't know what it is to New Zealand or Australia but next time—! Thank you for the good letter and the many, many cards. It is a joy to hear about the progress of the work, but even more to know how very satisfactory this trip has been for you and what a wonderful kind of fulfillment. And now you are a world figure! Nice to remember that some of us always stood a bit in awe of you—even in the early days—and not just now when everybody seeks you out.

This is my first opportunity to write in over a week and it is just as well, for the easy peaceful gently flowing stage, that lightness that comes with a relaxing in the Spirit, hasn't been reached yet—still swimming to keep my head above water, but it's all right, heaviness and all. "This too shall pass away.".…

Enjoy Japan, have fun, and may home be the sweeter to you upon your return. Always my deepest thanks and love to you,

Lorraine

December 15, 1955

Dear Joel,

Thank you for your letter from India. It was waiting for me upon my return from a day's jaunt to Champaign in regard to the new encyclopaedia.

Your trip must have been the highlight of your career—but isn't it wonderful to be home again? Was it ever so sweet?.…Yes, I hear you. You are all ready to turn your attention to the new book on meditation! A considerable amount of material, although by no means exhaustive, has been assembled for it—still lots to be culled. However, most of it has not been welded together into any kind of a unity. It has merely been allocated to the proper folder. There is more material to come that should be used. I am about ready to begin working now on one chapter at a time to bring unity out of a great variety of material that is taken from many different sources of your work....

How long is the book on meditation to be? What is the *latest*, last, and final moment you must have it? It's been slow going because the work is quite unpatterned, but now it is beginning to take shape, but you know how much remains to be done after that stage has been reached. I do try to meet deadlines and will endeavor to have it in your hands when you need it. I know you will want to do some work on this in the form of adding to and cutting out what has been included thus far. It will be helpful to have some time for me to mull it over after it is in tentative form so that it can be made as perfect as possible....

This must be an especially joyous Christmas for you for so many reasons. May your cup of joy be as full as grateful hearts can make it.

Lovingly,
Lorraine

January 10, 1956

Dear Joel,

Happy New Year! Wonderful days lie ahead—continued expansion and ever new and more beautiful experiences....

You ask me to help bring the assurance to the world that the things of this world are not power....You must feel how deep is that desire within me. Sometime ago I would have said, "This is my very life; this has my complete devotion," but it seems that there isn't a "my life" anymore—at least no consciousness of it, nor any opportunity to indulge it—just a continuous flow of activity, unplanned, but not without plan. True, no matter how continuous the activity, there is never the feeling of doing enough, no resting satisfied—the goal is so tremendous that any effort seems very feeble. I'm sure there is more I can be doing, so please tell me what it is so that love, devotion, and service may bear fruit richly.

Lovingly yours,
Lorraine

At this point Joel sent me the transcript of a tape which he asked me to make into a monthly *Letter*.

January 29, 1956

Dear Joel,

Here is "The Beholder."...   This article really has everything—it's a wonderful message and should have wide circulation.

Thanks so much for your letter relative to the income tax. I shall report the income from the practice [which consists of voluntary contributions. I have always considered these contributions *not* tax deductible, and therefore I report them and pay a tax on them even though no charge is made and no bills ever sent out] along with the other receipts from our room and subtract the expenses from this.   Doesn't that sound sensible?

You are a great comfort—at times. Thank you.

Lovingly yours,
Lorraine

February 9, 1956

Dear Joel,

A letter from Bettie Burkhart tells me she is transcribing *The 1953 First Portland Closed Class*. That is wonderful!...

Work, work, work. Now it is all so plain that there aren't enough hours to stay with it [*The Art of Meditation*] and watch it take form. I can see the whole thing finished now—but it is far from that. I expect to have Part I, about sixty pages, ready for you in New York, and also Part III. These will show the direction the book on meditation is taking so that you can see how you like it. As I see it now, the second part will consist of meditations, and they can be worked on later and will not alter the theme and development of the book. Love to everyone and thank you always.

Lovingly yours,
Lorraine

Another milestone for me came about through my going to New York in March to attend Joel's *First* and *Second 1956 Steinway Hall Closed Classes* and the two *1956 Steinway Hall Practitioners' Classes*. During this period, severe physical problems beset Joel; but despite them, he kept up his ever-busy schedule, so busy that none of the students was even aware of what a difficult time it was for him.

Often after the evening class, Joel and a dozen or so students including Emma Lindsay, walked over to Schrafts or Hicks, a short distance from the hotel, for ice cream or hot chocolate. On one such occasion Joel faltered and was urged to return to the hotel. But he went on ahead undaunted, refusing to accept the appearance of weakness.

In addition to the healing work, the two classes a day, the appointments, the never-ending mail, Joel made room on six different afternoons to meet with the "25" Group, which had been brought into being as the fulfillment of his dream of a circle of Christhood that would encompass the world and lift human consciousness out of itself into Christ-consciousness. By the end of the classwork in March, this group, which at its inception consisted of twenty-five people, was expanded to thirty-three, and by the end of the year after Joel's classes in England, Europe, South Africa, and Australia, it numbered approximately two hundred.

Joel was accompanied on this trip to New York by Emma Lindsay, who for some time had been responsible for making the Tape Recordings in Hawaii and who now, for the first time, had a real opportunity to meet the students on the Mainland. Although I had had correspondence with her and had heard a great deal about her from Joel, it was, of course, our first face to face meeting and our first opportunity to become acquainted. It was my privilege to have breakfast with Joel and Emma Lindsay, and Eileen Bowden whom I met for the first time. Eileen had become interested in Joel's work early in 1950 and was already involved in giving Infinite Way classes in her area. This activity has broadened into a world-wide activity that has continued to this very day, thereby making her one of the pioneers of The Infinite Way.The month in New York at the Barbizon Plaza Hotel also gave me an opportunity for many delightful visits with other students, who enthusiastically talked about how much The Infinite Way meant to them, how they had found it, and other experiences leading them to this Message.

One afternoon Joel called me to come to his suite where I found Paul Brunton and Emma with him. Long before I met Joel I had read every book this prolific writer had written, so it was a special pleasure to meet the man who had played such a significant role in my spiritual awakening. I told him how much his books had meant to me, to which he responded with a touch of sadness in his voice, "My works seem to get people started on their way, and then they leave them when they find the teaching which is for them."

Another morning when I went for an appointment with Joel, I found him with the proofs of *Practicing the Presence*[4] on which he commented, "This is the simplest of all the books," after which there was a long pause as if I were to digest that remark. It left me quite crestfallen and with a sinking feeling in the pit of my stomach that we had failed completely in assembling the material for the book, editing it, and preparing it for publication. Then he added, "But it is also the deepest."

April 12, 1956

Dear Joel,

Thank you for a very beautiful and deep spiritual experience in New York. It was a great joy to be there. The ensuing months will have to demonstrate its true depths....

You know, Joel, sometimes I think I'm a perfect fool to take your instruction so literally and follow each direction to the letter, especially when I notice how lightly and easily others take such instructions. All it does for me is to lose friends, fail to influence people, and give me a big headache, and a bigger heartache. It's not much fun.

A strange thing happened that last week of class, beginning early in the week. I, who never see visions and have inwardly bemoaned that fact, saw plainly and clearly an eye between your eyes and slightly above them—unmistakably "the third eye" or eye of Shiva. I gazed—stared is a better word—and every thing else was submerged save only this penetrating eye. Always the skeptic, I thought it might be an optical illusion even though it held me spellbound, until Wednesday

4 op. cit.

night at Hicks when you sat across the table from me within close enough range to preclude the possibility of illusion, and there it was again. As you talked, it seemed that eye was seeing through me—through every veil of illusion to the very center, and through it.

That night was very special for me. When you talked about actually seeing and companioning with Jesus Christ and the possibility of thus knowing any of the great mystics—past or present—a great longing came to me to have that experience, not only the "feeling" but the tangible reality. It seemed almost a possibility that very night. I went back to the hotel, got myself all cozy and comfortable, ready to sit up the entire night, if need be, waiting—waiting for the appearance of Jesus as a person. After quite a long time, I found I couldn't wait for that or for any form of God, even though I still want that experience. I had to wait only for God and nothing else—no person—and let God reveal Itself in and as whatever form or as no form at all. Did I miss the way at that moment? I waited a very long time, and what happened? Oh, Joel, it's awful, ludicrous, and disgusting. After several hours, I went to sleep in the chair! So close and yet so far. That's what I mean about my state of consciousness—I go just so far and then yield to some stupid suggestion such as sleep. What can be done about it?...

It was the desire for the mystical experience that brought me into The Infinite Way and if all the activity takes me farther away from it, I would give up all this work and go back to teaching school and spend every spare moment working toward that end. If there is any practice to be followed, please tell me, and at least let me have a try at it.

I know London will be a wonderful experience for you and The Infinite Way. Deepest thanks always.

Lovingly yours,
Lorraine

As I worked with Joel's writings, I came to see that the experience of seeing "the third eye" in him was the discernment of his Christ-identity. To make contact with any great spiritual light, whether someone since gone on or one living in this parenthesis, the contact must be made with God, and that contact will bring an awareness of whoever might be important to one's experience.

April 15, 1956

Dear Joel,

Your letter of April 12 just came and must have an immediate answer....

Strange that you would feel that you had offended me. The last day I was in New York I had a feeling of being a million miles away from you and not being able to get close at all—that you were completely inaccessible. I wondered what I had done to bring it about but could find no reason for the seeming barrier.

I know how great the demands were upon you. Everyone wanted to be "first" with you and to feel important and resented whatever stood in the way—a pretty little drama that unfolded before one's eyes. Perhaps I was so engrossed in watching it that you may have wondered at my detachment, but you know that I would not misinterpret anything you might do or say and certainly never feel slighted or hurt. There is too deep a bond for that. Surely you feel it, too. Of course I should love to have had more time to talk with you, but I didn`t expect that would be possible and so was not disappointed. So, Joel, no apologies—it seems that we have come to a place of understanding where words aren't necessary—that's always true when there is genuine understanding.

Thank you for liking the work done on the book on

meditation and for appreciating it. I have not done it for reward or recognition—to do a good job was all that mattered to me. That you were satisfied was joy enough for me. I'm very touched by what you say....

Do try to spare yourself a little on this trip. They will appreciate you just as much, and you have an important work to do.

Lovingly yours,
Lorraine

April 19, 1956

Dear Joel,

....In class that last Thursday night, the class that was just for me, or so it seemed, you said, "Your teacher will *never* leave you or forsake you." It is something not all the money in the world could buy, not all the wishing could bring to pass. You bring healing to hundreds, thousands of people, but this constant, continuous work you do, you do not give to many. It is what I used to dream of, pray for, and for seven years devoted every effort to finding until I met you—that someday there would be one who would reveal the hidden mysteries to me and lead me to realization.

But I could never have dreamed of the beauty, the love, and the depth of understanding of that relationship. It is unique, beyond human knowledge, and something no books have adequately described. There is the deepest love, but so different from the ordinary human concept of love that it is hardly the right word to use. It is a givingness of oneself completely, and the only reason one could ever want anything or desire to be or have anything is that there would be more to give. It is complete freedom in which no single trace of possessiveness enters. It is gentleness and sternness all in one, quietness and confidence in the midst of a divine unrest....I value what you have given me above everything in life. You have shared your deepest, most priceless treasures, the fruit of countless lives of effort, aspiration, and striving....

Lovingly yours,
Lorraine

April 20, 1956

Dear Joel,

Your last letter was so beautiful and lifted me so above this world that I neglected to take up a number of practical points:

Thank you for sending the people to me for help that you have sent. I'll try not to let you down. It's strange but sometimes I think I'm far better known away from home than on my own home ground. Often in one day there are as many and sometimes more telephone calls from out of town than in town.

I can't do a weekly talk yet—too busy. I think I'm avoiding it, dread the thought of it. If I just get sufficiently convinced of that, I'll *have* to do it—can't run away from anything.

Tackling the middle part of *Meditation* has been difficult. I guess I couldn't see how it could equal the rest of the material. I'm working hard on it—really sweating it out and yet it's tough going. The book you sent *Into God*, (thank you very much), did the trick and gave me quite a push forward.... It seems like such a labored attempt to be erudite and somehow it is quite "dead" for me. I love your directness and simplicity which have tremendous force. Yes, a boy with a grammar school education! I'll trade you!!! You could have all the education and degrees I have if you could give me what you have. Think of the thousands of Ph.D.'s who know one tiny segment of knowledge thoroughly, but who don't know how to live, how to face life's problems, and who are of no use to themselves or anyone else. Yes, it is the Christ of you which does the works. Yes, and it was this Christ in you which touched me almost seven years ago and changed the whole course of my life. Blessed Joel to be such an instrument—yes, and blessed everyone who recognizes it.

I don't think *Meditation* can be ready for fall publication. I assume you are waiting to see what Harpers will do and I'm glad. The middle part has to be loved and petted just as the rest of it was, and so I'll do it as fast as possible and maybe that will be faster than we anticipate. The pattern of this section will probably be a little different and just what form it will take has not yet emerged, but it will as I get deeper and deeper into it and as you continue your work with me. I know how important that last part is in the completion of this project. So don't give up!

But honestly, Joel, these last few days I have really been overwhelmed by my own stupidity and obtuseness. It's just beginning to dawn on me—what you were trying to tell me in New York, and I couldn't see it. How many times you must have said, "Lorraine, Lorraine, I'm giving you the answer. Why are you so blind?" You remember my dissatisfaction with the amount of activity evidenced here? This continued until this last Wednesday when in a flash the whole answer came through with startling clearness. It was so clear that I almost said out loud, "Oh, that's what Joel was trying to tell me all this time." You said to me, "One healing, one soul opened to the Christ is proof of the principle and that is enough." I thought those were very nice words, but certainly not a satisfactory answer to my problem and merely showed that you didn't understand what I was trying to say.

Then Wednesday this came: "If the presence of the Christ

is here, this meeting is complete. If there were only <u>one</u> person present, and this one realized the Christ, it would be a perfect, full, and complete meeting because there is only one. The Christ is fulfillment." I'm ashamed to admit it took this long of your oft-repeated words to register, but, so help me, I think they have, and for heaven's sake, bring me up short if I ever again talk about numbers. I never used to think you were rebuking me, but your patience this time is almost too much to have expected. I don't know how I could have been so slow in catching on. Aren't you surprised that I didn't *feel* this before?

I'm glad that you have arranged for the publication of the class books. They will be delivered as per your schedule. That you know. So happy to work on them. Now the work stacks up as follows: finish *Meditation*, next, one of the class books, plus what miscellaneous projects you think up, or if you don't, I probably will. Sounds simple, doesn't it? So clean and clear cut!!!

Working three periods a day with the realization of the Christ as you have directed is proving quite a marvelous experience. The scope is limitless. Also, attaining the realization of the Christ before attempting any healing work is the key.

Sunday evening, April 22:

....Thank you for your last letter which came Saturday. For heaven's sake, what is the matter with London? Every time you get there, you talk as if you would never teach another class. Is it that London fog that has you in tow?

I'm glad that Emma and W. kept you "hedged in." You can't possibly see all the people who want to see you and have anything left to give to the real work. People can wear one

down pretty fast. Right now, I'm very weary of people and
think the world would be such a lovely place if there were no
people....

Lovingly yours,
Lorraine

May 6, 1956

Dear Joel,

Thank you for your always good letters. It means so
much to have them. Three cheers for the new union. [Joel
proposed a union to secure a 30 hour day and an 8 day week].
That's a wonderful idea, and I'm for it 100%. Your goal is a
trifle conservative though, don't you think? But then I know
you are a believer in gradualism in matters relating to labor
and economics and so would not advocate striving immediately
for the ultimate goal of 1000 years as one day. Do let me go to
work at once on it—when do I begin picketing the sun? I
always thought it would be interesting to walk back and forth
carrying one of those signs, "Unfair to unorganized Infinite
Wayers! Stand still, Sun, because here we come!" When a
union is in full operation, such unfortunate incidents as the
enclosed correspondence evidences will not occur.

All kinds of things are happening in The Infinite Way
these days. I'm organizing a new business. You see, you don't
keep me sufficiently busy. My new business is called:
CLEARINGHOUSE FOR HURT FEELINGS, INC.—EXPERTS
IN THE PAINLESS DEATH OF BRUISED EGOS—MAIL
ORDER CASES GIVEN SPECIAL ATTENTION—OPEN DAY
OR NIGHT—CABLE ADDRESS: O-U-C-H! Our motto is:
OUR SHOULDERS ARE BROAD....

One other interesting bit, and I'll stop. While I was in
New York, I was sent a contract for next year from school with

a very nice increase. Of course, I knew the answer long before I received it, but it was a little bit of a temptation because, in retrospect, that life is so easy. However, I wrote to the superintendent turning it down. The point I want to make is that when my principal heard of my decision he was furious. I thought he would be so happy to be rid of me after the showdown I had had with him before the Board of Education three years ago. No, he was furious because I'm not going to be back and told one of my former co-workers, "I was counting on her." What I want to emphasize is the completeness of that healing. The last two years I was in school I spent every available minute praying for him and for the superintendent until I was *completely free* within myself. I remember I used to live with "The Wisdoms." Every bite of food I consumed during the blessed noon hour alone was accompanied by "The Wisdoms." And by that practice every trace of animosity in him was destroyed without a word from me, but in the silence.

May 19

I'd love to have seen the letter you wrote B.T. Surprising how such a sweet, gentle person as you are can let forth such terrific bolts of lightning and deafening claps of thunder. Isn't it marvelous to see how sure of themselves some people such as B.T. are? They never have any doubts, do they? I'm afraid I say that a little longingly, although I know better. I have a couple of characters here who are cut in the same pattern, and if that weren't enough, a promise (quite unsolicited, I assure you) from B.T. while she was in New York that she would be in Chicago this summer. The implication was that she would more or less take over and really make things hum around these parts! Of course we could use a little dynamite here with

profit, but I prefer your kind. Ah, me! How bright and rosy
school teaching looks by comparison—or retiring to a cottage in
the country. I begin to see that the real sacrifice is to remain in
the world rather than to leave it. The monastic life (not your
concept of it, but the ordinary expression of it) would be no
advantage, because it makes my hair stand on end to think of
the number of weird people who would be cooped up together,
but the life of a hermit—well, maybe it has something to
commend itself to us....

June 8, 1956

Dear Joel,

Your cablegram arrived just as I was getting ready to
mail your copy of the manuscript to you. Now I shall mail a
copy to B. at the same time. Thank you.

Into this book on meditation has gone your most beautiful
work—and that is really something! That is why it is so
inspiring—the highest moments you have reached have found
their way into print on these pages. I hope you like our
arrangement of material and are satisfied, *but*, and this is very
important, if there are things you do not like and which you
would like to have changed, please do not hesitate to let me
know and let me work on it some more. I love it as it is, but
with your deeper insight you may, and probably will, discover
ways in which it can be improved. It will not discourage me to
have to make any changes you may wish to have made.

Thank you for suggesting that I take a vacation, but I
don't really need one. I will take just enough time to get the
apartment clean—three days or so, and to catch up on the work
on the encyclopaedia—I'm five volumes behind on that, but
they were very understanding when I wrote asking for an
extension of time. A few days will take care of that. But I

guess the horse is so broken in that it knows only one way to go, for in spite of the above, I've already begun thinking about *The Master Speaks*[5], and am going to get started on that tonight—can't keep away from it. Isn't that something? I eat, sleep, and drink this—as it is the meat that perishes not.

I appreciated very much your first cablegram, too, and your kindness in trying to keep me from being disturbed over our friend B. That was very dear of you.

You know, Joel, one of the most beautiful things about working on this book [*The Art of Meditation*] has been the way the right material has always been at hand when it was needed. When I came to doing the last chapter which happened to be the one on relationships, I was stumped. It seemed that everything important on that subject had already been included in *Practicing the Presence*, and quite naturally I didn't want to repeat and use the same material. And then it began to come— first this manuscript, then that recording, and finally no one came down to our Center so that I had several uninterrupted hours when it just fell into shape, first one paragraph and then another and so on. An attempt has been made to have sufficient variation to each chapter so that the danger of sameness and monotony is avoided also.

Thank you for giving me the opportunity of working on this subject. It has been a great privilege and joy. Much love and devotion have gone into our small part in this work. Everyone connected with it has expressed unlimited love.

I'm impatient to get started on the next job and await your orders.

Lovingly yours,
Lorraine

---

5 op. cit.

June 12, 1956

Dear Joel,

No news, but just wanted to say "hello" and that I'm here....

Thank you for your card regarding group meditations on "Power is in Cause, not effect." We are using it for every meeting. There is tremendous power in that short statement; it brings closer than ever that vision of a united band of Christhood around the world. I would like some seed thought regularly or frequently for every student to work with. Who can measure what it will mean to have students around the globe pondering anything as potent as that! Thank you for this wisdom.

The last few days my own meditation has been powerful— it always comes in the degree of my being "nothingized" and feeling a complete zero and inadequate. There has been a wonderful sense of closeness, an ineffable peace, and Lorraine is very much in the background. With it comes an inward calmness and a conviction of a new step forward to be taken very soon— the next horizon is looming in the distance and I can't rest until I reach it. Until the last few days I was sleeping the sleep of the dead—not even awakening for a 3 o'clock meditation, only awakening when called during the night. But now for several nights there has been little sleep—enough, but with sufficient alertness for long periods of communion and an exhilaration that could come only from drinking of the water of life.

Lovingly yours,
Lorraine

July 4, 1956

Dear Joel,

This brief note to you is to mark the anniversary of a very important moment in my experience. It is just a year since I picked up the receiver, telephoned Chuck, my superintendent, and told him I was not going to be back on the job. I can still remember the complete vacuum of that moment and the moment when I posted the letter that would make it official.

A year has passed and one so full that there has not been even a minute in which to evaluate the effects of that decision, but there has never *once*, no, not even for one fleeting second, been a regret or a doubt as to its wisdom. There have been frequent periods of dissatisfaction with myself and my use of this opportunity. Well, I had to share this anniversary with you.

Just a few days ago, and writing about school calls it to mind, the superintendent at Park Ridge called again, asking me how the book was progressing and then, "We need a principal!" I told him that I wasn't considering such activity even though he was quite insistent. He ended the conversation by saying, "Well, next year, we'll have another one for you." Amazing, isn't it? Give up desire and the whole world comes— only then it is meaningless and we don't want it. The thing that makes me happy about this is that it makes it clear to me that I am giving of myself, not just when there isn't anything else to do. When the choices come to me I can turn from them without a moment's hesitancy and know that my life belongs to God, to serve in whatever way God gives me to serve. Guess it's wrong even to say, "I am giving," because I really didn't have any choice in it. Oh, Joel, if only I can be selfless enough to let God use me completely every moment! That's all I can ever pray for.

Thank you for reading this and please don't bother to answer it. I just wanted to talk with someone very close and near to me, and you're it. Yes, I have felt your closeness very much, especially during your flight across oceans and continents.

Lovingly yours,
Lorraine

July 16, 1956

Dear Joel,

...If you're concerned about the phenomenal growth of The I.W., I have news for you. Just put your little heart at rest—we have a nice little oasis in this tremendous upsurge of activity. We just chug along, remaining more or less stable, not that that should be encouraging for you, but if you are concerned about the opposite, you can take comfort in our lack of numbers. Nobody comes stomping down our doors. Golly, these other people surely must have the consciousness.

You would have been proud of your student this weekend though. When I saw the fine turn-out, and temptation would have me pleased, I said to myself, "What of it? Didn't you just recognize that the realization of the Christ is the infinity of all numbers? If there is only one person, what difference does it make whether or not that one appears as one, or 30, or 300?" So what was there to be pleased about! Once in a while an idea penetrates this thick layer of humanhood!

I do see the problem, though [The possible attempt of zealous students to organize The Infinite Way]. All I hope is that The Infinite Way never becomes too respectable, fashionable, or the thing to do! It's never been my lot to be on that side of the fence—just a born nonconformist. Can it be that there are many people really interested in *God alone*?

I wondered a long time about the people who come and then go to other teachings. Maybe it's because we inevitably draw a certain portion of malcontents and also the more adventuresome come seeking the excitement of new forms. They don't realize what it means to "die daily." When they glimpse it, they made a hasty exit.

Lovingly yours,

Lorraine

On July 24, 1956, Joel asked me to take over editing the monthly *Letter*.

July 27, 1956

Dear Joel,

...You know that I shall love doing the *Letter*....You can talk over the *Letter* work with me when you come in October and give me fuller instructions. Can it all be done as per schedule? It has to be, so I guess that's the answer. I'm very grateful for the pattern my parents established by their own example. Neither my father nor my mother knew the meaning of the word "impossible." In all the years Mother was with us, I never saw anything stump her; she was persistence personified. So maybe their example, and especially hers, penetrated a little, plus an understanding now of *why* the work given me to do can always be done and that, therefore, nothing ever is impossible.

Lately the only thing that has been slowing me up has been the healing work, much of which has been quite satisfactory. It has kept me busy, but more than that is the fact that severe cases of the world's incurable diseases in acute stages have been hitting up against me. It never makes me anxious, but sometimes it takes a long time for that peace to come and even then the effects have not always been forthcoming. You always say that these things don't come to us to be met unless we're ready for the experience, and it must be so. The fact that complete harmony hasn't been revealed, though, makes me realize that some way or other I'm falling down. Certainly there is a sense of helplessness and an awareness that I can't and don't do it, but there is also the necessity of staying on the job until *realization* of what *is* comes. I accept it as a call to go up higher, but sometimes it

seems as if I have an awfully long distance to go....
Lovingly yours,
Lorraine

August 2, 1956

Dear Joel,

Thank you for your letter and all that is in it. Your message on healing came before the letter and helped to break the spell which for a short time had me hypnotized into feeling there *must* be results. Of course, then, the next step is to look for them—fatal. I can see the reason these "deep" problems have been coming to me, because they really force me to go deeper and deeper within as nothing else does. The temptation has been to write to ask you to help me with specific cases, but it came to me very strongly that there was no time like now to fail if complete failure it was to be. Sounds crazy, but it had a wonderfully releasing effect....
Lovingly yours,
Lorraine

Through the good offices of Frances Steloff, who was the owner of The Gotham Book Mart, Harper & Row accepted *The Art of Meditation* for publication on August 9, 1956. To show the value she placed on the work and as an inducement to Harpers, she agreed to take 1000 copies.

August 10, 1956

Dear Joel,

So you're in! That is wonderful. And when Harpers

really begins to move, it moves!...When I returned home after our meeting Wednesday evening, the manuscripts were there. So I got busy right away, sat up most of the night, and worked all day yesterday making every last possible check. Now it is in the mail with my blessing. Have you a little blessing for it, too? Oh, a great big one! Yes, that I can believe....

The Infinite Way is well on its way with all the arrangements you have made for getting it before the public. I'm not going to take a bit seriously your statement "even though I should disappear from the human scene"—hope I'm not whistling in the dark. I'm going to look on it as a bit of the dismal philosophy I used to have and which carried me through some rugged experiences: Expect the best, but prepare for the worst.

I must make your hotel reservations. Will you give me the date of arrival? Three cheers for our side—I expect to have brand new tires on my jalopy when I meet you! In *Living The Infinite Way* you make the statement about a third-hand automobile not honoring God very much or some such thing. Golly, what about a five-year—no, a six-year-old one? And I like it and am quite satisfied! What would I do with a new one—just to stand out on the street and move from one side of the street to the other to satisfy the rule relative to alternate parking? I don't think I approve of that statement in *Living*.

You ask me not to become so involved in the human work that I do not have adequate periods for appointments with you. But you know how involved *you* become, how many demands are made upon you. I cannot add further demands on your time with everyone clamoring to see you—much as I should like to do just that. I accept whatever comes to me.

Lovingly yours,

Lorraine

P.S. Later—I think that I have followed all of your instructions to the letter—except for one. You wrote me from London that a page was to be included saying: "Dedicated with gratitude to Lorraine Sinkler." This I did not include. You see, I know the principle and know that it operates. I ask for no recognition and certainly desire no credit for doing the work that was given me to do. Whatever was done through me was a pure offering of love. My greatest reward, if there is to be such, is that the book has been accepted. You must know by now that my whole heart and soul belong to The Infinite Way; all I ask is the opportunity to give to it whatever God gives me to give, to serve in whatever capacity I may be most useful. Yes, we are both grateful—you to see this crowning glory of your years of work and devotion given such recognition and this greater opportunity to reach the receptive consciousness, and I to be an instrument to lighten your work by putting this matchless teaching in such form as would make it acceptable to a large publishing firm. Little book, go far and wide!

August 13, 1956

Dear Joel,

For the third time in my memory it happened. Saturday night, there was once again that pool of blue shaped like an eye. I had gone down, way down, because no matter how great the faithfulness and persistence, certain problems that had come to me would not yield—and then this came. The problems are still there, although there was an abatement of the most pressing one, at least temporarily. If this was the real thing, shouldn't everything have been wiped out? And yet I can't doubt it this time. It was real and with it came such a peace, such a release, that it seemed that I could never again have concern.

I have read enough occult literature to know about the Eye. Remember in the New York class there was the Eye visible to me in the center of your forehead? It doesn't happen often, and as I say only three times the electric blue pool of light, but what does it mean for me? Does it *have* a meaning? Why does it come always after stress and strain and a complete surrender (temporarily) of the self? You know how little given I am to anything of this sort, and yet this time I'm sure. Couldn't have been just an optical illusion because even though I tried later on I couldn't reproduce it, given the same physical conditions. It came twice that night within a short interval, and then no more, and it lasted only a very short time—how short I would not know. Thank you for listening.

> Lovingly yours,
> Lorraine

Almost before this letter was in the mailbox it was borne home to me that the Eye was the realized presence of the Christ and could come only after a surrender of the little self.

August 23, 1956

Dear Joel,

What can I say? Your letter was waiting for me when I returned home last night at 10:30. There isn't any way to tell you what it meant to me—a great wave of comfort, warmth, love, and gratitude swept over me. Please lead me to "spiritual victory and spiritual vision and spiritual glory," as you promised in your letter. No matter how long it may be, please stay with me. Even temporary failure is worth it all.

Since your last letter which came on Monday, I've been abiding so closely in God—just in that wonderful, peaceful contemplation of God, which brings me such contentment and joy—that nothing has entered to disturb. Ah, yes, I know I have no life of my own, and least of all the right to be downcast, which is a form of pure unadulterated selfishness.

Please, Joel, it wasn't about me—yes, I suppose it was, if I'm honest. What happened was that suddenly no help came through for those who called on me—even what seemed like the simplest problem didn't yield. It wasn't that I was afraid of so-called serious ones, but I felt that I was such a failure. I didn't want anything for myself—Oh, yes, I did want to be successful in giving the help because of the patients, but I suppose also, Lorraine didn't want to be a failure either. No use to lie to myself. I knew there were countless people who did a lot better job than I had been doing in the last few weeks, who actually had little or no sense of dedication, and it didn't make sense. The only thing I could see was that maybe that part of the work wasn't for me, and this was the way it was being brought home to me. Yet, if it is a principle, and it is, why shouldn't it be available to anyone who understands it? So I knew in some way the principle was not being properly applied.

The help that has come through me had always been so effortless. I always dismissed the problem very quickly, and this time when the same calls came back over and over with no apparent results, I thought, "I must learn to stay with these calls until harmony is revealed." It seemed that what was required was greater self-discipline on my part. What happened? In doing just that I began straining and struggling and lost the way. So now after this unhappy discursiveness I'm back where I belong, breathing free air once again. And it feels so *good*!

The Way is straight and narrow—rugged. I don't mind any of that; I don't "kick against the pricks"; I can take it; and there'sno reason to look back. Always I have known, since I was a child, that something like this would be my lot. The particular form it would take was not clear, but there never was a doubt that there would be some part of my life lived in and for God.

I used to be sad that I couldn't embrace Catholicism and give myself wholly to some such form of service, even though their outward display of sacrifice and the wearing of such dismal habits repelled me, and there were grave doubts as to the genuine spirituality of many such lives. So it was natural that this life should come to me, even though it was long in coming. Everything that went before was a preparation and, therefore, involved no sacrifice so far as I am concerned. Even when I am most tired—and that hasn't been mastered yet, but surely will come—and when pressed on from all sides, it is still a completely satisfying way of life. Yes, even the dark moments can be endured. It's good it is that way, because there is none of the martyr in me and little patience with so-called martyrs. Even being alone much of the time leaves, or carries with it, no sense of loneliness. There seems to be very little feeling one way or the other about myself as a person.

It was the failure to be an instrument for healing that threw me off the beam and now I see the reason for failure. Your other letter awakened me to that—looking for results, trying to realize God, then "peeking" to see if anything happened.[6] Now I'm staying with *Is*, and that is all, disregarding appearances, good, bad, or indifferent....

By relaxing more in the infinite Sea of Spirit maybe that hard shell which is unconcerned by appearances will develop. But speaking of hard shells, in spite of everything, underneath you're the greatest "softie" in the world. It's very comforting. Now don't get tough with me just because of that to "show me." I've felt you with me so much these last few days.

With much love,

Lorraine

6 Joel's letter to me is found in *Man Was Not Born To Cry*. (New York: The Julian Press, 1964). Pp. 89-90.

August 31, 1956

Dear Joel,

...Your sketch of your own valley experiences[7] was pretty moving. Yes, you had the Vision—and what is more, the courage to pursue it. You have a story the world should know. Can't you see how it would give others courage? I had such a feeling of awe—not a new sensation in regard to you, but accentuated. What a guy!...When I hear about you, I wonder if I have what it takes. I've had plenty of hardships myself— actual want of the barest necessities, and that for long, long periods. Funny, I never lost my faith through all of that—and it was tough—but when smoother sailing was my lot and I got "smart," agnosticism took over. But I guess that, too, was God, because it freed me from the superstitious fear of "wrong thinking" or somebody's malpracticing me or the virtue of performing any ritual such as reading a daily lesson.

I *think*, Joel, I'd be willing to pay any price for what I want more than anything there is in "this world," but only when the test comes would I ever be sure. I remember falling, falling endlessly, a year ago last Christmas—that was the toughest—but it was worth it. It was the beginning! Knowing that and what came from it, I should welcome a repetition of it—but I don't. You see, I don't like those dark moments.

Thank you for your little postscript about Hawaii's being in my teacup for next winter. This is very strange. Several days before your letter came, maybe a week earlier, I *knew* I would be going to Hawaii next winter—not the dates, but everything else was crystal clear. Guess you know the urge to go there was really never very strong or I'd have made it, but this time, this is it. So I have a double incentive to work like fury to get caught up, so that, although I'll probably work there, there won't be the pressure of deadlines, and I can haunt you. Honestly, it isn't Hawaii that I care two cents about—such an unappreciative gal—but the opportunity to work with you. I'd

7 See *The Spiritual Journey of Joel S. Goldsmith*, p. 24.

go farther than Hawaii for that.

Lorraine

September 11, 1956

Dear Joel,

...Last week I lost my first case. The patient had been making fine progress until about six weeks ago and then a reversal set in. Two operations came, one after another in rapid succession, and then she was gone. I missed the boat. If I had risen high enough, every appearance would have dissolved, and there would have been no obstacles. How I would love to have talked with you, but I know that you are always standing by, and that even though it would have been a great comfort, we can't seek comfort of any kind....

Lovingly yours,
Lorraine

The year 1956 involved literally hundreds of hours of classes and lectures for Joel, and thousands of miles of travel from Hawaii to New York in March, and then on around the world with stopovers for work in England and on the Continent, down under to South Africa, on to Australia, and then home to Hawaii in July, only to start again in October for a week of class work in Chicago. Emma Lindsay accompanied him to Chicago as she had to New York and then went on with him to Seattle and Portland but returned to Hawaii from Victoria leaving Joel to go back to New York alone for the release of *The Art of Meditation*.[8]

During the week of work in Chicago there was an

8 Joel S. Goldsmith, *The Art of Meditation* (New York: Harper & Row, 1956).

opportunity for several work sessions with Joel. He hammered away at the essence of the "New Horizon,"[9] the importance of not being satisfied with good human appearances but always reinterpreting them as more of the divine shining through and always the importance of pressing forward to greater realization. He came back over and over again to the point that we tend to rest back in the good with a complacency that is the death knell to spiritual progress. Our consciousness which knows our need has a way of jarring us out of such complacency.

I asked Joel again about the Third Eye which he indicated was the way in which the assurance of the activity of the Christ appeared to me, that Light that dispels the darkness and reveals the omnipresent Reality. Other "signs" could be given at other times or to other persons.

In one very special session he made it very clear that I had long since surrendered my life to God and no longer had a life of my own, so happiness or unhappiness could not enter in.

November 1, 1956

Dear Joel,

...You will note from the attached card that I don't have enough to do so have taken a new job upon myself. Actually, I am, as always, following out your instructions. You don't know how hard I tried to postpone having this forthcoming class on meditation until the first of the year—or not at all. As I told you, every time I meditated and our activity here came in, the demand came to have a class, but I wouldn't listen. But now Monday will be here before I know it and the class will begin. You wouldn't know that I had been a seasoned teacher, absolutely sure of myself in any classroom situation—but this

9 Joel S. Goldsmith, *The Infinite Way* (Rev, Ed.; San Gabriel, California: 1961). Pp. 192-196.

is different. I'm trying to be like Scarlet O'Hara and not think about it until tomorrow. But, honestly, Joel, I'm scared—terribly scared—maybe this will be my swan song in The Infinite Way—no time like now to find out. Please pause a moment and take me up to the mountain with you.

Thank you for your very dear letter and another generous gift! Instead of a weekend holiday, your last gift bought for me the most beautiful filing case in which are stored all the manuscripts so that everything is easily accessible. I don't yet know what this will buy, but it will be something very special.

November 11, 1956

Dear Joel,

Thank you for your two good letters. So glad to hear how beautifully everything is progressing—how could it be otherwise?

The class last Monday evening on meditation went very well—I was completely unaware of myself, which is, of course, the best sign of all. Thank you. There were twenty of us and this week three or four more expect to come in for the remainder of the class—they never got there this week on account of the "L" wreck; they were not in it but delayed by it. The consciousness of the class was beautiful—much depth. Of course, I'll be tickled to death when it's over.

News of your forthcoming New York class is wonderful. I announced it today. I'd love to be there, too, but this class in meditation complicates things a bit—plus a few deadlines to be met. Who knows? You say that the Father can do in 12 seconds what it takes us twelve hours to do, so I'm just being a beholder.

Sort of expecting you and Emma to stop off here. Do hope it's possible for you both.

Lovingly yours,
Lorraine

November 20, 1956

Dear Joel,

Surprised at how little you know me! Don't you know that I would gladly spend hours traveling to and from the airport to have 15 minutes with you? Bet you were just thinking about the work and that you didn't want to take me away from that. Well, it was good to hear your voice, even if I didn't get to see you.

It was quite a surprise to hear that Emma had returned to Hawaii. And so you are back to "aloneness." So it is. Probably my own "aloneness" is much greater than yours, although always immeasurable—because the world will not leave you alone and give you that opportunity—but I never regretted the sense of aloneness I feel. However, I know it was wonderful to have Emma with you and what a comfort and joy she was to you. I'm glad too that she got to Chicago; we were so happy to have her with us. Soon you'll be back in Hawaii— alone, and yet not alone.

I'm working away on a good many things at once. If they all shape up and I see them completed or sufficiently on their way to completion so that they will be ready on time, I may hop over to New York next Tuesday for a few days of the class and the lectures. That is still in the "iffy" realm and may not be possible at this time....

....How does it feel to be dined and wined by the heads of two important publishing firms? And living at the Waldorf! May I touch you, kind sir? I know all of it is a great experience for you—welcomed as a symbol of the fruition and fulfillment of your years and years of devotion and work—and at the same time pleasant while it is happening....

A very happy Thanksgiving to you—a cup overflowing with joy.

The latter part of November Joel had flown to New York for the second time in 1956 for the release of *The Art of Meditation*, an event which was celebrated by an autograph party at The Gotham Book Mart, given by Frances Steloff who had played such a significant role in getting Harpers to accept the book. The same week Joel gave a class at the Laurelton Hotel and fortunately I was able to fly there for a part of it. When I arrived at the Laurelton Hotel in New York, there was no room available. In the lobby I met two good friends, dedicated Infinite Way students, Martha Kittredge and Bettie Burkhart, who invited me to share their room. So I found a place to put my head when they secured an extra cot. Joel's surprise and pleasure were evident when I went down to the next session of the class and sat in the front row. His surprise and pleasure were evident. Afterwards when I expressed my gratitude for the deep message that came forth, he said to Bettie, standing beside me, "She's only thinking that it will make a chapter in a new book."

December 27, 1956

Dear Joel:

And now begin all the "thank you's"—so many to you. First, for the picture which I'm so happy to have.

[A copy of a large photograph Frances Steloff had had Joel take for a display in the window of The Gotham Book Mart along with copies of *The Art of Meditation*. On my copy Joel had written, "To Lorraine with love, Joel."] I like it very much. Your wearing glasses rivets attention on the eyes. It is as if they were a frame to draw attention to "the windows of the soul."... Thank you, too, for the Christmas check. As soon as I get an opportunity I'll spend it and let you know what my

Christmas gift is.

Am I supposed to get envious when you talk about barefoot at Christmas? Not me. Why, we have snow! It was lovely—just enough to make it Christmas. And Christmas Eve the streets were shining glass! But I like it. Actually in 1957 I hope to get started taking my morning walks again in the crisp winter air. I guess that's the Viking in me....

Now to come to Hawaii. I do want to go very much—you don't know how remarkable that is because I have little wanderlust in me. There are a number of things that should be taken care of before I leave....

Yes, it's been a rewarding year for you—so well-deserved. In looking back on it, it seems to be quite a year for me, too. The strangest year I have ever known and in spite of outward appearances and deep dissatisfaction with myself, there has been progress—great enough for me to know how much more there should be. Much of that "insulation" you talk about has grown up around me....

A joyous New Year to you and to Emma and my love to you both.

Lovingly yours,

Lorraine

7

"I See Hawaii in Your Teacup"

The relatively few direct personal contacts with my teacher made clear to me the importance of welcoming and seizing upon every opportunity to have time with him. Therefore Joel's joking prophecy, "I see a trip over here in your teacup," came only as a confirmation of what I already felt was inevitable. Little did I dream, however, that 1957 would see me taking three trips to Hawaii, 1958 one, 1959 two, and 1960 another one, as well as the final trip there for work with Joel in 1963, all landmarks in my own progressive unfoldment.

While it is true that all truth is within consciousness and must unfold from within, that withinness had translated itself into a kind but unbending guide without in the form of my teacher. What more natural than to seek to spend every moment possible in his presence? These moments became possible when in December of 1956 Joel invited me to come to Hawaii.

I arrived in Honolulu January 27, 1957, expecting to be there only a few weeks. But Joel and Emma were planning to be married on March 10, Joel's birthday, and asked me if I would be willing to stay on to be a witness at their wedding, to which I happily assented, leaving for home on March 12. Although this first trip to Hawaii, so

193

important to me, is described in further detail elsewhere[1] on this trip, as on all subsequent trips, I wrote in considerable detail to my sister:

Joel is putting me through a course of sprouts. He says when I leave here, I will be able to be an instrument for healing, and how! Darling, you have never seen anyone work with me the way Joel has. I couldn't have dreamed it would ever be possible. We meditate, and then he will sometimes give a full hour's lesson just for me. I can't begin to tell you what it all means, but it is far more than I could ever have dreamed of—far more. I go out to his house every day after the mail is in—so I can pick it up for him at the post office—and arrive by limousine (60 cents) at 12 noon. We either have some work and then lunch and talk or have some relaxation, work, or just living. Usually we go out for dinner and I am home about nine or ten o'clock. Emma is always there, too. Imagine those hours with Joel every day! If you think he's a good teacher, you should see him when he works with one or two really seriously. He is patience itself and persistence.

Joel was indeed patience and persistence. There seemed to be a special urgency about his work with me, as if he were preparing me for what my role in the Work was to be. He insisted that whatever else I knew or learned I must be absolutely clear on the relationship of mind and matter. He explained that matter is mind formed. Therefore, an activity of mind can change the form. Since the proper function of mind is as an instrument or facet of consciousness, the mind must be kept free of the myriad

1 See *The Spiritual Journey of Joel S. Goldsmith*, (New York: Harper & Row, 1973). Pp. 70-74.

suggestions of good or bad, health or sickness, and abundance or lack, suggestions floating around in the atmosphere. Only then can it be a clear transparency for the activity of consciousness which then shows forth as form and appears as renewal and restoration.

While in Hawaii, living at the Marek Hotel, I wrote the following letter:

Waikiki, Hawaii
February 18, 1957

Dear Joel,

Today you said that I looked like the cat that had swallowed the canary or a nice fat mouse. You were right because it was just about that time that this particular idea came to me—an idea which made me feel all glowing and warm inside.

When I stopped teaching a year and a half ago, I had saved out for myself a "cushion" of $1000 to be used for any contingency which might arise. It has never been needed or used and has remained intact. From that day to this there has always been enough and to spare. Now, at a time when it may be of use to you, it is my great joy and pleasure to give this "cushion" to you—maybe it will buy one square foot of the new home for you and Emma....

I have long since learned that no "cushion" is necessary when you have the Christ and that awareness you have given me in so large a measure that It has become my "cushion" and the whole meaning of life. Please understand that this little gift is in no sense a payment for what you have done and are doing for me. A thousand times a thousand dollars could not pay for that. For it, I would gladly sell all that I have even though you have given it to me as freely as the sunshine, "without price." There is only one kind of payment I can ever make that would be of real value—and that is to go and do likewise. I think the only prayer I have—the only desire—is just that: that I may be enough of a transparency for the Christ to be worthy of your work with me. Thank you always.

Lovingly yours,
Lorraine

Evanston, Illinois
March 14, 1957

Dear Emma and Joel,

This is really a "bread and butter" letter. Such a deep thank you for all the love, kindness, and understanding you showered upon me in such full measure and for giving me the true bread heaped high with butter and jam—yes, you saw to it that every added thing was included. The two of you are my "rainbow in the sky" which makes my heart leap up when I behold it. I thought I loved you both before with an immeasurable love, but now that love has grown to astronomical proportions. We're supposed to go from glory to glory, but how is that possible when one has had the most glorious of all glorious experiences? It seems to me Infinity is already encompassed.

Remember I reached Hawaii two hours ahead of schedule? Surely anticipation and joy gave added wings to the plane, but homeward bound it was a different story. There was a three hour delay in Los Angeles—engine trouble—and so for the first time in my short flying career, the plane was late. Guess reluctance and my nostalgic backward glances added chains to the plane. Nice flight, though. Of course I like being home, too, but it isn't quite the same.

We had such a wonderful meeting last night. We looked

like a little bit of Hawaii transferred to balmy Chicago—and I mean balmy, a warm 70 degrees. Over half of them sat there happily fondling the leis which were distributed as long as they lasted. T. B. came up with a choice remark, "I never expected to smell so good until my funeral." There was such a surge of love in that little room that I was almost overwhelmed. All that would come for our meditation—and quite enough to be sure—was "Except the Lord build the house, they labor in vain that build it." It was so clear that the Lord had built that house, and that therefore it would never be dependent upon any person.

We never did have our scheduled recording because I spent an hour and a half bringing them glimpses of my wonderful six and a half weeks. I wish you could have been there to witness the beautiful response to the announcement of your marriage. They were so happy about it. Do you remember that last day at the Pali Palms I said that in my meditations I had such a sense of Infinity, of the limitless nature of life? That was not mentioned in my talk but several of them caught it anyway because they said, "You have brought a feeling of Infinity to us."

And have I been busy! I'm swamped with calls—some just welcome home calls, but a good many calls for help. Nice healings and quick ones, too.

And how can I tell you what my weeks in Hawaii with you both have meant to me! I'm afraid it can't be done. No form can express the Limitless—no, not even as malleable a form as words. It was a limitless and boundless experience, the effects of which are immeasurable like the rock cast into the sea which sets in operation a continuing "rhythm" of motion upon the water. If I can remain as pliable and resistance-less as the water, that rock of deep Truth so gently thrust into consciousness will operate throughout all time to come—in all the days, weeks, months, and years ahead and perhaps grow in intensity and depth, moving forward from one horizon to another. As I have said so many times, only the grace of God could have brought this to me, and by the grace of God, the fruits will appear in their season.

My love to you both. How good it will be to see you again!

Shortly after I returned home, the latter part of March, Emma and Joel set out for Europe on their honeymoon, stopping a few days in Chicago for Joel to give *The 1957 Chicago Open Class* before going on to England and the Continent.

March 29, 1957

Dear Joel,

I'm still walking on air after the last two months culminating in this wonderful week! I wish you could know the number of people who have said that never has your message been so clear or meant so much to them. And for me these have been miracle days! Will write more about that phase of it later, but now just want to wish you and Emma *bon voyage* and give you the enclosed financial accounting of the weekend.

Lovingly yours,
Lorraine

April 4, 1957

Dear Joel,

Once again back to the old routine—if routine it can be called since always the unexpected is the rule. These days and nights are busier than seem possible that any days or nights could be.

One day such a barrage of crises and stark tragedies were thrown at me that I should have been a complete wreck if I had taken even a tiny portion of them in. But to each came the inward response: "My kingdom is not of this world. This is a spiritual universe." And some miracles were wrought or, more correctly, witnessed. I don't know whether or not I should recount them to you. The nature of any of them seems so unimportant: I've seen the principle work over and over again, and that is the wonderful part to me. You know I've never been happy about the healing aspect of my work, but now there is a certainty and a sureness that I never had before, and the signs follow. Oh, I don't mean that it is one hundred percent, but there is a large enough proportion to make me know that it just didn't happen. What I need now is to practice and practice, and this I am doing....

Lifetimes were spanned in these last two months. Life is lived in another dimension. With it has come an absolute conviction of the spiritual nature of the universe and of the powerlessness of form to be anything in and of itself. That conviction is like an unassailable wall against which all the suggestions of the world can hit, only to be thrust back without leaving the tiniest mark, even on the surface.

....My love to Emma and joy be with you both all the way.

With much love,
Lorraine

April 22, 1957

Dear Emma and Joel,

Since you wrote and said you were so busy and that I should do some work for you, I have had the most wonderful feeling of peace and joy, and then to top it all off, for the fourth time in my experience, early last week, that wonderful pool of blue came in meditation. I always feel when that happens that something very special has come to me and that great depths have been plumbed. I'm not a phenomenon gal, so anything like that is always an occasion, quite inexplicable, but surely an experience of Reality. Well, I really must get back to work. Writing to you is my recreation—and very pleasant.

Lovingly yours,
Lorraine

April 23, 1957

Dear Emma and Joel,

I'm so happy for you about *everything*—all just the way it should be. I loved every detail of both of your letters. The wedding gifts sound elegant. Some of that old Sheffield is so beautiful. And more ivory for your collection and an elephant of horn! The sweaters sound good, too. You've done all right so far, but won't it be fun when you can forget the work and just go leisurely poking around in all kinds of fascinating corners that only a town centuries old could produce?

Hawaii in August! That sounds better than Paris in the spring. What I really should say is that to see Emma and Joel any place, any time, sounds better in my ears than Paris in the springtime. Actually I am looking forward to it and expect to be there. You said you would put me to work, so when should I arrange to arrive in order to be the most help? Looks as if the rumpus room will be filled to overflowing....Whatever I can do to be of the most service, I shall be happy to do—even to trying to keep everybody happy. But that shouldn't require much doing in that heavenly place.

Much love to you both,
Lorraine

May 4, 1957

Dear Emma and Joel,

....*Consciousness Unfolding* reads very well. Everything is in it, plus the easy, fluent style you achieved in it. It's my favorite book. You outdid yourself on that one! Guess what I just typed from it: "This is a spiritual universe." See, it was all there, only it took a ton of bricks and years of study and even that didn't do it; nothing helped really until I could sit hours and hours in the silence with you—and that did it!

I'm keeping tuned in—at least I think so. Words don't usually come through, and, well, just nothing tangible, but mostly a great warmth and peace envelops me and that's it. All you ever taught me about doing this was to sit down and turn from the person I wanted to contact to God. So that's all I know. Maybe sometime, when I see you, you will tell me more so that I can develop greater receptivity to your inner teaching. Don't forget I'm a slow learner....

With much love,
Lorraine

May 20, 1957

Dear Emma and Joel,

Now, how do you suppose I can take care of such ordinary, humdrum things as doing the final checking on *Consciousness Unfolding* after receiving your letter. I am so thrilled and delighted that you will be here. How did I ever get to be such a lucky gal?

And now back to work: This is the way my mind runs: "Semi-colon or comma—oh, how wonderful to see them again! No, that's a dependent clause—I'm utterly selfish, not even concerned about the fact that Joel isn't going to talk—just want both of them for myself. No, that shouldn't be capitalized; it's

an attribute in the predicate—those dear, darling people."
With much love,
Lorraine

After the work in England came work in Holland, and then a holiday for Joel and Emma in Switzerland, Germany, and Italy. On their way home there was a three-day stopover in Chicago, not for any public work, but for a visit that was really like a family reunion. Furthermore, Joel brought news that an enlarged edition of *Practicing the Presence* would be published by Harper & Row.

June 5, 1957

Dear Emma and Joel,

Such deep and heartfelt thanks for your visit here....It was my joy and pleasure for you to be my guests....

I can't keep my itchy fingers away from *Practicing the Presence*, and I've already begun reading and sorting material to be used in the enlarged edition. Reading the book again, I see that there is a power and an urgency in it that will have to be maintained or the whole rhythm of the book will be destroyed....

With much love,
Lorraine

June 23, 1957

Dear Emma and Joel,

Thank you for your letters and especially for the last one....Your last letter about not playing God was a great help to me. Of course I would deny that I ever believed I could "play God," but it is a pretty subtle thing, and undoubtedly the thought crept in that there was something that I could do about these situations and wasn't doing. Well, I know I needed waking up and you were the one who could do it, because I do believe "the human scene is mesmeric suggestion"—but I suppose I must have been forgetting it or I should not have been concerned. The words you put into Jesus' mouth in *The Easter of Our Lives* kept coming to me, "Wherein have I failed?" And with them would come the answer. Yet the question persisted. Before your letter arrived—in fact the very day you wrote the letter—the awakening came. Thank you.

The following day Bettie and Warren Burkhart and Barbie, their daughter, were with me and although I had promised to take them to the aquarium, I had to beg off—just knew it was necessary to be home although my instinct as a hostess warred with the demands that spiritual integrity was making, but the former had to yield to the latter. Even though I felt that every call had been taken care of there was the persistent demand to go up higher. After a few minutes of silent listening, I opened to that wonderful passage in II Corinthians: "Henceforth know we no man after the flesh....therefore if any man be in Christ, he is a new creature: old things are passed away; behold, all things are become new." That was it—not good flesh and not bad flesh—my kingdom was no longer of "this world," but it was a spiritual kingdom, peopled only with the sons of God.

A few minutes later came the call which must have been the reason for my hesitancy in leaving: A woman had collapsed and had been taken to the hospital by the pulmotor squad.

Bettie and I were alone at the moment, and so we sat down together in a wonderful sense of peace—no struggle, no straining to do something, just a dwelling in that spiritual kingdom. The next day the woman was sent home in a taxi by herself and walked up the stairs to her home under her own steam, just as active as ever. But do you know why I rejoice? Because I had been sufficiently receptive and obedient to respond to the demand of Spirit to "watch yet a little while," and be willing even to appear ungracious in order to obey the inner call.

My conviction of the correctness of this principle is so strong that when there is no response my first thought is that there must be some point in which I have failed in my realization. In other words, the realization wasn't complete even though I felt such a sense of the Presence and it seemed that my mind was imbued with truth. "What truth?" I can hear you ask so sharply that I practically jumped off the chair—remember? Thank you, I'll never hesitate on that answer again: Every suggestion of a power, substance, law, cause, or activity other than God has been faced with the recognition of oneness.

I leave for Hawaii July 17 at 11:50 P.M. United and arrive Honolulu July 18 (Thursday) at 3:10 P.M. Flight 29.

My heart big? It can never be big enough to hold the love and joy I feel. There is so little I can do to express even a tiny measure of that. My only comfort is that you look beneath the surface and see with "seeing eyes." I'll be seeing you soon.

Lovingly yours,
Lorraine

For my second trip to Hawaii, Joel sent me an airplane ticket and again arranged for a room with a kitchen at the

Marek Hotel in Waikiki. The weeks there were busy ones, picking up the mail at Pawaa Station each morning, traveling out to Halekou Place by taxi, and staying there until nine or ten o'clock in the evening. Never a dull day nor a boring one. No, each day brought forth its special and varied activities, among which were working on the monthly *Letter*, helping Emma prepare luncheon and dinner when we ate at home, and helping her with some of the details in their new home—such as arranging Joel's extensive library on the approximately twenty-foot-long bookcase on one side of the spacious living room and interspersing it with priceless bric-a-brac, sent from all over the world.

Before I left for Hawaii, Joel had asked me to prepare an article for *The Seeker*, a magazine published in Australia. For that article, I selected material from *The 1955 First Kailua Study Group*, Reel I. When he read it, he looked up in amazement and said, "Why, this is just what I am working on today!" That was the first of many similar experiences showing the attunement in consciousness.

Joel went on to stress the importance of the principle of a power so great there was nothing against which it would have to contend. That power is spiritual power, and with it comes an understanding of true nonresistance. According to Joel this does not mean doing nothing but instead, through conscious awareness of this truth, actively bearing witness to the ceaseless harmonious activity of the one Consciousness forever functioning as fulfillment and perfection in the silence of pure being. In that awareness, there is no evil that can come to us and no good to be gained; we seek nothing and therefore no power is needed. We behold the rhythm of the universe as the first step, and then it becomes an integral part of us as we feel it flowing through us.

Earlier in the year, on my first visit to Hawaii, Joel had shared with me some of his experiences on his trip around the world in 1956. One evening at dinner in a small, quiet restaurant, this master story teller told how he had stopped off for a day in the Belgium Congo to change planes on his way to Johannesburg, South Africa, only to discover upon arrival in Johannesburg, that his luggage, much to his chagrin, was missing. He was sure it would be found but for three weeks until a day or two before he was to leave for India, there was no baggage. True, all his needs were taken care of without baggage, but he felt this should not have happened and that somehow he was missing an important point in spiritual practice.

It was then it came to him that although he knew *this is a spiritual universe*, here he was looking for material baggage, lost in time and space. In a spiritual universe there is no need for material baggage which is only a human concept of a spiritual function or activity. Shortly before he was to leave for India, his baggage was discovered in the hotel in the quarters where the crew was lodged on overnight stops. Something about that incident and the way he described it struck a chord in me, the music of which has grown stronger with each passing year. When I returned to my hotel, I realized that a physical condition about which I had had some concern was gone.

Whenever I shepherded anyone out to 22 Kailua, I asked Joel to tell the story of the lost baggage so that I could hear the principle pointed up again and again, each time a bit differently. At dinner at Halekou during the 1957 *Halekou classes*, I turned to Joel, "It is such a pity that we don't have your account of the lost baggage on tape so it could be used for a chapter in a book."

"Put a question about it up on the desk to remind me, and I'll talk about it." So the lost baggage became Reel II of *The 1957 Second Halekou Closed Class*, entitled, "Incorporeal Existence," and later the chapter "This Is a Spiritual Universe" in *The Thunder of Silence*.[2]

My main function in being there this time was to manage the two *1957 Halekou Classes*, each of which met for two-hour sessions on six consecutive nights with one week intervening between the first and second class. Most of the one hundred or more students from the Mainland, England, and Australia lived at the Marek Hotel, where I carried on the class registration. Every evening during the class, they all journeyed by chartered bus from Waikiki across the Pali (a ridge that forms the spine of the island) to Halekou Place. This gave the students an opportunity to drink in the magnificent view of the windward side of the Island. The two busses were unable to negotiate the narrow drive leading up to Joel's house, so the students had to disembark about a block away and trudge uphill and down over big stones.

The room for the class on the ground floor below the living room was large enough to accommodate all the students. It looked out on a lush tropical garden, where Joel's sonorous voice was often accompanied by the joyous, lusty singing of the birds and sometimes by a downpour of rain pelting against the glass doors. Such a sacred and holy experience took on the atmosphere of a pilgrimage having been undertaken and completed. A couple of weeks after the class, I returned home on the luxurious *Mariposa*, my first ocean voyage.

2 Joel S. Goldsmith. *The Thunder of Silence*, (New York: Harper & Row, 1961). Pp. 99-107.

Aboard the Mariposa
August 31, 1957, Sunday AM

Dear Emma and Joel,

Greetings from somewhere in the Pacific! According to the geographers, it would be longitude and latitude thus and so, but for me it's heaven. Today is a beautiful bright day, the water taking on the brilliance of the sun and glistening like jewels. I walked the length of the deck 24 times before breakfast. The food is delicious and unlimited in quantity. I'll really have to take it off when I get home! But I am enjoying this grand finale to a wonderful experience!

It was somewhat of a shock to me to discover that I wasn't as good a sailor as I thought I would be. At first it seemed the ship would never stop its endless rocking, resulting in a most uncomfortable internal churning. Elvis Presley has nothing on this ship! I could eat scarcely a bite of food the first night and the first breakfast, sleeping most of the first day with those most powerful of all words resounding in my ears: "Resist not." Yes, I must have been resisting—rocking and churning miserably because of a sense of "I"-ness, trying to keep my equilibrium—resisting—instead of abandoning myself to the motion. Then, I saw the ship had no qualities of its own, but only those qualities with which my mind endowed it—mental images—and I became very quiet, letting the Soul use the mind as Its instrument—and in that moment peace came....

(A long pause—) I am trying to find words to tell you just a little of my gratitude, appreciation, and love for all your goodness to me, and there aren't any. (Another long pause—). Yes, just guess I'm speechless. I know that the joy and privilege of being with you so much of the time came to me, not because of me, but because of the work, that I might be so steeped in that high consciousness as to be an increasingly better instrument. But even so, the joy remains undimmed....

And Joel, you couldn't be the great teacher and mystic

that you are and not know the depth of my appreciation. To be in your home, partaking of those matchless, impromptu lessons, dwelling in the atmosphere of pure Spirit—well, just to have had one hour would have been enough to make one feel blessed above all others, but to have hours, days, and weeks of such work!... The wordless teaching was being communicated to me effortlessly, so effortlessly that even now I marvel at it.

Today, sitting out on the deck in a state of meditation, the very first meditation you gave me and with which I worked unceasingly for two years flashed through my mind, "I and my Father are one." After all these years and the many, many hours devoted to it, a new level of meaning was reached. If I could tell you that I saw that I and the Father are one because that I is God and Lorraine a state of self-deception, I should be over-simplifying and fail to communicate the depth of meaning which was revealed.

It seems the desire that was deepest within me—the soul-hunger—has been assuaged. Always I longed for that ineffable moment of realization and illumination, but that has slipped into the background—at least for the time. My love for the Way is greater and deeper than ever, but I cease struggling and seem to have entered the stream of life and to be swimming—more like floating—with it. It will seem strange not to make that daily trek across the Pali, stopping first at Pawaa for your mail. But there is no time to spend on such thoughts—to linger on the past nor yet to anticipate the future—. I must get back to work or as you would say, Joel, "Back to the salt mines." Thank you both for giving me another beautiful, joyous experience.

Lovingly yours,
Lorraine

September 5, 1957

Dear Emma and Joel,

Home again and getting back into the old routine! Seems strange!

Valborg and George arrived home the same day I did, only a few hours later. And what do you think Valborg had done before she left for her trip and while I was away? She had straightened, sorted, and cleaned every drawer in my apartment; all the closets had been cleared out, washed, sprayed for moths; and all the dishes and cabinets washed and put in apple pie order! This she did in the evenings when she returned to the apartment after a full day's work at her own house. Did you ever hear of such a sister and such love? She said she knew how busy I would be when I returned and wanted to make it as easy as possible for me by freeing me from that responsibility. I don't know how one person could be so blessed as I am to be enfolded in so much love....

We had a lovely experience at our meeting Wednesday night. We never did get to the tape because I began recounting a little bit of our experiences in Hawaii and before I knew it over an hour had slipped by. The love and gratitude which filled my heart overflowed and enveloped them. For the most part it was a light, gay evening, interspersed with just an occasional very serious moment when bits that had really *registered* with me just popped out before I knew it and evidently affected them as deeply as they had affected me. The comment was that I was completely transformed, as if I had been reborn. But how could it be otherwise? No one had a greater opportunity and some of your consciousness must have rubbed off on me, just a little.

I keep saying to myself, "How strange it is to be here. Is it possible that I am really back in Chicago?" Yes, I miss you both—terribly! Yet I love it here, too, but it isn't what I might want, and I don't even know what that is, unless it is that I should be two, but whatever is given me to do, I shall try to do. I loved every moment of my experience in Hawaii—getting the mail, driving across the Pali, wonderful hours visiting with you, Emma, and other wonderful moments working, chatting, and enjoying those powerful silences with you, Joel; yes, and even registering students....Please let me help in any way in which I can be of the most use....Now, I close my eyes and see you both at beautiful Halekou Place, and I feel myself there too.

Lovingly yours,
Lorraine

On October 29, 1957, Joel initiated what he called an Inner Working Group, designed to provide the means and the persons through whom this activity would be continued on a worldwide scale as long as there was a response to this Message. It consisted of Joel and six persons, among whom were Eileen Bowden and I, who, Joel believed, were demonstrating in their lives the importance of living the life of spiritual illumination, and who had exhibited an interest in sharing it with the world as The Infinite Way. The instruction Joel gave was imparted largely through meditation. Whatever words came through were recorded on tape, and those tapes, which Joel instructed us were never to be played for anyone else, were sent to the group members. It is to this work and these tapes that the following letter alludes.

November 8, 1957

Dear Emma and Joel,
Thank you for your last letter. I'm so grateful for it. Even

before you wrote me about the daily work being undertaken, I knew that something was going on because of what was happening to me. I've been so consistently on the beam, completely indifferent to whatever the appearance was, and in most cases the result has been quick and effective. Our meetings have been quite wonderful—a very high consciousness there....All this is but the outward appearance of an inner certainty—a deepening conviction that permits no "ands," "ifs," or "buts." The peace and sense of soaring even in the midst of increasing activity are pleasant *effects*. I've been working with nonresistance and no power and *that is really it*.

When something happens to me personally in the way of a healing through the operation of that principle, I suppose it hits me with even greater force than to have others call up and say that now they feel fine. The other afternoon I was quite ill— might have been anything—and sitting at my desk working on *The 1957 Letters* was sheer torture, but I stuck at it. The next morning I longed so to stay in bed—since I've been in The Infinite Way I can count on one hand the days spent in bed and still have some fingers left—but how could I remain in bed? *If it had no power*, how could it have power to keep me from doing what needed doing? It could just continue, but it couldn't do anything. With that I got up and in less than an hour I was fine. I think one of the important parts was the getting up, that is, putting prayer into action a la our good friend Isaiah. If I had waited, I would have recognized it as a power.

Every day that I watch the principle in operation, I grow increasingly grateful.... I thought I had a conviction before, but this is so much deeper. Yes, I'm very grateful and I wait expectantly for instructions as to my part in the group work now underway. You may be sure that I shall hold it close within me so that the fruits will come forth. Thank you for giving me the opportunity.

Several times lately when I have been helping some

persons—and you know that I know enough not to hold onto them during meditation—I have had the feeling of their being nestled inside of me, held close and curled up as if in a womb. Please tell me—have I been off the beam on these occasions? In one case, the results were a real opening of the Soul and in another the healing of severe pain. But I don't want to go off on any by-pass, and if that was a digression into something other than the spiritual realm, I know you will help me.

Now don't brag about your weather, 'cause all I can do is tell you that we are promised snow for tonight. Snow is so pretty—when it first falls.

> With much love,
> Lorraine

November 17, 1957

Dear Emma and Joel,

....To be a part of the united consciousness of this group of seven, being taught the wisdom that has been gleaned by you, Joel, through your years of dedication and consecration, is an opportunity no other six in all the world have. At once the potentialities in such teaching and such a group are evident....

Since Thursday, every consideration has been submerged in the intensity of this prayer, "Please, let there be no rigidity in me, but let me be soft and pliable, ever responsive to Thy bidding."

> Lovingly yours,
> Lorraine

November 19, 1957

Dear Emma and Joel,

It is just seven o'clock in the evening, and I have finished an hour and half's work with you feeling myself right there at

Halekou with the three of you [*Joel, Emma, and another student*]. During the hour and a half, there was a very deep meditation, lasting for forty-five minutes in which I was stirred to my very toes with a tremendous force, but yet it was very gentle and peaceful. Then I listened to a small portion of the recording, up to the part about the cataracts, and meditated again. This came during the second meditation:

> *I* see—not eye—and *I* am the Light of the world. If thine I be single, no other identity but the one I, thy whole body shall be full of light....And the veil of the temple was rent, that which would enshroud the *I*, the Holy of Holies, and obscure It, was torn down.

I can see how the work of the Twenty-five [see above p. 126] is only nursery school as compared to the depth of this work. Already the practical work in various specific areas is proving valuable beyond words.

There has not been time for me to hear from out of town people whom I have been helping but in the city I have already had a very significant response to the work of this group....

I heard on Sunday that out in the Park Forest, a southwestern suburb, in Marshall Field's new branch store, they have a display of furnished rooms done by their interior decorating department. On the table in one of the rooms is a copy of *The Art of Meditation!* Maybe the cover fit in with their color scheme! Anyway, it's nice, isn't it? Also I had a talk with E.A. and T. the other day, and although T. is not one of your greatest admirers, he did say that he just couldn't understand about "that book. It's still selling and still getting notices in trade magazines.",...

I am most of all interested in the letter from the Triangles asking permission to publish excerpts from *The Art of Meditation*. And do you know why? The Triangles is the exoteric phase of the Arcane School to which I belonged for almost seven years, in which I was working or studying when I met you, Joel. I still remember the beautiful note I had from the Secretary when I wrote to tell her about you and that I was beginning to have a reading group of students of The Infinite Way and therefore wished to sever my connections with the School. Among other things she wrote: "It is heart-warming to hear from you, and I am so glad that you have found your particular niche on the Path. I'm sure that the practice of The Infinite Way fits into the hierarchical Plan and helps in preparing the minds and hearts of men for the reappearance of the Christ." This is the Alice Bailey group, you know. Isn't it interesting that they are going to publish quotations from some of your writings? They are a group of very fine people. Every day it becomes increasingly plain how each step of the way I was being prepared for The Moment. It was that group that had taught me a form of meditation which I was using when I met you and which you told me to drop and use in its place, "I and my Father are one."

Lovingly yours,
Lorraine

November 23, 1957

Dear Emma and Joel,

....The work of The Seven is really touching me and very deeply. I am trying to keep some sort of records of what transpired so far as I am concerned in connection with that activity—but they are very slight. You know the old saying that the baker never has bread, and I guess that applies here. But I am keeping a note here and there. Even humanly, my historical sense demands that. Since you are keeping a record on tape—such a wonderful idea and medium of teaching us—I wanted you to check my own notes. Below are a few things:
[Notes of my meditations:]

November 20: Whither shall I flee from Consciousness? If I ascend up into heaven, Consciousness is there. If I make my bed in hell, that same Consciousness is there. There is nothing outside and beyond this Consciousness which I am.

For Daisy: Held in Thy love I stand—unmoved, untouched, unassailable.

On Subliminal Advertising: The only activity that there is in reality is an activity of the Consciousness that I am. All activity is embraced in that Consciousness and that Consciousness maintains Its own activity in an integrity which knows no opposite and which cannot be reversed.

On November 21 - Thursday:

Much agitation—difficult to establish an inner quiet. Contemplation on the nature of God's love raised me a notch—even a couple of notches.

For Emma: And the glory of the Lord shone around about thee. Light so dazzling as to be impenetrable. Interesting how the idea of protection entered into the work for both Daisy and Emma.

On November 22 - Friday: Once again difficult to become settled and established in that unruffled calm which I usually maintain—at first quite a bit of agitation, but a joyous kind although none the less disquieting.

When inner silence came, there was a very deep realization of the significance of this particular activity as an instrument for freeing the world. Because it is an experiment, all data relative to it should be preserved. So many times I wished that I had kept a record of every step in some particular activity in which I had engaged which culminated in results far beyond my dreams, but now it is impossible to recapture all the steps. I have a very deep conviction that this work will be of major significance and its unfoldment should be preserved.... It is of untold value to me to go back to some point you have made over and over again until some part of it finally penetrates.

"My glory will I not give to another" is a powerful idea. That registers as much as "This is a spiritual universe." The word "fabrication" comes to me very strongly in connection with the advertising devise—no foundation, not a creation....

Lovingly yours,

Lorraine

In October Joel had invited me to come to Hawaii and instead of going to a hotel, to stay at Halekou Place for an extended period of time with him, Emma, and Sammy, Emma's son.

When I arrived in Honolulu in December, Emma and Joel were at the airport to meet me and drive out to Halekou. I was soon ensconced in my room on the ground floor, looking out into the garden, and adjoining the large room that had been used for the Halekou Classes earlier in the year. That room had now been transformed into an immense office where, on one side, I worked at a typewriter part of the day and where, across the room, Joel's secretary worked on the mail he had dictated.

Joel, Emma, and I constituted a closely knit family group that, together with the work, permitted little socializing with others. There were many hours spent with Joel, which included meditation, sitting with him and listening to him dictate his mail, and interludes in which he emphasized important points of spiritual practice.

Joel talked at great length about the healing and teaching work, emphasizing over and over that we are not trying to improve humanhood but rather to rise above it into spiritual consciousness. He cautioned me not to be concerned about the results in healing for that would be a negation of the entire principle. We are not dealing with a condition but with a mesmeric belief. Our work is the unfoldment of spiritual consciousness. We are not attempting to improve or change pictures but to see through the pictures of good and evil that are presented to us to the eternal, unchanging Reality that now is.

When I talked with Joel about feeling as if a patient or student were curled up inside of me, which I had written to him about, he told me that it was the realization of the Christ that was coming to me, the truth of spiritual identity unfolding within. During visits with Emma in the kitchen while we prepared the simple meals, and at many other times, she told me much about her children and her previous marriages to Ruston, Hightover, and Lindsay. Interspersed with these activities, I found time for my own work, so each day carried with it its own fulfillment.

This routine was broken by occasional jaunts across the Pali to Waikiki for dinner at some gourmet restaurant and once to see the movie *The Ten Commandments*. While I enjoyed the movie, watching Joel's uninhibited delight and deep interest in it was even more enjoyable. December 23, 1957, I wrote a letter to the students in Chicago in which I said in part:

And how can I describe life here at Halekou Place? The pictures will tell you a little of its beauty. The almost continuous rain has given the lush green foliage an even greater beauty and glory. Each day succeeds another in such a quiet and gentle way that it is easy to lose all track of time. Usually I awaken fairly early in the morning and as soon as I am dressed go into the adjoining huge attractive room. There I can sit and look up unto the mountains which are never quite the same, sometimes enshrouded in clouds, sometimes sharply chiseled against the sky, and always taking on different shades. After some meditation I begin to work and continue until breakfast.

Breakfast is at no set time—there is no rigid routine here—but usually it is around nine. Sammy is not always up for breakfast since school is in two shifts. He is in the afternoon session and does not get up early but stays up fairly late at night. Many times at breakfast Joel will launch into telling us about some particular phase of the work which he feels it is important to stress. Today it was the transcendent Self, the Self that is two and yet the two are one. He talked for almost two hours! And often it is that way and you must know how priceless these moments are.

Sometimes after breakfast we all have a meditation together and then I go on with my work....Dinner is about 6:30 and then at 7:30 B. and S. join us and we have one or two hours of meditation. Often in the evening there is coffee and cake before we go to bed. And that is a day at Halekou Place! Yet it certainly in no sense of the word describes what really takes place during the course of the day. Nothing can describe that, but peace and love and joy are expressed every moment of the day.

Sammy and Emma trimmed a beautiful Christmas tree last Sunday which is surely proving the law of multiplication because the packages underneath are multiplying by leaps and bounds. Sammy is particularly interested in that aspect of it. At night the reflection of the tree in the large plate glass window makes it appear as three trees instead of one. ...Yes, this is truly an indescribable experience. My only desire is to share as much of this experience with you as is possible so that you may enjoy some of its rich fruitage.

The evening of Christmas Day, after I answered a long distance call for help from Ohio, I almost apologized for wanting to pause briefly to meditate, saying, "I know I don't have to do anything." Joel's instant and firm response startled me, "Oh, yes, you do!" This was at ten o'clock while we were sitting in the living room talking, with Emma dozing on a nearby lounge. With that remark, Joel began talking and continued nonstop until midnight, when we all turned in for the night. Next morning at breakfast, as though there had been no break at all, Joel continued with the next sentence about what it was I was to do, while Emma and I sat at the breakfast table listening intently. Finally Emma realized it was time for lunch, so we quickly assembled a simple luncheon and again listened until dinnertime.

It was the most complete exposition I have ever heard of exactly how a person called upon for spiritual help should respond. It continued after dinner and was resumed the next morning—a priceless experience of a great teacher imparting to a willing and eager student the wisdom garnered through his years—his lifetimes—of practice. Every word was indelibly engraved in my memory.

During this lengthy, illuminating exposition in response to my apologetic, "I know I don't have to do anything," Joel emphasized that the thing we don't have to do is to change a so-called condition. What we do have to do is to work on ourselves so that we arrive at the conviction that there is nothing that needs to be changed because perfection already *is*, wholeness *is*, completeness *is*.

And how do we work on ourselves? By meditation on the principles, contemplating the nature of the Infinite Invisible, Its allness and inclusiveness, the Christ-identity of individual being, and the consequent nothingness of anything which is unlike the divine Reality. Because God, the Infinite Invisible, is appearing as individual being, there is no person to be healed or improved. The belief that there is, is just an impersonal, universal suggestion, having nothing to do with a person.

As I sat drinking in every word in my wonder at the clarity and authority of his words, I said naively, "Why didn't you ever say this before?"

"Why it's only on every page." And as I went through the books, I found this great principle of impersonalization on almost every page, but the impact of hearing him expound it to me in these priceless hours brought a whole new awareness or significance so the whole principle seemed new.

Joel continued to speak of the two steps in healing work. His sorrow was that students wanted to circumvent or bypass the first step and immediately jump into the second with no background of practice and reach what he spoke of as the ultimate of healing: healing without words or thoughts. Their unwillingness to work with the first step for long periods is why so many fail. In the first stage it is absolutely essential that whatever is presented as a problem be met with a statement of truth. When students are so well-versed in these truths that they become the very fabric of their consciousness, then they are ready for the second step: no words and no thoughts.

On another day, Joel talked at some length about the carnal mind or what he termed the fleshly mind which we have come to accept by virtue of having been born into this world. It is the mind that can think good thoughts and evil thoughts. He raised the question: Is it possible to so nothingize this mind that there is nothing left to hypnotize man?

A Spiritual Odyssey

He said that in dealing with this subject in my daily work, I should begin by recognizing that there does appear to be such a mind which perpetuates the good and evil deeds of humankind. But then must come the realization that although it appears that there is a mind operating as a person, it is not a mind, not a power, and has no avenue of expression, and is rendered powerless wherever this truth is realized. The secret is not to fight it as a power. Before the preparatory work that I do every morning is complete, however, he said that I must experience the omnipresence of a transcendental Presence and Power so that I can be assured of the fruitage in the form of the destruction of this belief.

During this period, one more person was added to the Inner Working Group, and on several occasions she came to participate in its regular and frequent sessions.

Emma no longer taped this work, so I sat with notebook in hand writing as fast as I could, torn between thinking that such pearls should not be just for the moment but for all time and my innermost desire just to sit and bask in an experience in which so much came forth—so much more than the words. Nevertheless, at this time I did have another experience of illumination. Is it not a spiritual principle that in forgetting self in the service of others the "bridegroom cometh"? In that unforgettable moment, there was a total merging in the Light.

Early in January, Emma and Joel boarded the plane for Australia and New Zealand for lectures and classes there. I remained at Halekou in charge of the household and Sammy, Emma's son and Joel's stepson, working and giving Sammy an ex-school teacher's close supervision interspersed with tender, loving care, fun and laughter all woven together.

Emma's first contact with Joel had been when she and Sammy went to hear him talk at the Unity Center in Waikiki. At that time, Sammy put a lei around Joel's neck, Emma introduced herself and offered to drive him around the island of Oahu. Thus a relationship which culminated in their marriage began.

Halekou Place
Kaneohe, Hawaii
January 23, 1958

Dear Emma and Joel,

....From what you sent me, Australia sounds wonderful. I knew you would stir things up there, but heavens, did it have to be a hurricane? Now couldn't you be just a little more gentle than that?

Sammy is doing beautifully, and I am really enjoying being with him. He is a wonderful little guy. Poor kid! He's so snowed under with homework that he hardly has had time to sleep or eat....We sit and work together. Some of the time I work with him and some of the time on my own work. Whichever way it is, he is satisfied so long as I am nearby to answer any questions....I talked to him the other day about school being the business of his life right now. "And what would you think, Sammy, if I stalled on the job when I was working for your Dad?"

The response was very quick and emphatic, "I wouldn't like it."

Sammy's appetite is wonderful. All my plans for reducing are fading into the distance in my joy in cooking for Sammy, and, of course, I do have to keep him company, don't I?

I've decided that all a prophet (I'm not really likening myself to that) has to do to be appreciated in his own land is to leave it. I'm still getting long distance calls from Chicago and from people who certainly never bothered to see me while I was there. Funny, isn't it? They wouldn't even spend carfare to go downtown to talk to me, but they will telephone to Hawaii! The human animal is surely one queer beast.

Last night I slept very fitfully. Finally, after being awake from 4:00 o'clock on, I got up at 5:00 and went to work. Was everything all right at your end?

With love,
Lorraine

Emma and Joel returned from their trip "down under" at the end of February, satisfied with the work that came through and with the reception the Message was given, but not entirely refreshed after a brief holiday stop on the way home in Fiji. The heat and the footlong lizards parading across the ceiling of their deluxe "grass shack" in Fiji were not exactly conducive to rest. But they were full of the trip and talked enthusiastically and animatedly about the great interest in the Message in New Zealand and Australia.

A couple of weeks later, as Emma and Joel drove me to the airport in Honolulu for my return home to make final preparations for Joel's two forthcoming classes in Chicago, I again spoke of my deep appreciation for having been a guest in their home and the wonder of it that three persons could have lived together so harmoniously without the shadow of a misunderstanding of any kind, but in perfect trust and understanding. Joel quickly gave us the answer, "That's because we've all made our demonstration. Not one of us wants anything from the other, for each of us is complete, and has realized that completeness."

Evanston, Illinois
March 4, 1958

Dear Emma and Joel,

I miss you! I feel like a stranger in a strange land....

Before I left I told you that I could never tell you how much my experience with you meant to me. You know the depth of my love and appreciation. You are very precious to me. I had to struggle to keep back the tears when I left and tried to be flip to cover up. You took me into your home and heart and made me one of you—not even a welcome guest, but one of you. I cannot imagine where else or under what other circumstances that could have been possible. Of the priceless hours of teaching, I dare not even speak, but must let the light ignited in me shine brightly enough to speak for me.

Lovingly yours,
Lorraine

Joel and Emma arrived in Chicago at the end of March for the Chicago work. At this time he was honored by being invited to lead the meditation at a regular meeting of the prestigious Conference of Club Presidents and Program Chairmen in Fullerton Hall at the Art Institute. This was an invitation Valborg had arranged with Myrtle Dean Clark, the president and founder of the Conference also known for years as The First Lady of Chicago.

One of the highlights of *The 1958 First and Second Chicago Closed Classes*, recognized by many as some of his most definitive work on mysticism, was the lesson "The Mystical *I*." For me it culminated in a deep mystical experience in which all form disappeared and there was only that one luminous eye. To this very day, listening to the recording of that session, I can still feel the impact of that work.

Emma and Joel took me with them when they left for the work in New York, and I remained there until they left for London. In addition to conducting *The 1958 New York Closed Class*, Joel was invited by Sig Paulson, the minister of the Unity Church, to give a talk at the Unity Center.

As always, there were lessons on spiritual principles that came quite naturally during the day-to-day experiences. Some of the clearest came at breakfast. It was on one such morning that Joel, in explaining the principle of living as a beholder with no desires, used the cake of ice floating in the glass of water as an example. So impressive was it, that as soon as I could break away I went to my room and wrote down all of it that I could remember. The essence of this incident was sent to Joel in my letter of August 11, 1958, and later incorporated into *A Parenthesis in Eternity*.[3]

Joel urged me to make an appointment to meet with Eugene Exman, the editor of The Religious Book Department of Harper & Row. Much of the correspondence I had with him involved changes the copy editor wanted to make in the manuscripts which would have altered the meaning. These changes I refused to agree to and elaborated at some length on my reasons for not making them and the spiritual principle involved.

For this first encounter, I dressed up in my best and most appropriate "bib and tucker." When I went into his office, we shook hands, and each sat looking at the other for a few moments. Then Mr Exman broke the silence. "You don't look at all the way I expected you to look."

"I don't? How did you expect me to look?"

Being very much of a gentleman he paused for a moment and then hesitatingly responded, "Well, perhaps a little thinner."

3 Joel S. Goldsmith, *A Parenthesis in Eternity* (New York: Harper & Row, 1963) Pp 278-282. Also see page 248 below.

"Oh, you mean the ascetic type?"

"That's it! And here you are a woman of the world."

Years later when I recounted this to a group of Infinite Way students they burst out in uncontrollable laughter, "You, a woman of the world? You are the most unworldly woman we've ever known."

After some conversation, Mr. Exman called on some of his assistants and together they questioned me about how the manuscripts were put together. I explained how the material was taken from many different tapes of Joel's recorded classwork and woven together into a unified whole. The comment of one person there who later found himself at the very top echelon in that firm, remarked, "You're not an editor; you're a collaborator."

May 18, 1958

Dear Emma and Joel,

Well, the wanderer has returned to find out what home sweet home looks like. And how does it look? Good, but dirty and neglected. Decorators are coming in this week to clean up the place and then I will be spick-and-span for a long, long stay at home....

The past year and a half has been such a wonderful immeasurable, really fabulous experience—well, there isn't a word for it. Now to settle down to let the little sprouts, so carefully nurtured, burst forth in all their beauty and abundant fruitage....

Letters and messages of gratitude greeted me when I returned home, and amazingly enough, although not amazing to you, there had been only the tiniest bit of "treatment" connected with any of these and some not at all....There was just such an assurance of a completed universe that I couldn't get excited. Now to let more and more of what you have given me, Joel, solidify within me by practice and eternal vigilance. There are still plenty of cases that make me realize how far I have to go, but these, and the way in which they were handled, make me feel that I've flown that "57 seconds" of the Wright brothers' first flight.

I still say that it is hard to evaluate the work in New York, i.e., to determine how much of what happened to me happened because of the class or because of the work you did with me directly. Those hours of direct teaching while in New York are some of the most important hours in my whole life, and there have been many important ones. Of course all the others before laid the groundwork that made it possible for these to be so important. It went deeper, much deeper than ever before and touched a chord which had never been played— plucked at a little—but not played....I have to tell you all these things, even though you must have known. I couldn't see myself but people said I was transformed.

Have mailed corrections for *The Master Speaks*. Most of the changes were relative to "Mind"—think all capital M's are eliminated and substitutions are made.

Being there with you at the St. Moritz, cut off from everyone else, and spending almost every waking hour with the two of you, made it the experience it was....All the difficult days and hours that are bound to come will be lightened by the remembrance of those precious days with my two most beloved friends. Thank you.

Lovingly yours,
Lorraine

June 8, 1958

Dear Emma and Joel,

You know I think I need some help! Everything under the sun seems to have come upon me this past week!....It began by my being horribly ill Wednesday morning....Then on Thursday I managed to fall flat on my face on State Street, but with the help of a couple of men I was able to get to my feet and proceed on my way. Pretty painful and I am still aware of such a thing as ribs, particularly when I breathe! Both hands were sprained, but I managed to get through two hours of class without anyone's knowing that anything had happened. I called Valborg when I reached home, and she gave me some really wonderful help so that I slept quite a bit of the night. Within two days my hands were comfortably usable, and it has not interfered with my activity in any way, but I still feel as if I have ribs! Strange, though, that the period after the class should be fraught with such difficulties—pardon me, "opportunities." But really I don't think I need such opportunities because the practice gives me plenty such.

Well, now my tale of woe is ended. Really I'm fine now—just a bit of pain but unimportant—and the reason I say I need help is that I must be off the beam to encounter such a series of situations in one week. Guess what I really need is some instruction as to where I am failing. I do see all this as impersonal error, personal sense, and that, I'm sure, is what has brought me through it all. I'm very grateful for the quick healings and lack of depressed feeling—not much response from me one way or the other....

Thank you for the book *Mirdad*.[4] It "speaks" to me. I love it. Also, I am finding much in Ernest Wood's commentary on the *Bhagavad-Gita* which you gave me. You know how much the *Gita* means to me. I always think of it as my preparation for The Infinite Way....

I would like to report officially, too, that this week's

4 Mikhail Naimy, *The Book of Mirdad* (Bombay, India: N.M. Tripathi, Ltd., Booksellers, 2. 1954).

experience caused a loss of exactly five pounds! See how we entertain angels unawares? How are the salads at 56 Curzon Street? Hope you are having a most beautiful experience and loving every minute of it.

Lovingly yours,
Lorraine

June 20, 1958

Dear Emma and Joel,

Thank you for your most welcome letter. Yes, I knew you had taken hold and were standing by and I'm most grateful. Really I wasn't too concerned about all the unpleasant happenings *as such*, but only as an indication of some failure on my part. I learned "The Wisdoms" too well to believe that anything can take place outside of my consciousness. I did have a strong sense of directed malpractice, but evidently was not sufficiently aware that my mind is my mind and my instrument and, therefore, can't be manipulated or be an instrument for world beliefs or suggestions to operate. Probably personal sense came in.

No, I didn't black out—have done that only once in my life, and very gracefully at that, in a college class in psychology.... What happened was that I tripped on the curb at State and Madison—those big feet of mine! It was the first time I had fallen in 20 years and it was a severe one, but although there is still a soreness in the region of the breast, I'm not conscious of it most of the time. My cheek is beginning to turn a chartreuse color like your draperies at home, much prettier there than on my cheek. Otherwise, there is no visible evidence. It really did bring forth some soul-searching and one of these periods of purging which in the end lifts one a notch higher....

Again thank you for your help. Have fun!
Lovingly yours,
Lorraine

July 3, 1958

Dear Emma and Joel,

Thank you, thank you—so many times thank you—for your dear letters and beautiful, thoughtful expressions of love....

I just received your note about the work you are doing for the Ten....I didn't know you were doing any special work, but for the past two weeks, the work of the Inner Group has been especially close to me, occupying a much larger portion of the day and night than heretofore, and I was going to write to ask you if you had any special message for us and that I would be happy to send copies of it to the others in the Group. Interesting? I have been doing more than the usual amount of work with a meditation, "Be still, and know that I am God."

On Monday, June 23, when K.B. was here, we had considerable meditation and, for the fourth time, the pool of blue in my forehead, shaped like an eye and which I interpret as the third Eye, came. Just before that, I had had such a wonderful feeling of freedom from all desire for any effect—I have to confess that sometimes after hearing about everybody else's experiences, I have longed just a little for some effect, some unusual effect—but this time I just knew that I am, and with such assurance what more could I possibly want? It was not necessary for me to feel anything, or have any kind of a sign given me, and then that experience came. A couple of days later there was a pool of blue in the region of the heart—lovely and peaceful—and then it expanded and I was in it. It is so seldom that visual experiences of this nature come to me, and it always seems to be of this same nature, but it may have no significance whatsoever, and yet it was very beautiful.

You know, Joel, when other people see lights around you, on rare occasions, I see the Eye in your forehead as I did on Tuesday and Wednesday of the First Class here in April. It has played a part in my meditation for the last ten days, and I have been so aware of it. Interesting, too, that just a day before yesterday the lovely book *Sun of Tabriz*[5] arrived, in which this Third Eye figures so prominently in the illustrations. Thank you so very much for sending it to me. I've had some lovely moments with it. Please tell me if you think my imagination is running riot—doesn't seem so to me because I wasn't hoping or seeking any kind of an experience. [*Joel answered this letter by sending it back to me with the marginal notes and for this paragraph he said, "Very good! Excellent."*]

S. and T. were over here on Tuesday evening. T. himself likes his review of *Practicing the Presence* and said it had been very easy to do—"Some of Joel's emanations must have reached me." T. had been so interested in the chapter, "Love Thy Neighbor," that I had promised to play him one of your recordings about the one Self, so that was their reason for coming over. He heard the first side of the *Seattle Private Tape*—the one you gave in 1955—on "Cosmic Law and Grace." He was surprised by the simplicity and directness with which you speak and by your lack of any attempt to "sell" an idea, the noncoercive technique. He said, "That's the longest period of time I've ever listened to Joel on a recording, and I am very favorably impressed—*very* favorably." He is enjoying the monthly *Letters* of late and wondered if they were not better written than before, or "perhaps I appreciate them more." He thinks *Practicing the Presence* a very, very good book, and added, "That's coming from someone who is not committed." He likes it much better than *The Art of Meditation*—me, too. Said he found it difficult to quote anything you write—couldn't remember it—and yet it became an unquotable part of him.

5 Jalauddim Rumi, *Sun of Tabriz* (Cape Town, S.A.: S. Beerman Publishers (PTY) Ltd., 1956).

You will especially love this part of our conversation: "I don't know whether or not I've mellowed, but when I first met you, I thought you were completely crazy—a wonderful teacher like you,—to have given all that up for anything so nebulous as this, but now I'm beginning to understand your motivation, and don't think it is crazy at all. I am surprised at how, without any outer compulsion, my whole attitude has changed during the last year and a half." Don't you think that is interesting? S. and T. are a real joy to me. [*To these last two paragraphs, Joel replied, "Really wonderful."*]

Have fun in Scotland—and more deep experiences. Thank you for the kindnesses you shower on me and for your work for me. I am "every whit whole" now—very deep thanks for that, too.

With much love,
Lorraine

July 28, 1958

Dear Emma and Joel,

Well, of course, you would wonder how I came by the picture [*of Joel when in the Marines with my brother-in-law and two other Marines*]. Actually, when I first saw it, I thought it was you; but when I explain certain circumstances, you'll understand my caution.

It all came about because Valborg, the sweet apple, first made a book of family photographs for me and then decided to make one for Swanhild [*our sister*]. We had gone through my storeroom and unearthed some charming pictures of Mother at St. Olaf College and while on her visit to Norway, and there was one of each kind for each of us. When we arrived at Swanie's, Valborg proceeded to get Swanie's book in order and naturally asked for pictures of Perry, Swanie's husband, so that they could be included in the book. Among the pictures was this one which I sent you. I thought it resembled you, but I couldn't make the bridge in my mind and so held my peace. However, when Valborg saw it, she said, "Why, that's Joel." Well, of course, we were all agog. Perry had a large picture which he had blown up from a snapshot and on it were the names—Goldsmith, the third one. Perry got out the program of a dinner the Masons had and on it was your name, but listed as Julius, and above all things as "trumpeter" or "bugler"—I've forgotten which. Well, that made us wonder if it might have been your brother, but there were certain facial features that were so like you that it was hard to believe that it could be other than you. As Perry told some of the incidents—how he never got overseas and so forth, I remembered some of the things you had told me and the two coincided, but as you notice, I proceeded with caution.

We were all quite thrilled that it is you, and isn't it interesting that it should be so? Perry—Corporal Wheeler of the picture as you say, and incidently the person to whom you have inscribed two books "To Swanhild and Perry, for their quiet moments—" is my brother-in-law. He was very much interested that there should have been such a connection and said laughingly, "Well, Joel may be your boss, but he's my buddy." I never believe things *just* happen and wonder what will come of this. They have never been Infinite Way students, but Swanie, you know, lives by the *Secret of the Twenty-Third Psalm.*[6] They are both pleased with what I am doing—probably thought I was crazy at first, not Swanie, of course, because everybody in my family always thought I'd wind up doing something like this, but they have been pleased to see my joy and sense of fulfillment. I hope they will have the opportunity to meet both of you some day.

With love to you both,
Lorraine

6 Joel S. Goldsmith. *The Secret of the Twenty-Third Psalm.*

August 9, 1958

Dear Emma and Joel,

...Thank you for sending the "Travelogs" and "Across the Desks." Loved the Thanksgiving and Christmas ones but wondered what had happened to call forth the one on Tape Recording Groups. It out-manuals the [*Christian Science*] *Manual*. Anyway, I'm glad you sent it to me when you did because I was just going to write you about some stirrings within me that were about to spill over into a six weeks class this fall on the subject of spiritual healing—I'm so full of it from the work on the book and the practice. I really hadn't wanted to do anything like that but have the feeling that I should, which shows how completely I misinterpreted you because I thought you were encouraging me to do that sort of thing. Now I see that not only do I not have to feel that I am shirking a job, but that I would have been going contrary to your precepts in doing it. Sometime ago you told me that I should talk for at least 15 minutes to our group preceding a recording to point up the principles, and this I have tried to do, but never for more than a very few minutes. However, I'll stop that and get back to the straight and narrow. I've certainly been in error and I'm terribly sorry....

This book on spiritual healing is to be a beginner's book— the ABC's of spiritual healing—simple enough to be understandable to a person who knows little or nothing about it and yet with enough meat to challenge the most advanced student. That sounds like a good enough straddle to be worthy of a political party platform! Always my thanks and my love to you both,

Lorraine

In response to that letter, Joel urged me to speak even

more at tape meetings and not to use that particular "Across the Desk."

August 11, 1958

Dear Emma and Joel,

I had forgotten to send you the enclosed summation of the lessons you gave Emma and me at breakfast at the San Moritz Hotel on Zen. I find myself referring to them constantly and have had some quite powerful—for me—unfoldments about a piece of ice in a glass. It has not been anything new, and I'm sure it is only a sinking into consciousness of what you told us—Emma and me—in those two lessons. May I share a couple of them with you?

The ice is individual, yet of the same substance as the water. It, however, is dependent upon the water for all its activity—"I can of mine own self do nothing." Every action is the action of the water itself.

The ice is embraced by the water, sustained and supported by it, upheld in its identity. Only a small part of it, the smallest part, is visible above the water; the rest is immersed in the water itself. So with us.

Then in connection with the Inner Group work:

Because this is a spiritual activity, it is not circumscribed by time or space; it knows no barriers, no bonds, restraint or limit to its scope. All nine students converge and merge in the realized *I* of them and of the one teacher. Then, as rays of light, each having become a body of Light, all go, each one his separate way, to light his particular world, but all united and upholding each other. In that oneness, each group can meet regularly, on the inner plane.

Today is our fourth anniversary. Just four years ago we

moved to 30 West Washington! We are celebrating by having the decorators in this week and sending out the rugs and draperies to be cleaned!

In the wee small hours of the morning I've been taking time out to work with the Inner Group material. Marvelous beyond words, and the few of us who have had this very great privilege are surely blessed beyond all people. Feel so little of what has been given to me shows forth, but I'm working on it, even though it may not seem so.

Thank you for your love, understanding, and patience.

Lovingly yours,
Lorraine

August 24, 1958

Dear Emma and Joel,

It must have been a wonderful five months that you had [*in England and on the Continent*] but I can well imagine how happy you will be to be home again, even though it is for so short a period of time. I should think you both would want to stay "put" next year—at least until the new book is off the press!

I will hold up material on the Study Center notice [This was for an "Across the Desk" mentioned earlier] for a rewrite for a later date. I know what you mean about these people who are aching to be teachers and be in the limelight. They think it is all glory! How little they know! I have come to the conclusion that the right course of action for me, at the present time, is to stand still right where I am and continue the work as it is proceeding at the present time, making a short introduction to the Recordings in which some principle is pointed up and doing the healing work which comes to me from far and wide. You did only healing work for sixteen years, and certainly I don't begin to approximate the consciousness you had even then, so the way is pretty clear for me....

You say the work of the "Ten" has not been satisfactory. Of course, that does not surprise me because I have never felt that I was functioning adequately as a part of it, but, to me, that work is very important—the most important thing there is and perhaps *the* reason for my coming into The Infinite Way. In some way or other, it holds fulfillment for me. It hasn't come, but it seems that if you ever teach me what is your vision in its fullness, I shall have learned what I came here to learn. I'm ashamed to confess this, but sometimes I become so bogged down in the day to day work—the *Letter*, the book, and the healing work which has been heavy and which has involved considerable correspondence—the work of the Inner Group does not receive as much attention as it should have. Actually, for a novice such as I to perform it satisfactorily would require hours and hours every day devoted just to that....Maybe someday a few of us will be able to devote all of our time to just such a purpose. In one sense it seems that my own pattern of life at the moment is ideal as a preparation for such work because in breaking material sense in specific cases which come for healing, consciousness, buttressed by concrete evidence of the nonpower of material sense, is being developed—albeit painfully slowly.

I'm not doing too well with myself right now—struggling physically. It came to me most forcibly yesterday that if you break this form of material sense for yourself, you will break it for thousands of others. Today I have done very well, maybe something cracked—a little shell or an onion skin peeled off!

So much love to you both,
Lorraine

On September 2, Joel sent me a telegram cancelling all public work for the remainder of the year. The ensuing months were exceedingly difficult for Joel and I understood how deep was the turmoil and suffering of this inner experience, which was to take him to the next horizon.

September 14, 1958

Dear Emma and Joel,

I'm still speechless at the magnitude of an experience which would lead to your decision, but trust that it portends the fulfillment you are seeking. For that, there can only be rejoicing. It was good hearing your voice over the telephone....

Do you remember that I asked you to retell the story of the Copernican theory and have Mary transcribe it from the dictaphone? Did you forget or did you know that I would find it? Shortly after I wrote you for it, I had a most interesting experience....Suddenly in the midst of playing the tape Monday evening, selected 3 months earlier for our quarterly schedule, I pricked up my ears because there you were telling the very story for which I was waiting, and when I returned home I turned right to it in my file. This is just a little thing, but such a clear evidence of the guiding Hand. Sometimes these little things are more thrilling than the big ones; they carry with them such a conviction of Grace....

The transcription of your Holland talk arrived. What a mess she (the transcriber) made of it. I've listened to hundreds of recordings and read an equal number of transcriptions but I never heard you talk like that before. How your beautiful Infinite Way is garbled....

Know you are enjoying being home. My love to all.

Lovingly yours,
Lorraine

September 19, 1958

Dear Emma and Joel,

Thank you, thank you for your prompt reply to my letter via cable. How kind and thoughtful of you!

....The pamphlet on *Parsifal* is a most beautiful interpretation of what to me is one of the deepest experiences possible in music. I had heard it so many times over the radio when it was performed by the "Met," but in New York in March of 1956 I had my first opportunity to see as well as hear it, and that was almost as deep an experience for me as the classes. You would have loved that performance because it was so mystical in its presentation and avoided association with any particular religious form—which horrified the people sitting near me. They thought it was sacrilegious. I am so happy that you let me read this interpretation of it—it was what I felt. I put much—I think all—of Parsifal on tape when the "Met" presented it one year, expecting to play it regularly for my Soul's pleasure. Must get it out and try it. There is nothing to compare with the Good Friday music of that opera.

Thank you for sharing your unfoldment relative to the cancer case that the omnipresence of Love holds everything in right relationship one to another. It helps, because it registers. It had come to me that divine Intelligence governs every activity and every thing, always maintaining it in its rightful place—not too much, not too little, no interference of one thing with another.

Lovingly yours,
Lorraine

Work on *The Art of Spiritual Healing*, plus meeting deadlines for the monthly *Letter* had involved months of work from early morning until long after midnight. And I was vulnerable. Joel too was at a very low ebb during this period of waiting for guidance as to the next step. Then he received my letter of September 14 along with a mass of other mail, he evidently read it in such a hurry and being "edgy" and weary misinterpreted it to mean that I was criticizing the talk he had given. He sent a blistering letter to me that threw me into the depths. In the following letter of October 5, I attempted to clarify my meaning, and one can read between the lines.

As I read my last impetuous letter to you, I realized that you might have inferred that in some way I felt competent to interpret your meaning or even pass judgment on what you say. That I would never dream of doing—I hope you know that, but if my spontaneous outburst had that implication, please forgive me. When I spoke about mistakes I did not mean in your presentation of The Infinite Way. Sometimes you do come down to the human level and are quite human in your judgments. However, I am not referring to your class or lecture work. If that is wrong, please tell me.

Thank you for your work with me. It has been tough—and that is the understatement of the year...The clearest thing that has come to me—and it is clear as crystal—after hours and days and nights of meditation and inner searching...is that opaqueness is the chief characteristic of a human being because a human being is a state of self-deception, and that as a human being I can never realize the Vision. I thought the human being in me had all but died because I am not aware of any desire for anything, but evidently it still haunts and plagues me....

Even though I no longer fear you, Joel, I stand in very great awe of you as a teacher, so great that I marvel that I could ever come to such a state of complete self-surrender.

In response to this letter, Joel and Emma both got on the
telephone and assured me of their love and confidence in
me and of the importance of this moment in my life and
for The Infinite Way. The net result of this inner struggle
brought forth that very loving response. Joel recognized
that I had been working at a fierce pace and needed a
change. He urged me to take a few days off for a vacation
so I could unwind and sent me a check for that purpose.

                                        October 16, 1958
Dear Emma and Joel,
     I act like a perfect fool, you turn around and shower love
and kindness upon me! I'm speechless! I shouldn't go away
with all there is to be done, but remembering that God has a
way of doing more in 12 seconds than we can do in 12 hours, I
shall follow through on your orders—imagine calling a vacation
an order! I'll get busy tomorrow and work out something and
let you know where I'm going. You said to drop everything and
so I shall do just that, taking off for somewhere next Tuesday
morning. I can't go before because I have tickets for *Il
Travotore* at the Lyric Opera next Monday evening after the
meeting. You wouldn't want me to miss that.
     Your signals really reached me because on Sunday I
decided I'd do a better job if all work were put aside for one day,
and Sunday after our meeting seemed to be a good time for
such a day of rest. All of your admonitions about getting away
from work to rest on Cloud 99 came back to me and, along with
the resolve to take Sunday off, I went over and bought tickets
for three operas—*Il Travatore, Tristan and Isolde,* and *Boris
Godounoff*, three favorites of mine that they are presenting this
year.
     Somehow, I, too, feel, as you indicate, that this is an
important moment in my spiritual ongoing and that a period of

quiet is very important for the next step. Do you know how I want and love to serve and be of whatever help I can be, to do whatever you give me to do? I am so ashamed to have been so much asleep that personal sense crept in. Of course, no one can be of any use or service if self is in the ascendancy. The body has been burdensome lately, and I know that you will help me to lay aside all personal sense of body and mind. I shall find out tomorrow about a reservation and let you know.

Lovingly yours,
Lorraine

October 18, 1958

Dear Emma and Joel,

Well, everything is all set, and I am leaving Tuesday morning for a quiet and restful time at Starved Rock Lodge at Utica, Illinois, overlooking the Illinois River and in Starved Rock State Park. It is supposed to be a really lovely place and not so far away that getting there will be arduous—about 100 miles southwest of Chicago. I want to drive so that I can take along my tape recorder and some books to read, and if there are any by-roads that look intriguing, it might be fun to explore them.

I'm not a bit sure that I'll know how to act—it's the first time I have ever gone off completely alone to be alone. It will be a time of drinking deep draughts of the Spirit and a great rising in consciousness—I trust. Think, maybe, I've learned that I can't take the kingdom of heaven by storm—I tried awfully hard and the results were almost tragic. So I shall remember my little piece of ice in a glass of water and rest in Isness.

Remember, Joel, when you asked Emma and me what the greatest sin was? Well, I'm not so sure it is stupidity as much as taking oneself too seriously. A good healthy sense of humor in regard to oneself is surely a saving grace on the spiritual path! Incidentally, one of the books that will accompany me

will be *Heavenly Discourse*[7]—yes, and *Mirdad*. Please be close
to me in the ensuing days—I shall be very near to you both.

With much love,
Lorraine

P.S. I would really like to return the check you sent, if it would
not seem ungrateful and unappreciative of me. I should rather
be sending one to you. Would you understand if I did return it?
I do have money for the trip and just your pushing me into this
period of renewal is wonderful, and more wonderful, bearing
with me, and even more wonderful, being close to me in the
forthcoming days. Thank you.

Lorraine

Starved Rock, Illinois
October 21, 1958

Dear Emma and Joel,
     The two and a half hour drive was restful and easy.
Autumn has never been quite so beautiful. The countryside is
ablaze with great huge bouquets of variegated colored leaves on
the trees, startling in their brilliance, and the air is a balmy 80
degrees. Makes me want to paraphrase Lowell, "What is so
rare as a day in October?"

October 22

     Twenty-four hours and I'm completely renewed. I have
that "born again" feeling I experienced during my first
meditation with you, Joel, September 28, 1949.

7 Charles Erskine Scott Wood, *Heavenly Discourse* (New York, N.Y.:
Vanguard Press, Inc., 1927).

I can scarcely contain myself as I sit in the dining room with the other guests, fairly bursting inside and marveling that they can't see that they are looking at a caterpillar who has sloughed off its skin and is soaring and soaring. Have had a very wonderful healing and release.

Last night, not much sleep, but a continuous dwelling in the Presence. This morning a tape in bed, a late breakfast, and a guided walk—for two hours up and down hundreds of steps to the top of Starved Rock, down into the Devil's Bath Tub, up Jacob's Ladder, and down into French Canyon.

This is a beautiful spot. Couldn't have dreamed anything like it could be so near Chicago. The Lodge is like the finest city hotel and far more attractively furnished than any I have seen. My room is knotty pine, looking out upon trees in all stages of maturity. The trees being stripped of their brilliant foliage only to make room for the new is a powerful example of what must happen to us—what has been happening to me— only I can't imagine a tree ever feeling bare.

October 23
There is a continuous song inside of me which says, "I now have no mind or body of my own. These are now Yours completely. They are only instruments for Your activity, instruments through which I function."

October 26
This has been a very rewarding and satisfying experience, a time to drink deeply of the Spirit and bask in the Presence. That's really what I've been doing. Much has come through on the *I*. Waking up several times each night, It sings within me.

All the materials of the Inner Group have been thoroughly reviewed and most assiduously practiced. It's just a year since that work began, and I can evaluate it only in terms of my own unfoldment. Particularly has it driven home [the nature of] hypnotism so that reinterpreting appearances as hypnotism has been practically automatic in the healing work: a clear perception of the substance of every problem and of all human good or evil as a mental image, and the importance of daily establishing myself in *I*. The practice of the meditation, "Be still and know that I am God," has been most fruitful. During the past few months I neglected it and, coming back to it again, its value is even more apparent to me. Seated at the top of my head, a searching light from the *I* seems to penetrate every portion of the body on which it rests.

Realization in the areas given us for work has varied greatly from time to time in intensity, from almost a deadness to reaching the heights. But I'm sure the work others have done and that I have done has been effective in my own healing work. Perhaps this year is but the prelude to more effective [*prayer*] work for the world. This Inner Work is still in its infancy so far as its practice is concerned, but you have given us enough to last throughout all time and to lead us up into eternity.

Much of my meditation has begun with "*I* am the Way." I found myself walking toward a marble building along a path which seemed to be a beam of light. There were shadows on the side and, when I looked, they were the shadows of self sloughed off bit by bit.

Since Friday I've been rested. I cheated a little, took some work with me, and began Friday reading transcriptions. Now my fingers itch to get back to the typewriter, and I think I shall go back tomorrow or Tuesday and then maybe come back again for a couple of days later on—might even do that once a month.

Lovingly yours,
Lorraine

Evanston, Illinois
November 18, 1958

Dear Emma and Joel,

Where to begin? Seems like centuries since I've written to you, so let me begin by answering your last two letters. First, about your invitation to go to Hawaii. It sounds very, very wonderful....I'm afraid I can't resist such an invitation. It seems each trip has been better than the preceding one, and I shall never forget the holidays last year and those wonderful days and weeks at Halekou Place! Priceless memories for me— so alive that they are not really memories at all....

Hey, hey! What do you mean by saying, "Please, please!" Surely both of you, who know the joy of giving so well, would not deprive us of that same pleasure! No matter what the monetary value of the projector you want, it would be inconsequential as compared with the love and gratitude of which it is but the symbol. Furthermore, Joel, you forget what a good teacher you are. Slow as I have been, a few of your lessons have actually registered so that they are second nature—just a few. My teacher surely would not deny me the opportunity of putting his lesson on the infinite nature of supply into practice? Well, I must get busy.

With much love to you both,
Lorraine

December 9, 1958

Dear Emma and Joel,

So sorry for you dear people having such a cold, cold spell! You poor dears! We had a mere 12 below zero this morning with a prospect of from 5 to 10 below tonight, plus snow.

It looks as if I should be able to make it by December 22....It will be wonderful to see all of you.

With much love,
Lorraine

So, on December 22, I set out on my fourth trip to Hawaii and my second Christmas with Emma and Joel. The Alexander Young Hotel in Honolulu, where my reservation had been made, was only a short distance from the bus stop and taxi service out to Halekou Place, where I usually arrived early, spent the day, and often waited until the last taxi left for Honolulu in the evening.

These days were exceedingly difficult for Joel. After his trip to Holland and his interview with Mrs. Hoffman, the spiritual adviser to the then Queen of Holland who had advised him to retire from active work for the time being, he had gone directly home to await further orders, cancelling all scheduled class work. Waiting was not easy for a person like Joel, who wanted tomorrow's work done today, but in obedience to inner guidance he remained at home, chafing a bit at the waiting, but nevertheless waiting for that longed-for next step in the fulfillment of his message that seemed to elude him.

Busy as he was, one sensed the inner turmoil and sometimes a quite obvious misery, which some of his letters indicated. This turmoil continued until his not-so-easily come by patience had its reward: a new ordination was bestowed on him, about which Joel wrote on April 15. With it, came a clear direction as to the nature of the work he was to do with the students: specific instructions on the principles of The Infinite Way. He realized that many of the students were simply "floating" on a rosy-hued cloud with none of the fruitage in their lives or their work that is an inevitable concomitant of spiritual realization. Immediately, he made plans for the remainder of the year, which included a class in Hawaii in July and a trip to England and Europe.

Before I left Hawaii on February 10, I tucked the following letter of gratitude into the midst of his mail:

Halekou Place
Kaneohe, Hawaii
February 2, 1959

Dear Emma and Joel,

Anything I might attempt to say about this wonderful visit would sound trite and inadequate, but surely you can read my heart and know what a joy and privilege it has been for me to be here....

The quiet, the peace, and serenity, the overshadowing kindness and love, the matchless lessons given with such patience and understanding have all helped to renew me in body and spirit so that I go forth with a new perspective, beholding "a new heaven and a new earth."

All of this I have accepted gratefully as a gift of love flowing out from the generosity of your heart. And now will you please accept this tiny gift which is enclosed in the same spirit? It does not begin to compensate you, even from a purely monetary standpoint, for all you have done for me—and it is not meant to do so. It is just my love flowing out into form, so please do not mention it.

Lovingly yours,
Lorraine

Evanston, Illinois
February 12, 1959

Dear Emma and Joel,

Home again, or shall I say home to my other home, because when I was with you I felt I was home, too?...

The weather had been so bad here that no planes were going in or out until the morning I arrived, so that nobody expected me to make it. But Chicago and Evanston really put on a show for my homecoming! Never have the trees been so beautiful. Can you picture a forest of diamonds? Every tree was covered with diamonds—drops of frozen water—polished to a dazzling brilliance by the sun. It was so beautiful it almost hurt. Furthermore, the weather had moderated and reached up into the high 30's or low 40's. But the streets are still [*almost*] impassable, deep ruts, snow, and ice.

Lovingly yours,
Lorraine

Under separate cover, Joel sent his private notes made during this period of waiting for the new message. In a letter of appreciation for this material I tried to convey how much it meant to me.

Thank you for sending me the notes you made last September. I didn't stop to read this material until late afternoon....When I did, the telephone cooperated and remained silent, giving me several hours in which I was lost in another world: "Release yourself now, completely, to *Me*. Release yourself from thought, and *I* will speak. This is the full surrender of the self." And "I experienced myself as life independent of form!" That stays with me—I cannot let it go. Of course I do not yet fully take it in, but just see it as a far-off goal—to *experience* it would be something! At least I can dream. I don't know how this material will be used, but it will probably find its way into a new book as a precious jewel in a setting which will have to be worthy of it.

The last days I have been haunted a bit, Joel, as the conviction grows that your full attainment is imminent. Please,

I hope it is not *too* complete! I like you visible.

Occasionally, I objected to a certain bluntness in the way Joel stated something which could so easily shock the reader. I had a protective sense about having whatever went into the books have a timeless quality since it was a message not only for today but for posterity. To that effect I wrote Joel on February 22, 1959:

February 22, 1959

Dear Emma and Joel,

I'm enclosing a copy of "Across the Desk." However, I should like to have you give serious consideration to the first sentence. I have not altered your phraseology as you will observe, but I should like to....

Okay. I've had my say. Remember this goes into a book that will be in print for a long, long time.

Do you know that it is tough to be the editor for your teacher? The student is not supposed to disagree with the teacher and the editor is supposed to be completely detached. Anyway, please think about it seriously and don't make it any worse.

Lovingly yours,
Lorraine

Two days later I wrote: "....Thanks for accepting the change in the 'Across the Desk.'...I make suggestions rather hesitatingly, but you notice I still make them. You see, I'm quite incorrigible! It's wonderful having you as my teacher and that was foreordained, but I think my job as editor might be easier for me if you were just another writer! However, I like it the way it is...."

April 10, 1959

Dear Emma and Joel,

I have in front of me I don't know how many notes, letters, and telegrams from you to answer so will attempt to do this as best I can. You've probably wondered why you have not heard further from me during this week and perhaps this letter will explain that, too....

Thank you for your most generous gift. I do hope the day will come when a couple of days in the country will be possible timewise. Maybe, but even now the June *Letter* is being neglected because of the urgent demands of this book [*The Art of Spiritual Healing*]. However, we hope to get at the *Letter* by the end of this next week. Thank you for "Across the Desk." Anyway, you are very dear to want me to take some time off and to send me a check to push me into it. Thank you.

Interesting and wonderful that April 1st was such a wonderful day in your experience.... When you said, "I take you with me," I had such mixed feelings—such deep, deep gratitude and the kind of humility that made me think I was reverting to orthodoxy because I felt so terribly unworthy and inadequate. I knew that you would have the will or desire to do it—take me into that higher consciousness—but would I be sufficiently responsive to be able to follow? That plagues me, especially knowing what hell you have gone through to reach those heights. I felt a million miles and eons of time away from it, and after this week, just multiply that sense of inadequacy by another million. But please, I'm waiting and trying to be in readiness. Having to come back into the business of this world even for the shortest of moments after reaching a state of consciousness, the sublime heights of which no human being can conceive and I can only speculate about, must be sheer torture, and surely must account for the subsequent gloom. If an outpouring of love and gratitude would help, you would now

be tabernacling in the Holy of Holies.
Again I say, "I am waiting and praying."
With much love,
Lorraine

April 12, 1959

Dear Joel and Emma,

....This was a weary and worn gal who opened her mailbox last night and found a letter waiting for her in that familiar handwriting—and such a letter! Of course I'd love to go [*to Hawaii for the July, 1959, class*] but just can't believe that I'm to go so soon again. I was just there! I've had no feeling that I would be there, and then along comes this wonderful letter. I can leave any time late in June. Probably Thursday, June 25, would be the best time—if that is soon enough to help with all the details of the class such as registration, etc. So far as I'm concerned it does not matter....Thank you again for being so dear to me always.
Lovingly yours,
Lorraine

At this time Emma's daughter-in-law and son became the parents of a daughter.

April 17, 1959

Dear Grandma and Grandpa,

Congratulations! I think it is just wonderful that after all the veiled insults to grandmothers, one in our midst is now a grandfather! Bet he'd be just as ga-ga about his grandchild as any grandmother....Yes, this is quite a spiritual demonstration—to be a grandfather without being a father. If you ever feel gloomy again, just remember that you have really exceeded the demonstration of all the great masters....

Well, to my favorite grandmother and grandfather, my love,

Lorraine

April 23, 1959

Dear Emma and Joel,

Thank you for your encouraging letter, containing such wonderful news: the mantle of Elijah! The Robe! [*Joel wrote of an inner experience in which these symbols of spiritual attainment were bestowed on him.*] Is not that the full and complete attainment?—the "he that cometh after me....whose shoes I am not worthy to bear: he shall baptize you with the Holy Ghost, and with fire....he will burn up the chaff with unquenchable fire." Yes, that's it....

The beatitude, "Blessed are the pure in heart for they shall see God," has been constantly recurring to me recently. Purity—not the world's concept which is fairly easy to achieve, but a purity in which all the dross of humanhood is burned away, leaving not a single trace of separateness. Out of an unrelenting urgency, I ask you to please help me speed that day when [for me] the chaff is burned up "with unquenchable fire."

My love to you both,
Lorraine

8

A New Emphasis

For the 1959 Hawaiian Village Class, several students came from foreign countries and well over a hundred from the mainland. During the long months of waiting for the next step, while Joel remained at home after cancelling his plans for classes and lectures in 1958 and early 1959, it had come to him that many students failed to make The Infinite Way a living experience because they did not understand the principles and were not practicing them. For that reason, in the July class, Joel specifically emphasized basic principles of The Infinite Way: 1) the nature of God; 2) the nature of individual being; and (3) the nature of error.

With greater clarity than ever before, he stressed the nature of error, emphasizing the importance of impersonalizing a problem as the carnal mind and then nothingizing the carnal mind as having no power and no person, avenue, or channel through which to operate. Although all of these principles are interrelated, impersonalization is one of the most difficult principles not only to understand, but also to practice. Perhaps that is because in one way or another, practically every problem involves a person. If that is true, then how is it possible to impersonalize?

To understand impersonalization it is necessary to be thoroughly grounded in the nature of God or Consciousness as infinite Being embracing all that is real, permanent, unchanging, and true, besides which there is no other enduring reality. That immediately makes clear the principle that there can be no being other than that one all-inclusive Being. Therefore, every person must be that one Being revealing Itself individually, with everyone the allness and fullness of the One. All that the One is and has is the truth about Its individualization as a person. With the third principle of the nature of error, the other two principles become believable, reasonable, and practical. If the one Being is all-in-all, then whatever does not measure up to the perfection, wholeness, and completeness of that One is to be understood as a misinterpretation, an incorrect perception of the perfection that now is and is all-encompassing. That misperception is sometimes described as the carnal mind or an appearance. Something can appear to be what it is not at all. When one sees with a sharper focus more of what is there in reality becomes evident.

If we accept the principle that Consciousness is expressing as individual being, then that individual must express all that is the nature of that one Consciousness. Anything else cannot be a part of the person. Therefore, it is impersonal - a non-person. I came to see that it was an impersonal suggestion coming to me, appearing as a person, but actually without a person on whom or through whom to function—not an easy leap to take, but a necessary one. A suggestion is a mental misperception, a conditioned mind called the carnal mind forming itself as a false sense of a person. Because of the basic principle of oneness, in reality there is only one mind, a pure instrument or facet of the one Consciousness, never misperceiving anything.

All this work had a familiar ring to me. These principles had been driven home day after day in Joel's letters to me and in the many hours of direct personal teaching it was my privilege to be given. His work was always to lift the student above attempting to deal with problems as persons or conditions, even though problems always appear as a person or condition. Instead, students were taught to recognize every problem as an impersonal activity of that nothingness called the carnal mind, which is only a *belief* in two powers.

Joel placed special emphasis on such terms as mesmerism, hypnotism, and malpractice. This latter term was a word seldom used because he felt it might lead to personalization, but one with which he chose to experiment with me. None of these principles was new. What was new was the emphasis. Before *the 1959 Hawaiian Village Class*, Joel had directed a few of us to work exclusively with the word "malpractice" in dealing with specific cases or problems that came to our attention. This was a word I had avoided because my understanding of it had been of some person who, through a kind of mental concentration, maliciously tried to influence or hurt another person. Joel was not using the term in that sense at all. My letter of May 15, 1959 sheds some light on the results of my grappling with the term from The Infinite Way point of view:

Heretofore I had been working from the standpoint of hypnotism or mesmerism, and, of course, not specifically dealing with person, place, or condition, which at my present state of consciousness seems approximately the same as malpractice. However, your letter focusing attention on malpractice, made me give the whole subject serious attention and reevaluation, and certainly it has clarified itself for me.

Every case in the past several days has been handled with the one word "malpractice," with the realization of the nature of malpractice as no power—as a mental activity based on the false belief that this so-called carnal mind is a power, that it can create and destroy, whereas all it can create is a mental image—a substanceless shadow. Malpractice is a product of the carnal mind which is not mind and has no intelligence and no life—it is a nothingness, the "arm of flesh." It cannot operate through thought-transference or thought-projection because only "*My* thoughts" are power. Malpractice has no law to maintain it, is not a cause, and cannot produce an effect. Since it is not a cause it cannot cause disease or inharmony—it is a nothingness. Malpractice has no life to sustain it, no mind through whom or upon whom it can operate, etc., etc.

Do you pinpoint malpractice more definitely and differentiate it from the term "hypnotism," by recognizing it as *directed* with a specific intent? I shied away from this, although I do know there are organized and concerted efforts directed at anything which would liberate men, and I'm sure we should be consciously handling this. However, am I on safe ground simply to identify malpractice as the product of universal or carnal mind and proceed as above?

For some time—particularly the last few weeks—I have felt that there was a great need to handle malpractice, and this I attempted to do. Your directive to limit the work exclusively to malpractice has been particularly valuable. Usually I have not felt satisfied until I have realized what body is, or relationships, or supply, depending upon the particular call. The person or condition, as such, was not dealt with except insofar as, for example, a call about some disease would usually bring forth a realization about body, law, and substance.

Perhaps that is desirable and necessary, but in one sense I can see that it could be a disguise, masking a deep-seated belief that there is something to be changed or healed. Anyway, for the last few days since receiving your letter, I have refrained from doing this. I shall be grateful for your comments but I do not expect a treatise on malpractice for my special benefit! Just tell me yes or no.

Since I just returned home, I do not know what the tangible effects, so far as patients are concerned, have been under this procedure. However, I, myself, have had a very great sense of freedom in regard to the cases with which I am working—absolute conviction. Thought I had it before but it seems deeper and greater. That has been the primary result for me, this absolute conviction and the ease with which I have been able to reach that state of peace and dismiss whatever the problem was that was presented to me.

Much love to you both,
Lorraine

May 17, 1959

Dear Emma and Joel,

Well, I really hit the jackpot Friday when not one, but five letters arrived from you!

So glad you have resumed talks to the Ten.[1] The May 10th talk is wonderful—very helpful, especially the work on treatment. Below is a report relative to cataracts. So far this has been about the sum and substance of what has unfolded to me in regard to the two cases referred to me:

> This is malpractice: the belief that man has a physical body which can be sick or well, grow, mature, age, deteriorate, and disintegrate. This is a spiritual universe and every faculty in it, a spiritual faculty—

1 The Inner Working Group of seven had been expanded to ten.

incorporeal—always governed by spiritual law. Sight is a quality and activity of *I* and, therefore, omnipresent.

Mind forms its own conditions of body. Since that mind is an instrument for the activity of the *I* that I am, it is subject to that *I* and forms itself as harmonious conditions of body. There is no mind through which malpractice can operate or upon which it can operate as cause or effect, as a law of disease, or as a law of karma or theology. God's grace is the only law operating, and that is not law, but love.

These are the things that registered recently enough for me to remember them. Is this what you meant by [*asking for*] a report on my unfoldment? I might add that with these meditations has come a complete sense of the nothingness of these claims, and, of course, the above is but the scantiest summary of what came through. This is a wonderful opportunity because you will instantly recognize holes in the work and I shall be so grateful if you will call my attention to them.

Much love to you both,
Lorraine

It came to me very clearly that Joel's emphasis on malpractice was another way of helping, almost forcing, the student to become more adept at working with the principle of impersonalization, that principle which came alive for me at Halekou during Christmas of 1957. In dealing with every problem presented as malpractice, it eliminated the possibility of lapsing into the trap of seeing the problem as a person and placed it exactly where it belonged—in that great void of nothingness: no thing and no person. It became increasingly clear to me that in reality there could be no person who could be guilty of directed malpractice, a fear many metaphysical practitioners entertained. That was but another belief, along with all the other suggestions of lack, inharmony, and disease.

May 23, 1959
Saturday evening

Dear Emma and Joel,

Just returned from the office to find your letter relative to malpractice. A class on malpractice would be a wonderful experience, but you are surely right when you say it would have to be highly selective. The whole subject is really ringing a bell with me!

I'm grateful that you have given the work of "The Ten" a shot in the arm. The lesson given to us has been thoroughly studied. Certainly, I recognize karma [*the law of cause and effect*] as a powerful factor on the human level of life...but can we accept it as law any more than theological or medical laws which are continually being proved to be of no power? Maybe the whole secret is in the word "forgiveness" insofar as karma is concerned. Certainly karma does not take such a word into consideration because it is the grim doctrine of paying to the uttermost farthing—even when the possibility of committing the sin has long since gone. And forgiveness is a state of Grace. Karma cannot operate in that Fourth Dimension of life where the only law is Grace, so to rise to a state of Grace is it.

Lovingly yours,
Lorraine

June 4, 1959

Dear Emma and Joel,

So much good news from you two in the last few days! First let me tell you how thrilled and happy I am that XA and her family are moving here. I know I shall love her just as much as I love you, Emma—well, almost! I hope that they will be at Glenview Air Naval Training Station which is just west of Evanston rather than at Great Lakes. Do send me XA's address so that I can write to her to welcome her here, and also to find out how I can be of help to them. I look forward to meeting her husband and those three dear grandchildren. Maybe I'll have Sam down this way yet, if he comes to visit them during the summer. You know that you can count on me to look after him. Well, this is really wonderful news, and don't you, Joel, go and spoil it all by making any of those nasty comments about our beautiful climate here! Anyway, you like Chicago, don't you, Emma? The news that XA will be here is just like hearing that a very close part of my family is moving near me. So happy and thrilled.

Well, of course we are thrilled that you will be here in November. I have already called the Congress, and the Pine Room is reserved for lectures...Can you give me a date for Chicago classes or class in the spring? It would be highly desirable to book space *now*. Of course, I shall be in New York for the class in November. Don't know about the lectures, but I'm so greedy, I can hardly bear to miss a word.

Oh, yes, I have arranged for lectures in Chicago for Friday, Saturday evening, Sunday afternoon, and Monday evening, November 27,28,29, and 30. You really choose the lulu's of time to come! Easter and now Thanksgiving! Can't guarantee a crowd then, but will do my best. Didn't think you would want to lecture on Thanksgiving—guess last Easter is too fresh in my mind—but if you should, it can be arranged. Actually, you will be here long enough for a class, if you should want to give one, but I'm assuming your program is rather to reach the general public during these lectures and thus launch another Art [*The Art of Spiritual Healing*] on its way.

Did you feel me calling out to you on Wednesday? Boy, I was sick as a dog—not critically ill, but miserable enough to wish I were. Anyway, about seven in the evening while I was waiting for our Wednesday meeting to begin, it began to subside. I didn't telephone because I knew I'd live through it! But I felt a quick lift about that time and so I thank you.

The work has been going along well here, but is it ever tough when I feel like a washed out rag and have to come up smiling. I think that's the only thing I regret about this work! When my Christian Science chapter closed, after 20 years, I vowed I would never again get involved in anything where I had to be such a Spartan! Please don't misunderstand me— most of the time I'm fine, but these bouts now and then are no circus! I haven't had a full day in bed for years and years now for which of course, I am so grateful. I'm really grateful for everything—you know that, but it is for something much more important than not being sick in bed.

Soon, soon, I'll be seeing you, and how wonderful that will be.

With much love,
Lorraine

June 12, 1959

Dear Emma and Joel,

Thank you so much for your letter of June 5 which was helpful beyond words.

The paragraph in your letter on malpractice has been invaluable to me—just stated in such a way that it really clicked. Sorry the work for S.S. and H.H. has been so fruitless, but I shall, and am, continuing and see more and more that all these names are as you describe them "a mask for malpractice." I can see that this is the only way a large healing practice can be carried on, or for that matter any size of a successful healing practice.

I have taken the lesson embodied in your letter very seriously and am trying sincerely to practice and live it. But first before I comment on your analysis of my difficulties, may I say that I know that none of us can really see ourselves as we are, and I guess that goes for me, too. When you wrote that I am humanly a loving person, I stopped abruptly, startled, because for some time it has given me concern that I am so unloving! But I won't argue with you, and if you see that as one of my weaknesses which must be corrected, believe you me, I accept your evaluation and will do my best to improve in this respect—and I know what you mean and how important it is.

I know that in the case of K.K., I did briefly become involved, but I interpreted that involvement more as an intense desire to witness this healing which is certainly no better if not worse, and which I should be way beyond. As a matter of fact, K.K. took another nose dive last week, but this time I did not attempt to see her, but stood fast in the principle. Last Sunday, before your letter arrived, I had a wonderful release in which it came with a bang, "Why, Lorraine, what are you trying to do? Improve or heal someone? 'My kingdom is not of this world.'" From that moment on I was free as a bird.

I really do love this principle supremely, but your saying it the way you did makes loving it supremely so much more. You have caught me up quickly and lovingly, and I'm so grateful. Isn't there a hymn, song, or something that says, "Count your blessings?" Well, I can't begin because they are more than the sands on the seashore.

Thank you and so much love to you both,
Lorraine

July brought an influx of students to Hawaii, clearly evidencing the beginning of the worldwide scope of the Message. To assist in the class and to work with Joel, I arrived on June 25 to be there for a month. This 1959 class was held at the Hawaiian Village Hotel because Halekou Place was not large enough to accommodate the many students who came. Obeying the inner direction he had been given during those seven long months of waiting, Joel hammered away at the principles of The Infinite Way, probably more specifically than ever before. Shortly after the class Joel left for lectures and classes in Europe.

On September 20, 1959, I wrote:
XA and the family were here for dinner yesterday and I enjoyed seeing them so much. They are so precious—hope they can stay here much longer than three years. Friday, XA, and I will be guests of Valborg for the opening program of the Edgewater Drama Study Club of which she is program chairman. The program, Val Betten, who does a one man show on the life of George Bernard Shaw, is supposed to be very, very good. I know XA is going to enjoy these new associations, because there are some lovely women in these groups.

Much love,
Lorraine

October 6, 1959

Dear Emma and Joel,
...Have had an idea. How does it sound to you if once a month I have an extra evening [at the Center] devoted to the

study of the monthly *Letter*? Don't know just how it would unfold, but feel it should be informal—and you may not approve of that, although I have always handled such situations with great ease and command—and perhaps a part of it would be spent in reading portions of the *Letter*...

Lovingly yours,

Lorraine

Joel was delighted with my idea. As a former teacher I realized that student-participation was a prerequisite to a real learning experience. I was hesitant about mentioning this to Joel because he seemed to feel that listening to the tapes of his classes and reading his writings would be all that would be necessary. What happened in countless cases was the students found Joel's voice so comforting and peaceful that they often dozed off into a sleep. At the end of the recording they had very little awareness of the depth of the message they had heard because it was a passive experience. They were not grasping the principles.

I knew that nothing really takes place except as an activity of consciousness. How much understanding of a principle is there if a student is not able to express in his own words what it means to him? So for years I have searched for ways to make the message more real and tangible to the student, a living experience. An understanding of the principles which at first may be a purely intellectual awareness, and is the barest skeleton of the message, takes on a depth of meaning through meditation. In order to reach the silence of real meditation the principles serve as a take-off field. Teaching *The Letter* was a first step in helping the unfoldment of the student reach those deeper realms within.

October 18, 1959

Dear Emma and Joel,

Thank you so much for your dear letters and of course, again you leave me speechless by the generosity of your gift and the love it expresses. Thank you, thank you—I'm so very grateful to you both....

The work here has been going along beautifully, and I am swamped with healing work, even calls by long distance from Arizona and Texas. As soon as I am settled a bit, I shall have an evening to study the monthly *Letter* since I have the go-ahead signal from you. I really feel this is the next "must" but how it works out or what the method, I have not the remotest idea. It will be interesting to watch what happens.

Can hardly wait to see you, and hope to make New York at least for the week of the class. Feels so good to think you are getting closer to home.

With much love,
Lorraine

To my dismay, I was unable to go to New York for class because, at that time, I was moving from Evanston to Chicago and was busy getting settled so that I could entertain Emma and Joel when they came to Chicago for Joel's four days of lectures early in November. I felt especially deprived because during the week of the 1959 New York Class my dear friend Ann Darling was being married to Alec Kuys by Rev. Sig Paulson, the then minister of the Unity Center in New York City. On this occasion Joel gave a talk about marriage which was recorded and later found its way into *The Spiritual Journey of Joel S. Goldsmith*[2]. After the New York work, Joel and Emma stopped off in Chicago for a visit and four days of lectures. I wrote Joel about this visit on December 6:

Such a long wait for you to come here, and now you've come and gone! It hardly seems possible, and your visit but a brief moment that flew by with the speed of light. Such short interludes only whet the appetite! But those days here were wonderful days for me.

The experience Monday night of bodilessness remains as a portent of things to come, and as you said, Joel, "It would speak to me directly" and It has. Last night I was so much in the Spirit that sleep was banished for most of the night in the awareness of the Presence. And yet, I cannot rest with that, and so I wait. It said so plainly, "I will give you the hidden treasures" and then "to him that overcometh will I give to eat of the hidden manna, and will give him a white stone, and in the stone a new name written, which no man knoweth saving he that receiveth it." I cannot doubt It, and yet it has been such a long time, so slow....

December 14, 1959

Dear Emma and Joel,

Such busy days! Before I know it midnight is here and 6:00 A.M. shortly after that. At least, if I haven't acquired any wings, time has. Think I'll have to make a better demonstration of unlimited time.

2 *The Spiritual Journey of Joel S. Goldsmith*, pp. 159-163.

Thursday we had our first meeting to study the monthly *Letter*. Because it was a busy time of the year and because there was just a casual announcement of it at the meeting, there were only a few—but a very alert and receptive group. I felt a great response in them and when the hour had passed and I said it was time to stop or something to that effect, there was a spontaneous burst, "Oh, no, not yet." This first time I permitted oral questions. Then as I talked about the significant points brought out in the Letter, I had different individuals read certain paragraphs, in that way giving them a sense of direct participation. Well, as I said, it is all in the experimental stage and I feel it is only a practice ground for me. Several of them asked if I would do this once a week, but at present we'll leave it at once a month. I spent much of the day in meditation so that the consciousness during the meeting was really marvelous. One student said to me afterwards, "It was no accident that you decided to do this. Could you feel the consciousness in this room?"

I've been staying very close to the work you gave "The Ten" this last year, and it has been most helpful and very effective. I know you are working for R.B. and every day I have been doing the same. A great part of the belief there is that the problem is due to the incidents of his birth, but last night it came to me sharp as a diamond, "There are no births and therefore can be no effects from such a belief." It certainly is not a new idea and one that you have been teaching from the beginning, but it registered with such tremendous force that I wouldn't have been surprised to have the heavens open up.

Know you had a beautiful time on Maui and hope that now you will both get some rest. My heart is very full of love and gratitude for you both.

Lovingly yours,
Lorraine

December 27, 1959

Dear Emma and Joel,

Happy, happy New Year! Wish I could think of some beautiful and original way to tell you that. Of course, you don't really need it because 1960 will be a tremendous year for you both, strenuous but wonderful. Loved hearing your voices over the telephone, but still missed you.

We had a very pleasant Christmas here. Since X.A. couldn't come on Christmas Eve due to driving conditions, I invited her and the family for brunch on Christmas Day, together with my other Christmas guests.... It was a busy but lovely day for me, and I was so happy that these dear ones could be around me on this special day.

Thank you so much for the beautiful book *The Life of Christ* by Chinese artists.[3] It is a lovely thing and they really have caught something I don't feel in any of the Renaissance work.

There is a great emptiness and void in me. It seems you could put all there is of me on the point of a pin, and there would still be ample room for something else there. Won't go into that now because it's not pleasant. More of that later. Have a happy holiday.

With much love,
Lorraine

January 12, 1960

Dear Emma and Joel,

...Still feel less than a pinpoint. What more is there to say? Yes, I do know the value of insecurity, and only in insecurity does one become that complete vacuum which is required of us. Don't know if it is possible to be any emptier than I am, but suppose it is. Am sure this is a necessary state

3 *The Life of Christ* by Chinese Artists. (Westminster, S.W. 1: THe Society for the Propagation of the Gospel.

for work on the new book, so that I can be completely receptive to inner guidance. There were long, long periods of emptiness when the work on *Spiritual Healing* was going on—real suffering. I ask now only to be a fit instrument and am willing to undergo whatever is necessary that the steel may be tempered. Would you do some really serious work with me in Los Angeles? I'm crying out for it!

Much love,
Lorraine

And Joel did just that! He had done relatively little traveling during 1959, but in 1960 he more than made up for it with a heavy schedule of work that included lectures and classes in many of the major cities of the United States, England, Europe, Australia, and New Zealand, plus a holiday and talk in Japan.

One of Joel's lessons for me while in Los Angeles had to do with the strong sense of love—human love—that led to a mesmeric kind of sympathy, causing unnecessary heartache, which was really a form of self-malpractice. My work, he indicated, was to learn to know people in their true identity which means there is still an overflowing measure of love but with fewer repercussions on me as a person.

Another lesson more or less on the same theme was the importance of non-attachment. We can enjoy friends and family as well as the good things of this world more if we are without undue attachment to them. Then, there can be no "hurt" from individuals because anything of a disagreeable nature is that impersonal carnal mind, that is, the belief that there is anyone other than the one Consciousness individualized. Any good that comes is from the one Source, God. Furthermore, Joel pointed out that just as my unfoldment had been speeded up by my close contact with my teacher, so would it be with those who came to me.

An overflow audience for Joel's lectures in Los Angeles awaited him, the first work he had given there since he had moved from Los Angeles to Hawaii in 1953. Joel was delighted with the warm and enthusiastic reception he received. His greatest joy came in a reunion with Esther, his only sister, and especially with his nephew, Charles Waldo, Esther's son. Charles was a younger carbon copy of Joel although considerably taller. After decades of estrangement, happy memories of the family's early days and Joel's great fondness for his nephew as a baby were revived. That Charles expressed an interest in Joel's message touched him deeply.

Over 200 students were enrolled in the 1960 Los Angeles Class that I had gone to manage, a class that developed into work on Transcendental Consciousness. My letter of February 16 gives a hint of the effect of that work:

The meditations in Los Angeles and since returning here have been deeper and more fruitful than ever before. Feel that I'm already touching something and it is all centered around *I*. I shall work and work until you come here in May so that I will be as nearly ready as possible for more. Know I have been given enough for this lifetime and many more if it were only realized fully.

I've talked with X.A. several times. She's too busy packing to come in until she comes to stay with me which will be Friday. [*She and her husband were separating and X.A. and her daughter stayed with me for a few days until she caught her plane for Hawaii.*] She sounds very, very happy and free. Friday, Valborg will pick her up and bring her down here [*which she did in a blinding snowstorm*]. She is going on a jet to San Francisco stopping overnight and then leaving for Hawaii on Monday. Will write more in a day or so. Wanted to send a brief thank you note and news about X.A.

With much love,
Lorraine

February 28, 1960

Dear Emma and Joel,

It really was wonderful yesterday to hear your voices again. I was so surprised that my human judgment and reason were completely in abeyance. Afterwards I thought, "Good heavens! What did I promise? October is just a hop, skip, and jump away." [The promise was to have *The Thunder of Silence*[4] ready for publication by October.] So it must have been the Divine in me making that promise and It will have to fulfill it.

It does look like quite a bit of optimism to think that the book can be finished by October. It means pretty consistent and concentrated work. The prospect of what is ahead tempts me to forget about giving those Sunday talks until fall. [*Students had asked me to give some weekly talks instead of playing Joel's tapes.*]
Is that temptation, cold feet, or just good sense? Maybe from a strategic standpoint it will be better to begin in the fall. For a novice such as I am, these talks will require preparation and that means time. How we human beings can rationalize!

Still dying to know how The *Art of Spiritual Healing*[5] is selling. The Hugh Lynn Cayce review comparing the book to

4 op.cit.
5 Joel S. Goldsmith. (New York: Harper & Row, 1959).

Zen is remarkable. He really caught the essence and spirit of it.

We have just finished a weekend session with *The 1959 New York Class*. Our group was the smallest we have ever had on such an occasion, but for all those who were a part of the group, it was a very deep experience and really worthwhile.

I'm sure the *Seattle Class*[6] has been another beautiful addition to Infinite Way literature, but I'm expecting something new to come to full bloom here in Chicago where you are "stuck" for three weeks! That will be *after* that nine month period has ended, you know.

Will let Valborg write you about *J.B.* [*a play by Archibald McLeish*]. We did not feel that it ended on a note of futility, but that it pointed out that we have to give up our reliances on everything and every person and rely on the Self within us.

If you think it will serve any purpose for me to go to Kansas City for the work, of course, you know I shall be happy to arrange to do so. Just suggest there is some place you think I should be where you two are going to be and instantaneity goes into operation immediately.

Love,
Lorraine

March 5, 1960

Dear Emma and Joel,

So happy to have your very dear letters—a heart full of thanks for them.

Thank you for sharing as much of your beautiful Sunday experience with me as you could. It must have been a little of that that rubbed off on me last Sunday when, during our morning session with the *New York Class*, I had a floating sensation as if in another world—but this was after your

6 1960 Seattle Closed Class, 3 reels.

experience between nine and ten your time.

Thank you for removing all sense of hurry about the new book [*The Thunder of Silence*]. Yes, it must be The Book, and to be certain that nothing of significance is left out does require a living with it over a period of time. I hope to be able to get it together before too long and then go over transcriptions to see what should be added to amplify and clarify it.

Happy to hear about The Infinite Way Reading Room in Waikiki. I am sure that it will serve a real purpose. We've had so little activity here in the past few weeks that I'm happy to know that other places are bursting forth in some real activity.... I was so grateful to be of some help to X.A. Every day I take her with me up on the mountain top.

Much, much love

Lorraine

March 13, 1960

Dear Emma and Joel,

What a gorgeous, beautiful, lovely, wonderful, super galopscious surprise it was when the package from Canada came with the luscious (running out of adjectives) blue stole. It is at once both luxurious and cozy—and I love the color. Thank you again for being so dear and sweet to me.

I'm cheered no end that you've done two lectures that can become two letters or a chapter in a book in the Canadian Class. [Note: Later they were incorporated as a chapter in *Consciousness Is What I Am*[7].]

Had another *Letter* meeting this Thursday night which was fairly well attended. Those who come seem to like it very, very much, but I can't say I'm any raging success. It's serving a purpose for me, though, and a very good one, giving me practice and a measure of assurance. I feel that it is very spontaneous.

7 Joel S. Goldsmith, *Consciousness Is What I Am* (New York: Harper & Row, 1976).

One student said a very interesting thing about it, "Somehow these Thursday nights are different—it's hard to explain, but it's as if there were another Presence in the room; it's so full of It."

Know you had a lovely birthday and anniversary. That was one of the times I wished you had taught me Brown Landone's trick of consciously leaving the body and traveling at will, because if you had, I would have been right there in your midst. Well, I was, in my heart anyway.

Thrilled about the Grand Commander or whatnot of the Masons writing you....

With much love,
Lorraine

March 17, 1960

Dear Emma and Joel,

I'm enclosing a copy of the May *Letter* for you to read and return to me after checking it so it can be typed in final form. ...In preparing the *Letter* I attempt to organize it so that all the material dealing with a particular subject is closely related. Furthermore, in order to deal fully with the subject, I have in some cases drawn on other transcriptions, in turn omitting some parts from the particular tape being used in order to use those parts in other *Letters*. Thus each *Letter* has a central theme.

If the *Letter* is prepared as you suggest, it is my conviction that while the first *Letter* thus prepared might read satisfactorily, you will find subsequent *Letters* would soon sound repetitious, have a sameness, and many times would lack a central theme.

At best the work is difficult, but conflicting directives make it well nigh impossible and tend to create an atmosphere which is far from conducive to creative work. One moment I'm instructed to follow a transcription to the letter, and then when that is done, I am taken to task for not including certain significant points. For example, in the February *Letter*, you did not understand how I could have omitted a discussion of the carnal mind, which of course was not in the transcriptions, but which I did mention, adding a sentence here and there, although I grant you it was treated in passing.

You frequently refer appreciatively to the fact that each *Letter* develops and focuses attention on one or more of the principles of The Infinite Way. If that is to be done effectively, it is necessary to delete, add, and in some cases reorganize. We discussed the possibility of a *Letter* on spiritual instruction and also one on government apropos of the forthcoming election. Another *Letter* contemplated in the near future on business requires dipping into four or five recordings for the material. It would be an utter impossibility to do any of these proposed *Letters* which I have already discussed with you, and carry out these last instructions. Am I to understand that you do not want anything of that sort?

Furthermore, if I have so completely misinterpreted the job expected of me, you must face the fact that *The Art of Meditation*, *Practicing the Presence*, and *The Art of Spiritual Healing* are all wrong, as well as the *Letters* you have urged your students to study: 1959 June, September, October, November, and December. Had I followed your directive to take it from the tape just as it is in order to keep the rhythm, even with the magnificent material you have provided—and who knows better how magnificent it is than I—there would have been no such books or *Letters*. These are a synthesis of your work, and I like to think of *The Art of Spiritual Healing* as a distillation of ten years of your work teaching the subject of spiritual healing. Do you remember, when M.B. had the brainstorm of asking that additional anecdotes be inserted in the completed *Art of Meditation*, Exman's response was that there was a rhythm to the book and to follow her suggestion would destroy the rhythm?

It was my impression that you were hoping Harpers would eventually publish all the class books including the San Francisco Lectures. Would you not like to have all of them in such shape as would be acceptable to them, or are you assuming that now that you are so well established with them—praise be!—that they will accept anything of yours, regardless of its form?

I know so well how your talks lift your audiences to hitherto unknown heights and that their natural tendency is to rush up to you and say, "Oh, if we could have a copy of this just as it is," but I doubt that you would want that to go into print for posterity just as it is. And when you have said to me so many times, "All I care about is to have it in print—especially with reference to *The Book*—so that it will be there when I am gone," was not that what you meant? Has not the scope of The Infinite Way become such that you must now think in terms of a larger, more important group and period than the groups that are for the moment gathered around you? Is not that the vision? Moreover, there is already a large, discriminating audience that you are now only beginning to reach and they should be considered.

Of course, it may be possible that you, Joel, feel just as you do, Emma, when you told me in Los Angeles that "we do not need any more books—we have enough already." Perhaps that is true, but I still long to see these other marvelous things that are coming through in printed form, because I feel that they could make such a unique contribution—such an original contribution—to the spiritual literature of the world. I guess it's natural for me to feel that way because of my unlimited admiration for your work—I love it so much...

For me to turn out something which, editorially, I know is

less than the best—even though it might satisfy you, which I grant is important—is to wither and die, and then my value to anyone or anything is gone. That is why I write at such length and call your attention to some of these points which you may have overlooked.

Certainly you know this work has always been undertaken in a spirit of dedication, selflessness, and a turning within for direction by both Valborg and me. How else do you suppose the plan and organization for these last books came through? Surely not humanly! There was no pattern for me to follow in working on them—no tapes that provided the schematic structure of the books. That was given me when I was able to achieve sufficient silence to be a transparency. It may be that I was not a very good one, but at least there was the attempt, and as I have been receptive to the Spirit, It has provided everything necessary for the completion of the job at hand—sometimes in miraculous ways—and the end product was not that of a person...

My love and devotion to you always,

Lorraine

March 25, 1960

Dear Emma and Joel,

Yes, I guess between us, words are not necessary, and even an encumbrance, because when one is enmeshed in words, the Spirit is gone in the tyranny of words, and what is communicated is not what is meant.

Your statement, "We will do better by recourse to spiritual interpretation. Let there be no strife between us—We be of one household," caused me to look back over the long period of your work with me and to realize how little of the work has been by verbal communication. Most of it has been done in the silence, and in the silence your instructions have been received more clearly than by any words. But I should be able to understand the words, too, and if I have misinterpreted any of them, I am sorry. Rather than cause you so small a moment's concern as to make it necessary for you to remember the word, "hypnotism," I would remain silent, fold my tent, and go quietly away forever.

Lovingly yours,
Lorraine

It was difficult sometimes for Joel to admit that he might be wrong in anything he had said or written. When he felt that perhaps he was mistaken, he would do something as a kind of peace offering. So, after my letter of March 25, he invited me to attend the lectures in Toledo.

March 29, 1960

Dear Emma and Joel,

Before I realized the Toledo lectures were April 8,9, and 10, I had scheduled your tapes of the *Los Angeles Class* for that weekend, and so I will have to go through with that. But I would have loved to have gone to Toledo to be with you two. However, it will be a joy to have even a couple of hours with you at the O'Hare Airport, and I shall be there to meet you Friday, April 8.... To paraphrase Paul, "All things work together for spiritual maturity—and so be it."

Lovingly yours,
Lorraine

April 1, 1960

Dear Emma and Joel,

Thank you for your letter and the new spare time work [*Joel appointed me historian of The Infinite Way*]. I will make arrangements to be in Kansas City for your work there. Wonderful things are surely happening in The Infinite Way.

Thank you most of all for the work you are doing with me. You are not an easy master, but I am grateful for that, too, and find myself echoing Job, "Though he slay me, yet will I trust in him." The prayer of David is continuously in my heart: "Search me, O God, and know my heart: try me, and know my thoughts: And see if there be any wicked way in me, and lead me in the way everlasting." And so the process of purification goes on, for I know that only the pure in heart can see God. I have reached deeper into the Center than ever, "dying" and yet living more deeply than ever before.

Thank you.
Lorraine.

Joel had talked at Unity Centers before he went to Kansas City in 1960 but he had never visited the Unity Headquarters in Lee Summit, Missouri. When he saw the Unity complex and the many facets of the work including the vigils at Silent Unity and the printing facility, he was much impressed. He was also pleased that a number of students from the Unity School of Christianity attended his lectures in Kansas City. His dream for The Infinite Way was that the principles he taught would be freely disseminated among churches of all denominations and act as a leaven. Because there was no organization to which one could belong, one could read and practice its principles freely without jeopardizing one's status in any church.

In May, Joel's lectures and classes in Chicago gave me an opportunity for a month of concentrated work with my teacher. This teaching in a very relaxed and informal way continued when he left for New York and then England and the Continent.

Before a class session, Joel ate very sparingly or not at all. In Chicago usually after a session, Joel and Emma went down to the coffee shop at the Pick Congress Hotel, where they relaxed with a few of his long time students over a sandwich and always a large dish of rum raisin ice cream, a great favorite of his.

Sometimes a greater clarification on some point made during the class was requested. At other times some aspect of The Infinite Way activity was brought out, perhaps something about world affairs from The Infinite Way standpoint, and then there was just every day talk about worldly things. On one such occasion after the session at the Chicago Class in May when Joel, Emma, Ann and Alec Kuys, Valborg, and I gathered for a snack after an inspiring class, Joel was extolling the advantages of married life, speaking especially to the newly wedded Ann and Alec, saying, "Everybody ought to be married." With that Ann, with her usual forthrightness and directness burst out with, "How come you told Lorraine that she would never marry?"

"Oh," Joel responded, "You ask that because you don't know how Self-complete she is."

9

The Disciple Steps Out on the Waters

The long years of discipleship—ten years, not counting the many years before of searching to find the one who was to serve as a guide on the way—had been marked by an emptying out of old concepts through one inner struggle after another, and outwardly by a burgeoning spiritual healing practice simultaneous with the time-consuming work of editing all of Joel's writings.

This increasing outer activity never brought a surcease from the inner dissatisfaction with myself which continued to be a perennial experience. Now, however, Grace had given me a way of handling this spiritual unrest, which made it possible for me to emerge from such periods quickly. In the early years, I had felt that there was some virtue in wallowing in the mire of spiritual self-depreciation because I believed it signalled the "death" of the personal sense of "I." Working diligently with the principles of spiritual identity and of mesmeric sense as the one temptation gradually brought a depth of realization that made it easier to recognize that the only struggle lay in releasing the shadow which is the personal sense of "I."

The demands of editing Joel's work and the healing practice required the wise use of every waking hour and a restriction of any other form of activity to a minimum. But the Spirit has a way of opening ever new areas of work when the student is ready. The Infinite Way Study Center was in full swing by this time, involving five meetings of meditation and Tape Recordings a week, and additional blocks of time for appointments with individual students. Nevertheless, along came the next very simple beginning, which eventually led to embarking on a ministry of lectures and classwork, first in other parts of the United States and later in the rest of the world. As the outer activity increased, the inner instruction given by the teacher intensified, boiling over in minor crises that left the student empty and sometimes desolate with no sense of satisfaction in the outer achievements.

June 22, 1960

Dear Emma and Joel,

...Well, the die is cast... I have just prepared our new quarterly schedule and on it have scheduled five Sunday morning talks during the month of July by Lorraine Sinkler. I finally got pushed into it, but if you only knew how I hate the thought of it! Anyway, it seemed the easiest way out, because I won't be free in August, what with trekking off to New York to see you, so that these five talks make a nice little trial balloon. Then if it is just too awful, I have a good reason for not continuing in August and can let such a miserable idea die a natural death, bury it, and never resurrect it. Anyway, please pray for me July 3. Ugh!

With Much Love,
Lorraine

A report on this first attempt of the disciple to step out on the waters was sent on July 3:Today was my first talk. We teachers always used to say on Friday afternoon, "Thank God, Friday." Well I thanked God for 12:00 Sunday. We had the largest group we've ever had and it really went quite well. The subject was "Spiritual Freedom" and before it was finished, I had us all doing impersonal work for the forthcoming nominating convention. Anyway, they all seemed to like it, and even the most noncommittal person actually waxed enthusiastic. But I'm really in a very bad spot: I've told all I have to tell! There isn't anything left, so I don't know what I'll do on subsequent Sundays.

The first days of July bring with them very tender memories. It is just five years ago on July 4 that I resigned my position in Highland Park. What a lifetime those five years have been—full, rich, and satisfying! Whenever those happy years of teaching have been brought to my attention, it has always been with affection and warmth and love, but never with a longing to go back. That chapter closed with a finality, and the new one is still being written. These five years have been another wonderfully satisfying experience, the "to-this-end-was-I-born" kind of experience.

July 8, 1960

Dear Emma and Joel,

...We're at a very frustrating stage in the book [*The Thunder of Silence*]... the final polishing and cutting stage, a very slow process. We're still on Chapter One. Think there will be an Introduction telling how and when this revelation came to you and a few other bits. In that event I will send it (the

Introduction) to see whether or not you agree.

Thank you for your very good letter. [*Joel likened the giving of a class to a mother having a baby.*] I've never given birth to a baby, but now I think I know what it is like—only I can't be as much in love with my baby as are most mothers. Always there is the feeling that it could have been so much better....

The roof of 1360 [*Lake Shore Drive, Chicago*] is much nicer than heaven could ever be. I was up early this morning for a bit of air and sun and marveled at how all this goodness could have come to me. And I've been walking to the office at least twice a week.

With much love,
Lorraine

On July 14, another report: Well, another Sunday has come and gone, and each time it gets worse for me. But they seem to like it better and better... I practically die before it begins, and then when the meeting opens, it just flows with great ease. I've made some notes, but so far have never had to refer to them—just a crutch in case I deserts me as It seems to beforehand. Well, back to the salt mines.

July 23, 1960

Dear Emma and Joel,

Thank you for all your wonderful letters. Feel so rich and blessed to have them. When the first one came from Lausanne, I had a deep peace and sense of release about you and your work, Joel, but since then I have taken up daily work for you and it's probably blessed me more than you. Know Manchester will be wonderful. Glad to hear news about the German publication....

I shall not be tempted to make these Sunday talks a regular feature—just a series now and then. I always felt for you when you went on the platform and before, but now I know...

With much love,

Lorraine

In August I flew to New York to greet Joel and Emma on their return to the States after Joel's classes in England, Germany, and Switzerland, arriving almost simultaneously with them. In the days preceding the *1960 New York Closed Class* the meditations with Joel were deep and fruitful for both of us, and the talk informal and instructive as always. Joel was happy about his contact with a German publisher who arranged for the translation of his writings into German and agreed to publish them, as well as a German edition of The Monthly *Letter*. This publisher, Heinrich Schwab, told Joel that while many wrote about mysticism, Joel was the only one he had met who was a real mystic.

During this trip, while in England, the Maharishi asked him to come to see him. In addition to their meditating together, a lively conversation ensued in which Joel talked about some of his unfoldments such as the one about the mind forming itself as matter and, of course, about the activity of The Infinite Way and the deadliness of organization. I asked Joel what his impression was of this man who had done so much to popularize meditation in the Western World. His response was that the Maharishi was "a very sweet man."

Those who do not take on the burden of sharing their enlightenment with the world cannot know what an inner turmoil is sometimes set up by trying to live out from the Center in the midst of the world with its unceasing demands. Joel's whole being cried out for the quiet, away from people, that he needed to be able to continue abiding in the inner kingdom that was his true home. So great was his love for these spiritual principles, for which he was the transparency, that he gladly sacrificed himself to share them with the world, that the world might be awakened. From time to time, Joel's letters showed the inner struggle he experienced as one creative message after another came forth.

The strain of the heavy program of unremitting work undertaken in 1960—one flight after another with the endless waiting at airports; in and out of hotels and all that connotes; an endless procession of appointments with students; all in addition to the demands of giving one class after another, which always involved that apprehension and concern that the message really would come through, although it always did—took its toll on Joel, despite his protestations that he never experienced fatigue or weariness. When he reached New York for class in August he was testy, irritable, and short-tempered, a state of mind that he did not hesitate to vent on me as well as on Valborg, who was in New York for her first class away from the responsibilities involved in helping to arrange and manage the classes given in Chicago. To his credit, his own recognition of having reached a low ebb was best summed up in a letter to Valborg asking her forbearance.

September 2, 1960

Dear Emma and Joel,

Now you are home once again, and I know the joy that must be in your hearts, for I know what was in mine when I opened the door of my apartment and felt myself embraced in warm, tender, gentle, loving arms—the more real because invisible.

My heart ached for you in New York as I saw the strain and fatigue. It ached so much there was no time to think of my own aching, and that is good. Thank you for all your kindnesses to me in New York, for the beautiful class, and for some precious hours with you. Through it all, I learned some valuable lessons—the hard way.

You both should be walking on the water by now. I am surprised you had to fly across the Pacific, but I'm sure it was only because it was a quicker way until instantaneity comes into full activity. Last Monday night, in my work for both of you, I really reached *It* and was living in *It* throughout the night—and this has continued. A glimpse of how to meet this whole claim of karmic law was given me, and this I'm sure came as a deepening of the New York work in my own consciousness. So there must be fruitage. And I continue.... Please let me know when you begin those "deep meditations."

Sometimes I think that the most profound statement in the whole Bible is: "Opened he not his mouth." To some it is given to speak freely, continuously, and even egotistically, with never a repercussion of any kind, but that grace has not been given to me. And so I have become almost inarticulate. Maybe it is necessary to become completely so. Years ago—seems like lifetimes ago—I was given a mantra: "I take refuge in serenity; I take refuge in order; I take refuge in universality." On my morning walk that would sing within me. Perhaps it is time for a new song: "So opened she not her mouth."

I have been going a mile a minute, sixteen hours out of

the day, through unbearable heat... Anyway I now begin to glimpse the possibility of meeting all these deadlines, and that gives me a sense of peace.

I thought you were going to rest, Mr. Goldsmith! And here you have eight talks scheduled! You just don't know how to stop, and that's something I can understand. Rest is not in the cards for this incarnation. Wonder if next time I'll be a nice lotus floating blissfully on top of the water with nothing to do all day long but bask in the sunshine.

Lovingly yours,
Lorraine

September 13, 1960

Dear Joel,

Something happened to me this morning, so sacred that I dare not share it even with Emma—only you, my teacher. Did you have some deep spiritual experience between 2 and 3 o'clock Tuesday morning? I felt I must be receiving the fringe benefits of it because [*the experience*] could only have come through your deeper awareness.

As I sat meditating, establishing myself in the Presence in preparation for the day's work, a scene unfolded to me. Before my eyes danced grotesquely the false faces called human beings, and I stood in the midst of this macabre dance. As I stood there, It said, "I will lead you by a way that ye know not, and in paths that ye have not known. Be not afraid! My peace envelops you. All these are but false faces: *I* am the only being. There are no friends and there are no enemies—there is only *I*." Then the flat level ground on which I was standing rose up and became a cone-shaped peak like a picture-book volcanic mountain and *I*, mounting higher and higher on top of it, growing in brightness and brilliance. That *I* was not a person—

it was a light. All the faces disappeared by being drawn to this *I* as to a magnet and merging and dissolving in It.

This whole vision is inadequately expressed, but the peace and freedom which followed it were unmistakable. Thank you for this vision of Reality.

Lovingly yours,
Lorraine

September 20, 1960

Dear Joel,

Thank you for your beautiful letter. I'm humbly grateful to you for sharing this experience with me. Also, I'm so grateful that it was given me to be receptive enough for your work to flow through me as such a deep experience.

The unfoldment continues. Once again there was the *I* shining like a torch—there is no physical sense of light, and yet it is light—and this time—around it were all the "me's," all the false faces of the human personality called Lorraine—some good, some indifferent, some unpleasant. These all gravitated toward this torch, drawn there irresistibly and magnetically, just as in the case of the moth being drawn to the flame but to be destroyed, so as they drew closer and closer, their very forms became less and less distinct until finally they touched the torch and disappeared in its flaming light.

Ah, me! How this vehicle has to be hammered and pounded before it becomes a fit instrument! Sometimes in spite of all this flowing of the Spirit, there is an undercurrent of despair, hopelessness, and utter aloneness, but these I hold in strict rein and whenever they would engulf me, work steadfastly with the principle of impersonalization and nothingization until an utter indifference as to what happens to me is achieved. I pray that no matter how painful the refining process, it go on until all the dross is burned away and there remains only the perfect instrument of tempered steel—strong and pliable.

I thank you so deeply for your work with me. Little as I know, I know enough to realize that this must be one of my great opportunities to go deeper and deeper until that Center is reached and there is no *me*, only *I* dwelling and eternally being. Will you please continue?

Lovingly yours,
Lorraine

September 28, 1960

Dear Joel,

...You suggest "A year of refreshment!" Now I know why there's to be less work—although I'm from Missouri. It is what I've longed for, but I thought I was one of those who had to have the greatest enlightenment in the midst of the greatest activity. I'm sure this will mean a great deal.

I am to talk in Washington on Monday and Tuesday evenings, October 24 and 25, and in Cleveland, October 29 and 30. Then you will note from the enclosed schedule there will be four talks here on Sunday morning, beginning this Sunday. Already my feet are so cold that fire wouldn't melt them! Not an idea for this series here. Maybe all of these will be the talks to end talks for me! It all seems like a dream—nightmare would be more exact!

The example [*you give in your letter*] of removing a live goose from a narrow-necked bottle is a wonderful illustration of not solving the problem on the level of the problem. I see that trying to work from the standpoint of trying to get *rid* of personal sense might only intensify it, just as bemoaning one's failures would keep one mired in the dream, and that the secret is to dwell only in the *I*—in Being. I have had a glimpse of this, but the depths of its import in full and complete *realization*? No, or there would be no "me"—and if I am honest, I know there is. So I shall live with it and live it.

When I speak of this sense of aloneness, it is merely a statement of fact—no sense of complaining or wishing for some other state. I love it as it is, with all its dark threads. Why else was it given me to be completely alone and to have such a freedom from human ties and human responsibilities as few people obtain, if not for this one great purpose?

You say, "One finds one's Guru—or else." But I have found mine. You are my Guru. Yes, I know my Guru is within me, but are you not the *I* that I am? It took seven years of ceaseless prayer to find my Guru, and in those years that was my only prayer—never a prayer for anything or any person— and now eleven years have passed since that fateful September 28, 1949—eleven years ago today, my spiritual birthday.

There isn't much I fear, but I do fear that I may fail so miserably in some test that you will decide it is no use to work with me any further. It is not even right to ask for the assurance that you will continue because that would be resting on some *thing* and there have to be those periods of feeling utterly bereft of all comfort - even the joy of feeling safe with one's teacher.

I missed it in another life because of my rebellious nature. That's why I discipline myself to be obedient—even subservient —and this is not my human nature. Oh, no! So you will never know how I have worked on subjecting the ego and the silent struggle and how well I know the struggles that lie ahead.... There could be no struggle if there were no ego, could there? But this you say is all part of Initiation. Yes, yes. This is the moment; this is the time. Please help me through so that I do not fail again....

"But you will still have some struggles because there is

still a Lorraine seeking a goal and trying to hold on to some of yesterday's manna." What is it that is holding me? I would brush it all aside. Please tell me how I am holding on to yesterday's manna and let me try to loose it. I am not aware— of course I would be the last person to be aware—of any reliance on anything.

There is an absolute conviction that nothing is stable; nothing is permanent; so to rely on any thing would only be to be deluded into thinking one had a tower of strength when it was only a straw or even less substantial than a straw. Maybe this is just an inveterate skeptic talking, or maybe it is a tiny bit of spiritual perception coming through. Does it mean I should give up *all* the work—and go away alone and just *be* for a time? Please help me to let go of every encumbrance, and with your help I will try to jump off the cliff.

Lovingly yours,
Lorraine

October 5, 1960

Dear Joel,

Yesterday I really hit the jackpot when all your letters and the packet of your jottings over these last years which you sent me arrived. These are priceless, and I treasure them. [His diary and the notes he made, some of which were embodied in "The Wisdoms" and also in *The Spiritual Journey of Joel S. Goldsmith*.] I've had some wonderful hours with them already and am so humbled that you would share them with me.

Thank you for your beautiful letter. Thank you for it and the reassurance in it. Knowing I have found my Guru, then I shall never doubt—but my doubts have never been about him, just my own readiness. To know that you are watching over me and tending my spiritual unfoldment is worth all the treasures in this world. Please take me into the deeper and deeper strata of consciousness. I know so little. There is so much to be realized—depths I have not even glimpsed.

The prospect of work with you in January is so wonderful that I am trying to keep my feet on the ground, but knowing how busy you will be there, how many demands on your time, and how many things you always have to take care of—all of which would eliminate the opportunity for the work for which I hunger—adds a little to holding me in restraint. Anyway, I'm preparing by living each day and going deeper and deeper in meditation. Today, very deep—yesterday, no depth at all—tomorrow?

Lovingly yours,
Lorraine

October 7, 1960

Dear Emma and Joel,

Well, Mr. Goldsmith, dear sir, I never thought that my revered and honored teacher would turn out to be a sadist. But what else can I call anyone who would enjoy my misery? Sympathy for you and understanding? And how! I do know what you go through when you talk, only it must be a million times worse for you because you are giving birth to spiritual principles, whereas I'm just taking those spiritual principles that you have nurtured until they are now full grown and trying to talk about them. Do you know that from Saturday afternoon to Sunday evening—a mere 24 hours—I lost five pounds? Sadly enough, I put the pounds right back on the very next day, but that actually happened. I don't sleep, and yet I am wider awake than if I had slept 20 hours, and my stomach just churns around in the most awful fashion. Furthermore, after Sunday was over, there was no feeling of elation—just terror at the prospect of what lies ahead. Well, there you have all the boring details!

You two make me envious—down eight pounds. How wonderful! And from what Joella tells me, your next trip [*to Japan*] should be a cinch what with the food there. I'm on the Stauffer [*an exercise machine*] every day and have begun walking to the office frequently, but my appetite knows no bounds.

Don't think the Yerbana tea is for me. [*An herb tea Emma sent me.*] It made me want to sleep all the time so I gave it up. Evidently my metabolism, which was low enough to be at the moronic level when it was last measured over eleven years ago, doesn't need any such soothing potions.

I had quite an experience with A. last week. I could feel something going on in her, and then last week she slipped way back—a curtain dropped which I could not seem to penetrate. She came over to see me at my request, and I pointed out to her that she had a responsibility now to stay on a high level of consciousness because what would she do if someone called her for help? The only response was a laugh that indicated that that was the craziest idea ever—that anyone would call on her. So she left with the curtain still shutting out any awareness. Unconditioned mind was the one thing that kept coming to me. The next day she called, a completely new A. Shortly after she had returned home, an urgent call for help came to her from someone who had never called her before. It lifted her right out of the darkness and to a much higher level than she had heretofore achieved. I'm so grateful for that. She said that it came to her so clearly, "There are no people." And the guy who called her had an instantaneous healing!

October 16, 1960

Dear Emma and Joel,

The Japanese *Art of Meditation* is beautiful—love to look at it. Nice to have your picture in it, too. Thank you so much for sending it to me and for the very beautiful inscription. Thank you for the instruction on the work for the Prayer Circle in Washington. Will approach it from that standpoint.

Thank you, too, for "Be not afraid; it is *I*." There has been a much greater sense of release the last two Sundays—not easier, but a certain freedom. Guess it's really a freedom from personal sense, because Lorraine has been practically nonexistent.

I'm living pretty continuously in meditation these days. There's nothing spectacular to report, but I feel your work—an experience in depth. Very, very grateful

With much love,
Lorraine

October 22, 1960

Dear Emma and Joel,

Thank you for your beautiful letters and cards. What a paradise Japan must be. Already feel as if I'm there. That's the kind of country I would like—particularly the serenity of it. Well, maybe in my next incarnation.

Mr. Hattori's introduction to *The Art of Meditation* is magnificent and certainly is a must for the January *Letter*. As you say in your December "Travelog," this is but the sowing of the seed. I feel a tremendous fruitage which may not be immediately apparent, growing out of the work you have done there this year.

What an experience that first talk there must have been. I'm glad to hear the comments on your "scholarly presentation"—the last thing I would ever call what you do—not that it isn't beautifully presented in a most dignified way, but it goes so much beyond that. Anyway, Harvard will show. [*Joel, with his education limited to grade school, had at one time, in what seemed a miracle, been permitted to take a course in Sanskrit at Harvard.*]

Tomorrow I am off for Washington immediately after the talk here. Valborg is accompanying me, and although I can't imagine it will be very relaxing or much fun with these talks hanging over me, at least next Sunday at 12:00 noon I can enjoy myself unless I feel too miserable looking back over the week. Thank you for your encouraging cable. Whatsoever is accomplished will certainly be on your consciousness—I'm drawing heavily on that. If you feel someone crying out to you, you will know who it is. I noted that about the time you must have sent the cablegram I had a most wonderful meditation and great sense of release—so great it is hard to believe. That worries me, too, because I know the best work comes out of those inner struggles. Please be with me, and thank you.

Love
Lorraine

A report on the Cleveland work was sent on November 1:

Cleveland was a real experience. Ann Kuys has probably written or will write you about it.   Throughout the day surprises came in the form of unexpected people arriving, and then the frosting on the cake was the beautiful buffet Bettie Burkhart had at her home on Sunday afternoon for all the out-of-towners....

Ann did a most beautiful job...dignified and so sincere. What she said preceding the talk was done so beautifully—just the right words and with a love and sincerity that carried a conviction. You would have been proud of her.

As for me—well, it was the same old story which you know so well, only more of it, and to add to it, in Cleveland I had a throat that had sharp knives stuck in it. However, none of that was apparent to the audience, not even to me, once the talk began. Up on the platform, there is no awareness of body, nor even much of persons. I see them, and yet I don't.

Everyone was most kind and generous in his attitude, but it leaves me sort of numb all over—glad it's over, but not especially happy or elated. I suppose that is because of this feeling of detachment about this whole thing—knowing I'm just the mouth out of which It comes, not that I wasn't plenty worried that my mouth wouldn't be good enough.

Sunday, November 13, 1960

Dear Joel,

Thank you for your beautiful letter and for the spiritual ordination which makes me tremble at my own insufficiency when I read it.

I could wish that I were worthy to wear your mantle, but I am only your obedient and loving disciple and seek but to serve you and, in serving you, to serve God. I know you, who you are—"Whose shoes I am not worthy to bear," and so I can never aspire to wear your Robe, but only to be able to come close enough to touch Its hem—so far am I from the ultimate goal. And so, please be with me and gently lead me so that some day I may be worthy, never to take your place, but to remind the world of the truth you have given it.

It will be a sad, sad day for the world when you cease to

be as much in evidence as in the past. It cannot yet be time for
that.   The world is unresponsive, but it needs you—the
awakening which only you can bring about. There is much—so
very much—for me to learn, things you have yet to teach me. I
know so little—"I know not how to go out or how to come in."
Perhaps if I continue to work I shall be ready for the deeper
lessons.

These days I am living almost constantly in meditation to
be as close to my teacher as possible and so that I may ever be
responsive to his instruction, that his light may shine in my
heart and illumine it.

In deepest gratitude and humility,
Lorraine

10

The Middle Path: The Secret of Mystical Consciousness

Step by step the consciousness of the student was being prepared under the watchful eye of the teacher so that she would be sufficiently pliable and receptive to partake of the unfoldments coming to the teacher. And now he was taking her into the "effort of the effortless," a relaxing in Beingness.

Although the full and complete revelation of The Infinite Way was received by Joel during his two-month period of initiation in 1946, the meaning and implications of that revelation were ever deepening in his consciousness. New unfoldments continued to pinpoint certain aspects of the message, and different approaches to the principles were highlighted from time to time.

In 1959, the emphasis had been on the healing principles of impersonalization and the nothingizing of the carnal mind. In 1960, the work stressed the necessity of rising out of material sense to the transcendental consciousness of oneness. In 1961, throughout the work ran the theme of raising up the son of God in individual being. Of course, none of these aspects of the work was completely independent of the others, but all were interwoven into one whole fabric. The difference was in emphasis, but all of the work was designed to enable the student to reach that effortless state of resting in pure Being, accepting neither good nor evil but looking down the Middle Path to what eternally is, which no amount of work or effort can change.

December 2, 1960

Dear Emma and Joel,

Welcome home—as if you needed any welcome!—

Thank you for your note telling me of your unfoldment emphasizing that prayer, to be fruitful, can come only through the transcendental consciousness. You may not know it, but you have taught that for years. When that must have struck you so forcibly, I seemed to be knocking up against a stone wall in all the healing work I was doing. So I dropped it all and just basked in the Presence for a long, long time until I was really in that transcendental consciousness. And when I came back to the work the next day, you know what happened. Miracles! Magic! So I know...

Lovingly yours,
Lorraine

December 15, 1960

Dear Emma and Joel,

First of all, my heartfelt and grateful thanks for your generous Christmas gift to Valborg and me. We haven't yet decided what to buy with it, but it will be something very *special.*

I think I am most grateful of all for the cable and for your beautiful letter. You must know how deep is my gratitude that the healing for you came through and was instantaneous.[1] Through this work, I reached such a high state of consciousness that there were some other quick and beautiful healings, so you can see that the primary benefit was to me—guess that is always true.

Thank you for the clear-cut dissertation on cosmic law. With that clarification, obviously it is karmic law with which *Thunder* deals...

Well, the crucial days in December have come and gone for you, and once again the carnal mind has been proved a nothingness!

The busy-ness of the last few days has kept me marking time spiritually, but now I trust that I will be able to get back to some more intensive meditation—just for me so that I can be close to my teacher's consciousness.

Lovingly yours,
Lorraine

December 27, 1960

Dear Emma and Joel,

Thank you for the beautiful Christmas greeting via cable—worth getting a cable address just for that.

A couple of things have hit me over the head recently—packing a terrific wallop, but so simple I wonder why they never came before. One of my "pets" and one which seemed to have yielded a maximum realization is: "Thou couldest have no power at all against me unless it came from on High," and yesterday like a bomb it hit: No power, unless it comes from *I*—*I* am the power. It never came quite like that before. And then: "Creation is complete, so no mental imposition such as lumps or things like that can be added to an already complete and perfect creation." This may not sound like much to you because

1 See *The Spiritual Journey of Joel S. Goldsmith*, Pp. 99-101.

I know you've said it before, but it meant so much to me at this particular moment.

I'm so grateful that my home is in your consciousness. That is really dwelling in the "many mansions"—all of them.

With so much love to you both this New Year.

Lorraine

January 1, 1961

Dear Joel,

I'm grateful to you for telling me about Emma so that I can get busy. Could it be that she is suffering from boredom? That would seem incomprehensible to you who are always seeking new horizons and giving of yourself, but actually, how much really purposeful fulfilling activity does each day hold for her?

I'm taking up daily—almost hourly—work for her. The first word that came to me was karma, and it has kept recurring. Perhaps that's because I've been working with that quite a lot lately and it has broken quite a number of things so I'm working from the standpoint of "My kingdom" in which no karmic law operates—where there is only *I* infinitely expressed, living eternally under Grace. In My Kingdom, there are no barriers to the activity of Grace which knows no past and no future—only now. Evidently this is one of those arid periods for her, but she is so surrounded by springs of living water that it can't last.... I will stay with it faithfully.

Lovingly yours,
Lorraine

January 8, 1961

Dear Emma and Joel,

...Enclosed is a copy of a weekly bulletin [*with an excerpt from the recordings being played*] which we are making available to our students here. Those who attend meetings receive a copy when they come and then we are sending out copies to some of the others on our mailing list who do not attend—a few each week so that every month or so everyone on the list will have received at least one of these bulletins.

One woman has already called and reported a healing as a result of what she read in the first bulletin when she received it through the mail, and a man who does not come to our meetings called from a book store to ask me the names of the books referred to for study so that he could purchase them—he did not have the bulletin with him. So it seems to be serving a purpose.

Glad you approve of the New Year's letter we sent out to students. One night several weeks ago, I was awakened out of a sound sleep at 3:00 A.M. by a fuzzy voice on the telephone, "Miss Sinkler, I can't sleep." I'm afraid I was annoyed—she was obviously stone drunk or however drunk one gets—and the result was that I couldn't go back to sleep. Usually this is no problem, but this time it was—my reaction undoubtedly. So I decided to get busy, and this letter, which Valborg and I polished up a bit later on, began to flow. Surely God appears in many forms—even an intoxicated woman waking me up!

Interesting that you should be reading the *Aeneads* of Plotinus at this time. I just bought a copy of *The Essence of Plotinus*[2] about a month ago and I'm looking forward to quiet hours with it sometime....

Sorry, the ducks we sent you for Christmas are not geese. [*Joel had spoken glowingly of how beautiful the geese were that we had sent.*] But ducks fly, too, and maybe they'll come to have special meaning. One reason we sent this piece of Royal

2 *The Essence of Plotinus*, compiled by Grace Turnbull (New York: Oxford University Press.)

Danish is because you, Emma, said that the only thing you had brought back from Europe this time was a bird of this particular ware, so we thought you might like it.

With much love,
Lorraine

On January 9, Joel wrote and invited me to meet him for some special work in either Tulsa or L.A. where he would be for a few days, . He left Hawaii on January 15 at 2:30 P.M. for California. In accordance with his invitation, I arrived in L.A. January 16 and stayed until January 20, working with him throughout the day on the *modus operandi* of impersonal Christ-healing. This involved recognizing every problem coming to us in the guise of a person needing help as an impersonal suggestion. Discernment of the true identity or Christ-identity of every individual eliminated the possibility of there being any person with a problem, thereby lifting the one apparently needing help above the problem. Such a realization brings a sense of detachment and non-reaction.

January 22, 1961

Dear Joel,

I'm grateful that between us no words are necessary for I should find it difficult to put into words what the last week has meant to me. The only thing at all possible is to tell something of its effects; the Experience itself defies description. There is a state of the most intense aliveness. It is being in the world and not of it—seeing it really for the first time. I seem to see through everything and everyone, not through them physically, but through them in the sense of going right to the heart, seeing all the outer forms as so many pictures and discerning the *Reality* of all form. So much is coming through. There is a steady flow from within, an *I*-Amness revealing Itself. And this is real! The world seems but a dream, a play in which I am moving, but of which I am no part. Such detachment—such freedom—such unconcern! It is *My* kingdom, not of this world.

Even so, the temptations still come. It would seem that after initiation and that deeper awareness, there would be just a continuous living in it, but the world is still so much with all of us. As the calls for help have come in, I have answered most of them with a kind of don't-bother-me-I-am-resting-what-have-I-to-do-with-thee attitude, but already I have been faced with the temptation to do something [*to the appearance presented*], to react. However, it has been possible quickly to return to this *I*-Amness, to rest in Being, and to let consciousness be a transparency for the activity of the Christ, the *I*. The Invisible is becoming the real and permanent, and with that comes that detachment from the world which makes impersonal Christ-healing a living reality...

This is all very inadequate to describe the Soul-stirring impact of your work with me. But because you are my Guru, you know. You know, too, my love and gratitude. You have led me gently—and sometimes not so gently—to this point. There must be a purpose in all this, and whatever it is, I shall need your guidance and instruction more than ever, and perhaps I shall be more responsive to them. I thought I knew the meaning of humility before, but this is different—there is not even a person to be humble: there is only *I*, pure Being.

Thank you for giving so generously of yourself that I might be lifted to this point, refined and purified—not for me, but that the work may better be served. May I be a clear transparency, a ready instrument, and a faithful servant.

January 24, 1961

....This last week has seemed like a brief interlude with eternal undercurrents. Yes, it was good—really wonderful—to have those few days with you in Los Angeles. I'm sure the effects of it will be with me for a long time to come. The real communion and the deepest teaching can take place when only the student and teacher are present, and I suppose that is the reason for the importance of individual instruction. The fire in the teacher sets aglow the fire in the student, communication is instantaneous and understanding complete. So I shall live on those days for a long, long time to come for such periods are rare, but I'm ever so grateful to have had such an opportunity— the first in years, and in some ways the very first such opportunity.

So, thank you again. Mayhap that Presence which has provided for me every step of the way will provide another such period. At least, I can hope. I would go anywhere and make any sacrifice for it.

With love and gratitude,
Lorraine

February 9, 1961

Dear Emma and Joel,

The April "Across the Desk" is really magnificent and just what is needed to supplement this series on the contemplative life—another classic along with last June's "Travelog." I'm so grateful for it.

The April *Letter* will be ready for you as soon as I can type up a copy for you—probably Sunday. It seemed that it should contain an Easter message, so it is from *The 1959 Maui Advanced Work* on "Maundy Thursday, Good Friday, Easter— Esoteric Meaning." This has been jealously guarded for just such an occasion, so I hope you approve. [*Joel returned this letter and wrote in the margin, "Typical of you. Thanks."...*]

I've really been working—spiritually I mean. I've spent more time than ever every morning establishing myself in the Presence and trying to realize that all those who reach out to my consciousness must receive instantaneous help at that very moment. There is something I am trying to catch in respect to that and feel it coming through more clearly—but not enough—so I'm working with it. [*Joel said, "Good, good. Another step."*]

Emma, darling, I'm toying with a new diet—Low-Cal, the dairy version of Metrical, only I like it much better. Even so, the weight just hangs on like the ton it is. I think I'm going to have to have help. [*Joel added that Emma was 140. Joel—one ton.*]

With much love,
Lorraine

February 12, 1961

Dear Joel,

How is Emma? I have been so aware of her recently that I wondered whether or not she's completely free. You haven't mentioned how she was feeling in your letters, so that probably means that she is way up there on top, but because of this strong feeling, I must inquire.

Every time I can snatch a few minutes, I am loving *Dionysus, the Areopagite*[3]. He really caught the essence of the deepest spiritual wisdom. I feel so at home with him.

Thank you again. There is no way I can really thank you for the blessed privilege of being a part of your consciousness. I am very grateful.

With love,
Lorraine

3 *The Mystical and the Celestial Heirarchies* (London: Unwin Brothers, Ltd., 1949).

February 16, 1961

Dear Emma and Joel,

How I would have loved to have attended the tea you gave last Saturday.

The April *Letter* is sufficiently Easterish not to need anything more about it in "Across the Desk"... The *Waikiki Tape* "Preparation for Beginners and Advanced Students" must be out of this world because the transcriptions show how important it is. You ask me what its disposition should be. It would be a wonderful *Letter*. It would also be a marvelous chapter in the book either on practical mysticism or on advanced spiritual healing—whatever their titles are to be. I find it very, very helpful, and I'm working with it every day and since I find it helpful, maybe it would be good to make it available to all students in the form of a monthly *Letter* because I'm sure it would mean a great deal to them... *[It became chapter nine of The Contemplative Life⁴].*

The impersonal approach tricky? And how! I'd like a post-graduate course on it—no, I don't mean that at all. I'd like a first grade course because that's about where I feel I am, but I'm working with it. Whenever I'm really *there*, the results are too. At my stage, it takes lots of time—lots of time to just dwell in *My* kingdom. Have a feeling California will bring out a lot on that.

Guess I have to break down and do some of that talking here as well as in Detroit. We have thought a little of renting a hotel room here for a lecture or two because it would be less crowded, and we have also thought of putting an announcement in the paper. This might attract the attention of some of the people who are reading the books, but who know nothing about any activity in this area. Any objection to my using as the subject *The Thunder of Silence? [Joel returned this letter with a notation that indicated he heartily approved.]*

Lovingly yours,
Lorraine

4 Joel S. Goldsmith. *The Contemplative Life* (New York: The Julian Press, 1961). Pp. 141-158.

Joel had made the trip to Los Angeles in January, primarily because his brother appeared to be mortally ill. Although the brother had little interest in spiritual matters, Joel hoped to be able to break through the claim and witness his awakening. Together we worked with the principle of impersonal Christ healing, recognizing no person as needing help in the realization of spiritual I-dentity. While Joel was there, his brother experienced such marked improvement that Joel felt the problem had been met, but within a few weeks his brother had made the transition.

During these weeks Joel was going through an inner turmoil and frequently asked me for a lift.

February 20, 1961

Dear Emma and Joel,

So glad you enjoyed the flowers. It is so difficult to find any *thing* that can add to your pleasure because it is already so complete.

Boy, Mr. Goldsmith, dear sir, you surely don't give a guy a chance to coast—not for a second! I think your letter about the weekly class on Bible quotations is a wonderful idea—really do. I can see what is back of it; and knowing that it is the outlet your first group teaching took I can also see the wisdom of getting us to work in that very area. However, I need a little light; please give me some suggestions as to the following:

1. In view of the attached already very heavy scheduled program, when would you suggest that I do it? Would you eliminate one of the nights or would you add another devoted to this? As it is, it keeps our students pretty busy.

2. You know I never let much grass grow under my feet when it comes to carrying out your directives, so I should begin it the first week in March, but how do I handle it during the

time I am away? For example,I had hoped to be in California for much of your work there, but it would be impossible to carry out this particular job at the same time.

If you can answer these questions for me this week, I will get a notice out for the next week. You're just building a little fire under us, aren't you?

With Love,
Lorraine

P.S. One really needs a sense of humor in this work—pressed down and running over!

February 24, 1961

Dear Joel,

These arid periods are hellish times. I remember what that waiting was like for you through those last months of 1958 and early 1959, but look what things came out of it! So it would seem that again you have to go into that wilderness before it can blossom as the rose.

A passage from *The Doctrine of the Heart*[5] comes to mind as descriptive of such periods: "The 'deadness' *[experienced by all aspirants at times]* stands to acute pain in very much the same relation as solitary confinement to imprisonment with hard labor.... Positive, intensive suffering does not either test or repay or bring into play the same capacities and merits as a dull, dreary void within. Patience, faith, devotion are far better developed under a mental gloom than under an active hard struggle."

Anyway I have to tell you that whenever I do very consecrated work for you, the lifting of consciousness that I experience is so tremendous that there is no more earth. So it was last night and today—only indicating that I touched the "mind" *[the unconditioned mind]* that was in Christ Jesus—

5 *The Doctrine of the Heart, Extracts from Hindu Letters*, Foreword by Annie Besant (Adyar, Madras India, 1947).

your mind. Yes, always it comes, "This is the very mind of Christ Jesus"—absolute perfection and infinite wisdom. So again I have to say that whether or not it helps you, it helps me!...

I was thinking about your comment on Valborg's and my being loving—this in relation to the bouquet of roses we sent you. It is something of which I have no awareness as being a quality of mine. For so many years I have lived with and striven to achieve—but fallen short of—this little passage, also from *The Doctrine of the Heart*. "The sternness to the lower self, spoken of above, is a condition of this helpful service; for only the one who has no cares of his own, who is for himself indifferent to pleasure and pain is sufficiently free to give perfect sympathy to others. Needing nothing, he can give everything. With no love for himself, he becomes love incarnate to others." That to me is its essence and surely that is an accurate portrait of you—so I can't accept your estimate of yourself.

> With love,
> Lorraine

March 16, 1961

Dear Joel,

Thank you for your very important and deep lessons. The lesson especially for me is one that came to me before I received your letter. On Saturday, as I was meditating, it was so clear that I could never expect *anything* of the students—not even any real understanding of the Message—and that those on whom I poured out the most—and I have poured without stint—might easily forsake it all and turn and rend me. I must admit that a sadness swept over me, but then ever so quickly it came, "What is that to thee? Follow thou me." It brought me out of it quickly, and I could see so clearly the way I must walk. Why, in checking your letter again, that must have been about the time you were giving this lesson to me way out in Hawaii! Wonderful that there was enough receptivity to receive it. Thank you.

No, I have few illusions about people, and little about their capacity for spiritual unfoldment, but there are times I do hope and think "Ah, this one really has it," and then I'm so surprised to see the feet of clay. I guess the reason for that is so that I will never fall into the error of seeing any good in a person, as such. I love them all, but it must be a spiritual love because it is very impersonal. I try to be warm and kind, but there is an area within me into which no one can penetrate, an inner aloofness that I cannot break down, and an uncommunicativeness. Maybe that's my insulation against too many heartaches from the world. Thank God, I've never had any delusions that I am important to anybody, can do very much for anyone, or that when the chips are down anybody cares too much about me.

All this should make life completely unendurable, but way back in the deep recesses of consciousness Something keeps reminding me, "Your joy no man taketh from you," and so the joy comes in the pouring—and for myself I need nothing that is not abundantly supplied. The joy is in the work—the fruitage is not my concern.

The impersonal nature of karmic law is the message the world has been waiting for and so sadly needs. Have I glimpsed a tiny bit of what you are telling me when I say as we sow ignorance of spiritual law, we reap the fruits of ignorance in the form of becoming [victims] of world beliefs, but that actually there is no person through whom ignorance can operate because the only person is I—infinite Intelligence and Wisdom individualized?

I think I've told you before that I have worked a lot with

karmic law as nonpower in the healing work—and very effectively at times. It seems very important at this stage of unfoldment, and your revelation on its impersonal nature should once and for all do away with the tremendous sense of guilt under which men labor...

With love,
Lorraine

The latter part of March and during April, I joined Joel and Emma in Los Angeles for the class work he conducted in southern California. It was an important period for me because Joel spent a considerable amount of time working with me.

Emma had insisted that I be given a room adjoining their suite so that I would be close to them. She popped in from time to time and when Joel took a "breather" from the mail or appointments, he would also come in for a bit of "shop talk." In talking with students in California I was constantly amazed at some of the "experiences" they purported to have had, some of which seemed truly awesome. On one occasion, when Joel came into my room for a few minutes, I told him about this and asked, "How come I don't have any experiences like that?"

"You have had the real thing, what people would give their life to have."

In a letter to the students in Chicago, March 31, 1961, I wrote as follows:

Well, here we are. The first night went off to a beautiful

start with almost a thousand present in the beautiful, spacious Pacific Ballroom of the Statler Hilton. Running through the message on the first night was the theme of the one Father and the brotherhood of man, also that "Ye have not chosen me, I have chosen you." The other two lectures stressed: Not armament and not disarmament, not war and not peace, not sickness and not health, but My Kingdom. Woven into the talk on the final night was the theme of impersonal love; no practitioner can really succeed who is not a bundle of love.

> I had to introduce Joel all three nights of the lectures. I thought it would only be one night and that others would be asked to introduce him the other nights; but no, it had to be the three, according to Joel.
>   On April 11, 1961, I wrote to the students in Chicago that the theme of the Closed Class was:

Resurrection, Lifting Up the Son of God in Us—and It really was lifted up. To achieve "My Kingdom" there are three stages:

1. When God becomes more and more of a reality and when we live more and more on that reliance.

2. When we are awakened to our failings and try to live up to a higher degree of humanhood, doing benevolences and loving our neighbor.

3. When there is the actual experience of the Christ in which all the work of the first and second stages is left behind. We no longer live by human standards. Now Christ lives our life and material and mental laws no longer have power. We enter a stage where we do not have to fight or resist error. There is none in the transcendental consciousness, that God-

consciousness. A new factor enters our experience, a joy which is not dependent on anything in the outer experience.

From the Mission Inn in Riverside, California, again I wrote on April 11, 1961, to the students in Chicago:

The class has dealt a great deal with degrees on the spiritual path: the first degree is attaining a greater awareness of God within us, beginning to perceive that we are living more by Grace than by conscious thought. Thus our faith and reliance shift from the material to the spiritual. In the second degree we discover a great principle: A mind imbued with truth is a law of harmony to our experience. Truth is the substance of the harmony of our experience but truth does not dangle in the air: truth must be incorporated into consciousness. Wednesday night we had the principle of no power, and Thursday: "I have meat."

Joel talked to me somewhat sadly about how students reach a high point in spiritual unfoldment, but are not able to remain at that totally centered degree of awareness and they slip back into good normal humanhood. That can cause grief to the teacher unless he or she is alert and has attained the necessary degree of nonattachment and an understanding of the impersonal nature of Christ-healing. We are not doing things for persons in the sense of feeling that our mission is to help them. Rather, our work is the demonstration and proof of

the truth of the principle. Therefore, we never hold a
student in bondage to us or look for gratitude, although
gratitude is one measure of their spiritual unfoldment. It
becomes a lonely way for the teacher, and the deeper
insights go unshared except to those of sufficient inner
perception to receive the silent teaching. How grateful I
am for all that Joel shared with me even sending notes on
his unfoldments as they came to him and also sending his
most treasured papers to me for safe keeping.

The demands of the series of classes left Joel tense
and short-tempered. The night before I was to leave for a
lecture tour in Portland, Seattle, Vancouver, and Victoria,
I asked Joel if he would clarify for me the principle of God
as the substance of all form. It had been difficult for me
to explain to students how God could be the substance of
all form and yet to see deterioration and degeneration in
the form. I had wrestled with this idea for a long time
and finally resolved it after months of meditation in what
seemed right for me; but I wanted to be sure I was correct
in my understanding. I had been working on the two
chapters on mind in *The Thunder of Silence* to get them
ready for publication and it was important for me to be
very clear on this subject. Joel, weary from all the work
and demands that were made on him, became angry. His
patience was wearing thin and he lashed out at me about
asking such a stupid question which he felt I should have
been way beyond questioning.

Nevertheless, the teacher-consciousness in Joel was
operating even while the human sense of impatience at
what seemed to him my obtuseness was in full sway.
That forced me to find the answer within and with that I
was satisfied. As I flew on up to Portland, total
clarification came to me so that it was plain that God was
the substance of all form—*spiritual* form, since God is

Spirit—and that what we see and know as deteriorating, dying form is the mental misconception of the spiritual universe. That spiritual universe is forever intact, always expressing the divine perfection. So many students get trapped into believing what the human picture presents.

Shortly after returning from lectures and classes in the Northwest I began giving a series of Sunday lectures at a downtown hotel in Chicago.

June 5, 1961

Dear Emma and Joel,

Thank you for all your wonderful letters and for the telephone call. It was good to hear your voice again. Bless the Telephone Company!...

Well, one down and three to go! Yesterday was my first talk at the Conrad Hilton Hotel. We had a lovely room—one of their private dining rooms and beautifully air-conditioned. How did it go? Well, there were more than twice as many people present than we have had at most of the talks I've given heretofore in Chicago.

And how was the talk? To begin with, it was just as tough beforehand as it has ever been—if not more so. I lived in a state of suspended activity for 24 hours preceding it, but when I finally got going, it seemed to flow. The subject turned out to be "How to Practice the Presence," a sort of around-the-clock with The Infinite Way. The consciousness in the room was really beautiful and the love that flowed was heartwarming. This is really punishment, though. I spent hours getting myself as completely out of the way as possible. And thank you for your help and support.

So wonderful to know that you are standing right beside me.

With much love,
Lorraine

June 12, 1961

Dear Emma and Joel,

This has turned out to be a beautiful week beginning with a great sense of heaviness—just sheer physical heaviness, mostly—and merging into a quiet joy that has been carried along on a wave of Spirit.

The fruitage from the talks at the Conrad Hilton has been sufficient to make me know that I am going in the right direction—and am so grateful for that. Yesterday was the second of these talks, and this one was good, I know, because of what happened to me. Almost from the beginning, I had the strangest feeling that the voice that was coming through just couldn't be mine—and I'm not talking about phenomena. I found myself listening and marveling at the depth, the quality, and the resonance that had never been there before. It was a strange experience. I know that this is the thing to be done, that I *must* do this, and I want so much to run away—but, of course, I won't.

I do feel that you are right—*[these book reviewers]* are instruments for an "inner working externally made manifest." I can feel and almost see the seeds sprouting—the feeling of being on the brink of something tremendous, not personal, but tremendous for The Infinite Way. It is as if, for the first time, it is coming into its own. I've been working a lot with the idea of the omnipresence of activity—guess I shouldn't because my own is certainly omnipresent. Seem to be resting in deep spiritual awareness.

Much love to you both,
Lorraine

Dear Joel,

...I told you that I *felt* Sunday—the talk—inside and in my voice.   There was one interesting comment a woman made when she called me for help on Monday.   She said something about my skin, and then, "Did you know what happened to your forehead? Just between and above the eyes it became pink and then a vivid red as you proceeded." She added that she had read about such things but had never witnessed anything like that. Obviously she was the only one who noted it because no one else spoke about it.   Strange, though, isn't it?   Seems to happen, too, when I'm alone and deep in meditation.   I recognize it as an *effect* and drop it there, but thought you, and only you, should know that it is becoming more pronounced. *[Joel's response: "This we understand."]*

One other thing.   I've been working with J.S. for a long time now but I'm obviously not cracking the case.   What should I do? Will you give me some help on this, please?   Feel it should be met one way or the other.   Thank you very much.

Lovingly yours,
Lorraine

June 27, 1961

Dear Emma and Joel,

Well, happy days! The final Sunday lecture in the series of four has come and gone, and knowing that it is all over is such a *wonderful* feeling... Thank you for your help and your instruction on the J.S. case.   Before your letter came I called on L.B. to give me a little help on this.   Last night *[J.S.]* called around midnight, worse than ever, and then I found myself in one of those sleepless nights, with the word "hypnotism" going round and round in me and becoming of deeper and deeper significance.   Such complete freedom came to me as I have rarely experienced, an absolute indifference to the appearance, a complete unconcern, all of which I obviously had not achieved heretofore in dealing with the case.

This morning...notable progress... L.B. has written to me about the unfoldment that came to her about this to the effect that "*I* will make a new heart." And suddenly during the night it came to me with such a bang: I'm not dealing with hearts or lungs—I'm dealing with hypnotism, and there is no hypnotism *and*. There is just hypnotism. This is your lesson in the *Thunder of Silence* tape, and that really is the healing principle *par excellence*. So now, Lorraine, stay there!

Lovingly yours,
Lorraine

July 3, 1961

Dear Emma and Joel,

Thank you for your notes, the clippings, and thank you for your thoughtful check for typing services. Yes, we will be having quite a bit of that to be done, and so this will come in handy.

You say that a few of us will have to take the next step of transcending mind, as you come close to that horizon which looms before you in the distance. If I may be permitted to be one of those few, I stand in readiness for whatever is to come and wherever it will lead me. I await your instructions.

Even in the midst of great busy-ness here, I feel an inner instruction from you going on. I am so grateful for that and try to keep myself as receptive as possible. There is so much for me to learn. The attempt to give this forth in the form of lectures and teaching has only made me realize more than ever—if that is possible—how little I know, really nothing. I'm not thinking about knowledge now, but how I can learn to be more and more of an empty vessel so that I can be receptive to the inner teaching.

Know that you all are having a wonderful time. How richly you deserve it! Really this period of comparative quiet and rest in what would be a heavy schedule for most people—this rest is important. Out of it will pop what you are waiting for. No news? This semi-quiet is itself the news.

All of you have fun!

With much love,
Lorraine

July 15, 1961

Dear Joel,

You did not ask for help, but you are being given it anyway—maybe not getting it, but being given it. The meditations for you have been good. Always when I work for you it comes, "This is the mind that was in Christ Jesus—the unconditioned mind. This mind forms itself as a perfect, complete experience—with nothing missing—a body that is a ready instrument and an experience expressing the infinite abundance and boundless joy of spiritual fulfillment."

Disappointment? How well I understand! And yet could it be otherwise for anyone with your highly developed sense of Infinity, coupled with the impatience of wanting to embrace It in one magnificent moment? Any achievements, no matter how earthshaking, must seem infinitesimal when measured by the Infinity you have glimpsed. Yet in my meditation it came: This disappointment and frustration is sheer hypnotism. You exist at the standpoint of fulfillment; you are fulfillment.

August 31, 1961

Dear Joel,

Every time I sit down to meditate, and even when I don't, over and over again it comes, "This is the anti-Christ, an attempt to impede the progress of the work, and that is an impossibility.   When   it   hits   up   against   the   Christ-consciousness, it can only blow up and be gone." With such a complete recognition of the non-power of this whole situation *[whatever the problem]*, I should be able to do as you say, "Turn over and go to sleep." But with all of this work—and it has been both consistent and persistent—there has not been a release, not the feeling "It is done", and that I could stop.

It is as if there is an undercurrent which must be brought to the surface. So great has been that sense that many times I have almost called you, but I knew that if I did, there was nothing to be said. When I work for you, there is a sense of your being deeply troubled and peace not coming...

I am sure all of this is only the outer stirring which is the evidence of a new high mountain you are about to attain. I am trying to be very still so that I might tail along far down below, but close enough to know what is happening to you, and maybe catching a tiny glimpse of it.

With love,
Lorraine

September 3, 1961

Dear Joel,

Yesterday I had a very deep spiritual experience which began during the day, but culminated in the night. For a couple of days there has been a sense of aloneness, being cut off from everyone, including you. Now when these experiences come, I have learned not to give way to a senseless dawdling in the mire of human emotion, but quickly to begin work with malpractice and the principle of impersonalization. This I did during the "lonely" days, but the heaviness did not lift until the following experience came.

I found myself standing alone on a dark and gloomy road. Far ahead in the distance was a dim light, but so tiny as to be almost imperceptible—one little ray of hope—and so far away it seemed completely inaccessible. A hissing noise made me look down, and there close to my feet were snakes stretching their heads—bloated heads—to reach me, but were not quite able to do so yet. It was frightening, and I yielded for a brief second to the temptation to turn and run, only to find myself surrounded and unable to move a step. As they squirmed around me, I could see them as the personification of the hatred of the world, its envy, jealousy, lies, and deceit, attempting to strike at me.

Then from within came the words: "Stand still in being!" I closed my eyes and listened as the words kept repeating themselves: "Stand still in being!" I breathed a little more freely as the fear abated and then a light seemed to go out of me from the topmost part of my head. It was a light that lighted the surrounding region, not bright and not dim, but a light defying description which rose up out of my head, was connected with it, and stood above me almost like a miniature umbrella.

Way in the distance, emblazoned across the horizon in an arc, were the words: "No weapon that is formed against thee shall prosper; and every tongue that shall rise against thee in judgment thou shalt condemn." There was a great stillness, and when I looked down, there were no longer squirming, writhing reptiles, but only beautiful cattails swaying in the breeze. A lightness and a quietness filled me with peace.

With much love,
Lorraine

September 9, 1961

Dear Joel,

Thank you, thank you for being my teacher! No sooner had I written my last letter to you than a great freedom came, and today the experience has been indescribable—not in this world at all. Right after I wrote, the calls began coming in of healing of those cases which had not yielded... But all of that seems relatively unimportant when I am dwelling in *My kingdom...*

It seems that always when you have these relatively quiet periods, a tremendous upheaval takes place in me—highly effective learning experiences. It is a learning, too, that goes on without words or specific thoughts. Please, please continue to work with me. It is so important—oh, I know not important to anyone except me, but tremendously important to me. I am so grateful, but I can never be satisfied with half a basket.

All day long it has been singing in me that *My* consciousness is the consciousness of all—your divine Consciousness is really my consciousness, and my divine Consciousness is the consciousness of all those I worked with today. This realization of *My* consciousness as the consciousness of all is a clearer or deeper unfoldment for me than your realization of "my conscious oneness with God is my oneness with all spiritual being." It eliminates any person or thing separate and apart from consciousness—it is the complete at-one-ment. I'm flooded with a warmth and love that has nothing to do with people—just being.

My gratitude knows no bounds for the clarity of your consciousness. Once you said that I had made my home in your consciousness, so don't forget it or I'll knock so hard you can't.

With love,

Lorraine

September 10, 1961

Dear Emma and Joel,

...For about the last six weeks, we have been devoting fifteen minutes preceding our meetings to world work...

Over the Labor Day weekend it occurred to me that our work should be more localized and deal specifically with the problem of accidents on the highway. The meditations were very powerful, but afterwards I dropped it and forgot all about it—but not so the group. They came in to the Thursday *Letter* meeting and asked me if I had observed what had happened in this area over that hazardous weekend, and then they reported that there had not been a single traffic fatality in the Cook County *[Chicago and environs]* area and that the accidents reported had been the lowest since 1954. I was grateful because I'm sure it gave them a sense of the importance of this work on a larger scale and of the possibility of its effectiveness *[even though we make no claims and there is no way of proving its effectiveness]*.

Thank you again for everything.

With much love,

Lorraine

September 13, 1961

Dear Emma and Joel,

... Sunday must have been a most wonderful talk. I sat in meditation for an hour before your talk and during the talk, and had quite a beautiful experience. I was completely resting in Being, and this is what came through:

Oneness: One Consciousness, the Consciousness of every person and all life. The Self of me is the Self of every person I meet and of everything I encounter. There is no giving Self and no getting Self; there is just Self being. I cannot give to another because there is no other; I cannot get from another: there is no other! That Self is the essence of Truth, flowing forth into expression as wisdom...

All this week, the response to every claim that has come has been complete nonreaction—almost instantly dismissed. It's very sharp. So grateful. Thank you.

With much love,
Lorraine

September 19, 1961

Dear Joel,

Life on this plane is a matter of one release after another. I suppose there will be no permanent release until that final moment of complete illumination when we become pure white essence. So for the past two weeks the work for me has been to maintain and hold steadfast to a state of consciousness which evidently was not attained but only glimpsed. The suggestions to take me down from this high state of consciousness have surely been legion.

Always the most diabolical form such hypnotism can take for me is a sense of separation from my teacher.... I have tried to look at myself with as much detachment as I could muster and with complete dispassion. The errors were sufficiently glaring to make me stop and try through a severe inner scrubbing to see them dissolve, and to pray that the purification would continue until the blemishes are removed.

I knew that I could not become emotional about this—that all sense of aloneness, failure, and unworthiness was illusion, personal sense, a universal hypnotism which would make me believe in finiteness, limitation, and separation.

So it came to me so clearly that the mystical state of

consciousness is possible only to the person who can impersonalize, that it was the only way one could possibly attain the realization of One. And this realization of only the one *I* came to me very forcibly in reverse order: It was brought home that all people I see—good, bad, and indifferent—are but facets of myself, the "imaging" forth of a personal sense of life, appearing to me as some other person, only for the purpose of dramatizing for me what I myself must work on in myself, what I must recognize as the mask hiding the *I* that I am. Every thought of criticism I think, every judgment I make is a judgment, not of someone else, but of myself—and I have been guilty.

So it was strongly impressed on me that as long as there is personal sense there will be people separate and apart from me, but in proportion as personal sense is destroyed, so will the great heresy of separateness go with it. When every quality in myself or in some other suppositional person is recognized as impersonal, there will be no judgment—just instant dismissal.

The aloneness has been all-encompassing, greater than ever before experienced—a sense of being bereft of everyone, even in the midst of many people; and the greatest aloneness of all came, that of being far from the teacher—not in distance, but in consciousness—as if he had left me.

Out of that came a second release last Saturday evening, and it came as the blessed *I*. It said to me in no uncertain terms—It welled up from within me: "*I* will never leave you nor forsake you; *I* will go before you to make the crooked places straight, and the rough places smooth. *I* am your teacher and *I* will never leave you—*I* in thee and thou in me, eternally one. You cannot be separated from me, because *I* am your very being. *I* am the words your teacher speaks, and the silence when he does not speak, for *I* am he."

I suppose it is because I have never had the sense of being "worthy" or deserving of your effort in teaching me that I never have the certainty that you will not at some moment decide that I am not worth a second's thought and turn to more receptive channels. You, I never doubt; your wisdom I never question; and your discipline, I accept now and always.

But after Saturday night I knew that *I* was one with that teacher, because that teacher is the *I* of my being, and It said to me then, "*I* will *never* leave you." Since then, that *I* has enveloped me continuously. There was a complete merging—gentle, peaceful, and beautiful.

Monday night, after sleeping little more than an hour, I was awakened and this time urged to get up for my meditation. Gently but insistently it came over and over again: "Seek *Me*!" Seek *Me*!" and It told me to open the *Baghavad Gita*, and when I did, there was the final chapter—the eighteenth:

> Precious thou art to me; right well-beloved! Listen! I tell thee for thy comfort this. Give Me thy heart! Adore me! Serve Me! Cling in faith and love and reverence to Me! So shalt thou come to Me! I promise true.

So I was to seek "right" abstinence, "true" knowledge, "right" action, and be the "rightful" doer. I knew that any pain was but the breaking of the shell of my awareness, the shattering of the shackles. It said to me so plainly, "Have you forgotten *Me*?" And then, "*I* will give you the work you are to do, and whatever *I* give you, *I* will do through you. Do not seek the approbation or praise of men, for that is transient and unpredictable, but *I* never change."

So great was the longing to be closer to that *Me* that I wanted to write you right away to ask to be released from all outer activity for a month, but before I could, It said, "You will find *Me* in the work you do; you will find *Me* in every struggling Soul you meet. Where can you go where *I* am not?"

This was the bliss ineffable, indescribable. When I went back to bed after what seemed ten minutes, I discovered that three hours had passed, and it was four o'clock in the morning.

Even then there was no sleep—I was loath to give up that sense of peace and lapse into the apparent unconsciousness of sleep.

Last night, it was not as long, but this came: "Never again will it be your work, but henceforth and forever after this, it will be *My* work you perform. You need have no concern. *I* take you with me all the way."

All this you probably already know. Thank you for these experiences.

Lorraine

September 26, 1961

Dear Joel,

Your letter came as a confirmation of the comfort that had already come. Thank you. Thank you. It means so much to me—beyond all praise and all evaluation.

Please know that I do know you inside and that I have never doubted your discernment—but within me there is no confidence in my ability spiritually to measure up to what is required of me.

Nevertheless, ever since a week ago I have been living in a wonderful quietness and peace—hope that isn't the danger point. Guess, though, that there is enough unrest in me so that there can never be complacency, and furthermore the memory of the beating one takes at these times is never completely erased.

You say that what I have been going through is like "a one inch stream of water getting through a ¾ inch hose." The vehicle—and I'm not speaking of the body—just is not adequate, is it? How can I expand it and make it more adequate? How can I be more and more responsive to your consciousness—effectively responsive?

The inner work has continued and with it comes this

feeling of being so far away from people—and wanting to remain at that distance. It must be something like what an astronaut experiences on his flight into outer space—still the remembrance of being one of the little earth-bound ants, but far enough removed from them to hear the music of the spheres.

This letter will probably reach you on my *real* birthday, the anniversary of my spiritual awakening when I had my first meditation and interview with you on September 28 twelve years ago...I can still feel the lightness in my step as I walked out of that funny little room and hear the waitress congratulate me at dinner on my birthday and her insistence that if this were not my birthday it was something special because "there is so much joy here."

What eons of time have elapsed since then—how much and how little! When I went to see you I was completely reconciled to another 1000 births and deaths before the goal of illumination could come—the great illumination that would forever free me from this earth—and when I left you, I knew it was possible here and now. When I see how much other people accomplish in a much shorter period of time, I'm not so sure it will be possible for me to achieve it in this life-experience, but every step forward is that much of the journey behind me, and always the great experience looms before me as a possibility. So I continue in patience to work...

Thank you for these twelve wonderful years of working with me...

Lovingly yours,
Lorraine

October 5, 1961

Dear Joel,

Thank you for your wonderfully helpful letter. I know

that there must be deeper and greater preparation before the ultimate goal is realized—that it is all a matter of preparation—and so every hint you give me is seized upon and put into practice in order to "break down the middle wall of partition." You say that there is one more step to be taken by me on this plane—although to me it seems that there must be a million more, but in this as in all else, I trust your judgment implicitly. Will you please continue to help me become ready for that step?...

"Be not afraid; it is *I*" has been with me constantly ever since Los Angeles. Now I take "Peace, be still," carry it with me day and night and abide in it. It is the last thought at night and the first one in the morning and throughout the day it comes up to me as a reminder. Thank you for this mantra....

Lovingly yours,
Lorraine

October 11, 1961

Dear Joel,

Thank you for your beautiful letter..."Peace, be still" continues to be my abiding place—and there are times when the storm does rage without—but quickly the "Peace, be still" overtakes me and silence comes and quietness. There is no doubt but that something is going on in me, so peace and its realization must come—to make way for whatever is working through me.

I know that you would never withhold anything from me, and that means more than it is possible to say. I guess it is just an impatience with myself that makes me keep asking you to stay with me. But thank you for always being there.

With love,
Lorraine

A letter from Joel, October 13, written at 5:00 A.M. brought an invitation to spend Christmas with Joel and Emma in Hawaii.

October 20, 1961

Dear Emma and Joel,

A great nostalgia swept over me after I finished talking to you and I almost called the airline company and made new reservations *[to go to California]*. But it is true that if I am to see you in December, it would be unwise to make that hurry-up trip out to the coast for the brief glimpse I would have of you.

What a thought, Christmas in Hawaii with you! Hawaii itself is pleasant and delightful, but to be in Hawaii with you, ah, what is that about "paradise enow"? Well, that is it. You let me know when it is best—sometime in December—and I will try to get way ahead of the work here so that I can take off with a good conscience...

Will be at the Statler Hotel in Washington for class until Sunday night, possibly Monday morning, but more likely Sunday night and then at my sister Swanie's until Friday evening and then home, and to work, and how! I shall miss seeing you in the Northwest—had my bag all packed for that trip, too but I'm sure that it's best to forego that pleasure in view of the greater pleasure to come. Then, too, I really do need every minute to keep up with the schedule of work ahead.

With much love,
Lorraine

Camp Hill, Pennsylvania
October 27, 1961

Dear Emma and Joel,

Well, the vacation is almost over—just a few hours and

Valborg and I will be taking off for home. It's been a good rest, a complete change of pace, so that now I'm ready to go back to work with new zest.

Washington was a beautiful experience...Thank you for being with me.

Swanie and Perry have been wonderful to us making every minute delightful. And such food! We have lived on the fat of the land and I'm afraid some of it has rubbed off on me.

Love,
Lorraine

November 11, 1961

Dear Joel,

Last Wednesday I really reached out to you. Your beautiful and illuminating letter of instruction and comfort is concrete evidence that you heard, but I knew that, even before the letter came, because almost simultaneously with the reaching out, a response was felt. Thank you. Thank you...

I've always known what my lot would be, and is: to serve—and I always wanted just that. But I'd like to be a better servant! Perhaps that is why I do as you say, "Make too much effort to be what you are and to accomplish what is accomplished without conscious effort." I'm guilty—and what a sin after all these years! But Wednesday night it came to me so clearly: "What are you trying to do? Improve an already perfect universe?" So your lesson did come through to me, and with it a real release which was needed...

Yes, I know it is a lonely life—but I've been alone really all my life. No one has been able to get really close to me, except perhaps, Valborg. There is always that wall, and yet I don't build it—it's just there. Sometimes it is easier to be alone than to be with others and attempt to maintain the fiction of comradeship with one's associates. That is what wears me out!

But there is no need to describe it to you. You already know that state too well. I'm willing to give and give of myself and all I have freely, and yet I feel so detached about everyone, so really unconcerned, that I chide myself for inner aloofness and lack of love—and then bend over backwards to make up for it. How paradoxical it all is—to be one with all life, to be the Life Itself, and yet to be separate and apart from Its forms.

When I go to Hawaii, may I have some time each day for specific meditation with you, some real work? And so in the meantime, I will try to make the only effort necessary—"the effort of effortlessness," as you have so succinctly put it...

Lovingly yours,
Lorraine

November 20, 1961

Dear Emma and Joel,

Happy, happy Thanksgiving! If just a little of the joy you have let loose in the world comes back to you, it will be an especially joyous one and you will be engulfed with a tidal wave of Grace—nothing of less proportions.

Thank you for sending me the ticket to Hawaii. So very dear, kind, and generous of you! Saturday, December 2, dinner in Hawaii with you! You teach me not to be grateful for any *thing*, but I am really grateful, and I'm awfully grateful, too, for this beautiful opportunity that has knocked at my door, and to you who are making it possible for me to have it. I have always said that no one has been so blessed as I, and always the blessing is tied up with you! Thank you.

I'm really living this minute, but there's just a tiny area way, way back that is always in Hawaii. Seems that this is an important time for me—very important.

With so much love,
Lorraine

11

A Deepening Spiritual Bond

Three flights to Hawaii in 1957, one in 1958, two in 1959, including Christmas of 1957 and 1958, and now a third Christmas in 1961! Hawaii was getting to be a habit. For me, such trips were not merely a matter of going from the wintry blasts and snow of blustery Chicago to the soft, gentle, warm ocean breezes and liquid sunshine of tropical Hawaii. No, it was not this exotic land surrounded by a turquoise sea with stark mountains rising up out of the middle that drew me to Hawaii. Such beauty provided but the setting for an ever-deepening and closer contact with my teacher, a priceless opportunity to watch him at work, and to revel in long periods of being a willing listener as he recounted many of his personal experiences with colleagues of the past and gave interesting sidelights on family relationships, and to have the rare privilege of sharing some of his deepest feelings, thoughts, and concerns. That was what Hawaii meant to me—an experience in consciousness.

At no time was that experience more significant or deeper than during the month of December, 1961, culminating in the Christmas and New Year holidays. Joel seemed to be in a less burdened mood, far happier than usual, and with a greater degree of inner peace.

337

As always, Emma and Joel met me at the plane and drove me to my hotel, The Rosalei, where I lived in a one-bedroom apartment on the windward side of the building. Emma welcomed my being in Hawaii because of a closeness that had grown between us. It also gave her more freedom and time to spend with her children, two of whom were living at 22 Kailua Road.

At this time I talked to Joel about some of the students with whom I was working when I was not exactly sure of what steps to take. He explained quite forcefully that in doing healing work, of course, we never take a person into our thought but always recognize whatever the problem seems to be as the carnal or conditioned mind, impersonal. He added that in dealing with students, I had a responsibility to point out that, although obedience to moral codes such as the Ten Commandments, did not make a person spiritual, a person who had developed a degree of spiritual awareness would not grossly violate them. In our spiritual healing work, however, we must never try to change or improve a person even though in teaching we point out the importance of spiritual integrity. He told me to encourage patients to study the writings, so that instead of dwelling on the problem they would be dwelling on the things of God. As teachers or practitioners, we are the instruments through which that light that has been given pours forth to a darkened world.

Listening to Joel dictate mail, engaging in in-depth talks with him, especially about the direction in which The Infinite Way was moving, and discussing projected new books filled every day from morning until into the evening hours. Ever since he had first envisioned a book on advanced spiritual healing, I had begun to assemble material for that purpose and had brought with me the first four chapters. But already, his mind was filled with new ideas, especially because of the way the message was developing in his meditations and public work.

So as we sat at the dining room table one warm, sunny day, going over the chapters on advanced spiritual healing, he said, "This is fine, but let's drop this for now, and instead, let us do a book on mysticism.[1]" Since it was the mystical aspect of The Infinite Way, with its specific principles to aid the aspirant in attaining the mystical consciousness, that first drew me to the message, a silent hallelujah rang out in my heart.

Because the subject of how better to clarify the mystical life and its nature, a theme that ran through all of Joel's work from the very first book, was uppermost in his mind, it was natural that a considerable portion of his work with me on this trip should center around a discussion of time and space and how to surmount the tyranny these would impose. New vistas opened up for me with a glimpse of "beyond the Beyond." I seemed closer and closer to the realization that there is no "There" and "Then" but only "Here" and "Now."

January 4, 1962

Dear Emma and Joel,

My first letter just has to be to you, just as my first thought is of you.

And how can I tell you what these days have meant to me—the joy of the hours and hours with you? Can't be done. Your developed discernment is my only assurance that you have any understanding at all of my joy and gratitude. Giving me this trip was such a beautiful thing to do, but much more beautiful was the giving of yourselves, your sharing of so many

1 This became *A Parenthesis in Eternity*. (New York: Harper & Row, 1963).

precious hours with me.

The only way I know of saying "thank you" is to dedicate myself each day to this work and specifically to daily work for you both... Thank you for the most perfect and beautiful month I've ever known which will forever extend itself as the now.

Much love,
Lorraine

January 7, 1962

Dear Joel,

Ann and Alex Kuys drove over from Cleveland late Friday night to have a first hand account of my beautiful experience. They were almost as thrilled as I was. Unfortunately, a blinding snow storm blew in so that they left early Sunday morning. The prediction is ten inches of snow!

We had an overflowing house last Thursday when we had our *Letter* meeting which consisted mostly of tales of Hawaii. There was a beautiful response from them, and I was happy to see so many turn out.... When I reached home it seemed that the whole world was about to collapse right on my hands. So many calls came in within the first two days that I hardly had any sleep, but now things have simmered down a bit. Tomorrow begins the noonday meditation work. It will be interesting to see what happens.

How is Daisy? The meditations have been good, especially on the plane, and the non-power so clear, that I am continuing to stand by until I hear from you to the contrary, taking up work daily and sometimes a couple of times a day; for you also.

The memory of my month in Hawaii is still with me as a perfect jewel to be cherished, more real than what is here, and it really isn't a memory, but a continuing experience. I feel that I'm about 90 percent there and 10 percent here. Hope nobody notices the faraway look in my eyes. Seem closer and closer to the realization that there is no "There" and "Then" but only "Here" and "Now." So much was absorbed in those hours and hours with you, Joel, that it will take a lifetime to express. For me there is no greater gift than to be able to sit in your presence. The experience has been beyond price. My heart overflows with love and gratitude.

Lovingly yours,
Lorraine

January 10, 1962

Dear Emma and Joel,

Brrrr! But it's cold! Last night it was 15 degrees or more below zero, and when I was coming home yesterday in the middle of the afternoon, the warmest time, it was eleven below at the Palmolive Building right near me.

This is certainly a blistering kind of week in which to initiate our noonday meditations, but we're doing it even though nobody wants to stick his nose outside unless absolutely necessary, so we had all of six at each meeting. That, in itself, is a tribute to the devotion of those who came. How I would have loved to have stayed home these days instead of going out, and even a taxi was not to be had, but hardy Norseman that I am, I weathered it. Just ready to go down now for the Wednesday sessions....

I just don't believe that cheesecake can be on your diet! That is too good to be true. Let me know how you make out on it. I went haywire on my eating yesterday—so cold I had to console myself some way.

Know you all had an elegant time on Saturday and with food that was out of this world.

Much love,
Lorraine

January 11, 1962

Dear Joel,

You must know how much joy your last letter gave me.... I really worked for freedom and release from all this hypnotism for you both all the time I was there and every day since then.

Grateful, too, to hear about Daisy and that she had an instantaneous healing. When you spoke to me about her, instantly it came that just as there is no power in malpractice, so there is no power in the fear of malpractice. I do not know if you are aware of the deep-seated, unholy fear she has of malpractice, a fear which, I gathered, has communicated itself to others, too. I don't understand it, but then maybe I don't have enough respect for malpractice, that is, the personal sense of malpractice. It was one of the things that drove me away from my earlier teaching.... Anyway, please do not mention this to her, but maybe it is something for you to watch....

Again my heart is singing with joy at the good news *[that Emma is waking up a little]*.

With love,
Lorraine

January 21, 1962

Dear Joel,

It's uncanny—positively uncanny! Do you remember that I wrote you that I had worked on the tape "The Mystical *I*" all last Tuesday and part of Wednesday, and how deeply moved I was by it? Do you know what the theme of it is? Reincarnation, pre-existence, and the continuity of life! Yesterday, your two notes from Maui came in which you spoke about that very thing—how these ideas were percolating in your consciousness on Tuesday—and probably before that—and then how it came through on Wednesday. Isn't that interesting?

I had dozens of transcriptions laid out for me to work on, and yet out of all of them I picked just that one which was certainly not the logical one from the standpoint of sequence because it is not the next chapter coming up, but only a chapter in the book some place. Now, I ask you, was it my attunement with your consciousness—my oneness with it—which led me to that particular one at this time? It must have been. Also,was it the impact of the transcription I was feeling, or was it the direct contact with your consciousness which made it such a tremendous experience? Until your letters revealed what was taking place in you, I thought it was the consciousness I felt in the transcription, but now I wonder if it were coming directly through you—and this time I was able to catch it. This sort of thing has happened to me before, but I never cease to wonder and marvel at it when it does.

The suggested title of the new book, *A Parenthesis in Eternity*, sounds pretty "superscalopious", really powerful. Hold it close! This latest book is going to be so wonderful that it deserves a title that will arrest attention—and that surely will—lovely, beautiful, wonderful. You can't know the joy I am finding working on it. I'm home in it, and it's such a beautiful home. There's a fire burning in me now---a warm, bright glow—and such peace.

With love,
Lorraine

February 4, 1962

Dear Emma and Joel,

Thank you for your good letters which have meant so much to me.

...Your experience with the wind storm must have been a

top-notch one—one of those moments that stretches into eternity. So grateful to hear about it. The oneness of consciousness is always an underlying awareness, but these moments and experiences which give concrete evidence of it such as in the experience with "The Mystical *I*" and your "Parenthesis in Eternity" are always such precious things....

Your last paragraph in that same letter on the new body and that every new elevation of consciousness is really a new embodiment is something to live with and embody. Very wonderful... Yes, I have been busy. It seems that the world has dumped all of its problems right smack in my lap. And if there is an incurable disease that has not been laid on my doorstep during the last two or three weeks, I haven't heard of it. There have been some very critical cases which have kept me going night and day. Consequently I am way behind on everything else. The big solution is for me to get to the point where there is just healing with a smile and no treatment involved. Sometimes it is that way, and I am completely in the Spirit, but then again, there are times when I really have to go deep, deep within. I'm learning so much from all this and am so grateful for it, and for the opportunity this gives me, even though I certainly do not succeed with every case, by no means.

The possibility and prospect of going to California seems further and further away.... The new book must go forward. There is still so much to be done. Valborg and I need time together to work on it and not feel that we are working against time.

With much love,
Lorraine

February 13, 1962

Dear Joel,

...I can understand how you feel about the work that you have already done as being a thing of the past—dead, but dead only to you—and that now you are entering a new phase. That, I think, is evident in the recent work. If you were dreading the past or coasting on its laurels, satisfied and complacent, nothing more could come through. Surely complacency is the lot of humankind and its curse, accounting for many of its problems. It is that eternal brushing aside of the past and the reaching out into the beyond, "beyond the beyond," that makes possible the ever new and fresh work that comes forth from you.

When you say that you would like to go away and meditate and write, you strike a responsive chord in me. That would be so wonderful for you—and is so important! You have become such a perfect instrument, such a willing channel, that you must have this period of retreat in which to let this new Soul-stirring within you be "birthed." It would be wonderful to be near you at such a time. I think so often—many times a day—of those days in Hawaii when I had so many hours in your presence, and how priceless they were. It should be enough to last me forever.... It was as if the "parenthesis in eternity" had been rubbed out for that little while and only eternity was there.

Love,
Lorraine

February 15, 1962

Dear Joel,

Thank you for your letters—for sharing your sorrow with me, for that I want most of all to be a part of. It is sad and disheartening to see the very people whom we thought had the clearest vision of this teaching turn away. When I hear about such things, I wonder why you ever try to teach anyone, and yet I know the reason is that you are compelled to do so. But it is a thankless task. I know you don't look to anyone for thanks but only to see if the seed has taken root, and that is what I mean by thankless task—it takes firm root with so few out of all the hundreds.

I see the same thing here on a smaller scale, and my reaction is to want to leave them instead of devoting hours and hours to them, and to what purpose? Then I remember that the only reason this means so much to me is that I must have touched it many, many times in previous life-experiences and that eventually the steady dripping of the water wore away the resistance. So I think that sometimes maybe I'm just another little faucet through which the water is dripping bit by bit on the stony soil to help make it fertile—if not in this incarnation, then in some future one. And you are a mighty river wearing deep gorges in human sense! It helps me most to remember that this is all hypnotism and that no one has ever really left the bosom of the Father.

Thank you for letting me be a part of your joint mission. I shall work steadfastly and consistently with the principle of the nature of spiritual power.

Valborg came over yesterday for a couple of hours. She looked so weary and weak that I was shocked. She is still not on top of the hill. It's been a rugged time for her. I realize that I have pushed her much too much, and must not do that any more. I can't let her work under pressure any more and must mend my ways. She is such an angel that she would wear herself to the bone to get everything done. In all the years, she has never once let me down. That's quite a record....

With love,
Lorraine

February 20, 1962

Dear Joel,

...Working with spiritual power has given me as the first fruitage a wonderful sense of relaxing in the Presence, and the immanence of the kingdom of heaven. My response to every call since your letter has been a confidence that no power is necessary, and that this spiritual power, which is using me, is a gentle Spirit, a Light in which is no darkness.

The calls have been coming so fast and furiously that this is just what I needed to remind me that no might and no power are necessary. Have you ever felt a heaviness because of the continuous reaching out of the people of the world for help? "Letting spiritual power *be* the power" has given me such a release from that. It breaks the hypnotism.

In pointing up this principle of "My kingdom is not of this world" or "This is a spiritual universe," incorporeality is the word I have been working with in this connection. Incorporeal being can be neither sick nor well, rich nor poor—it is above and beyond all human concepts. *I*, Consciousness, am unfettered, limitless, and free, pure being.

It means so much for me to be working directly with you...The one question I had when I went to Hawaii was to ask for greater enlightenment on time and space, and now that has been given, and it remains for me to let the seeds sprout and grow in silence and secrecy....

Good sailing to you both....
With love,
Lorraine

In my response to a letter from Joel on March 1, I commiserated with him:

... Yes, I'm sure that most people—even those who talk about wanting God-realization—have no real interest in the spiritual path, and just want this world improved without exerting too much effort on their part. Discouraging, isn't it—and disheartening? I remember that you once wrote to me that if I had one real student in my whole lifetime, I would have done better than the average. Well, it doesn't look as if I'm going to beat the average. Hate to be just that, just average!

It seems as if I should be taking off for California tomorrow to be there to greet you... Only the necessity of making inroads on the book holds me here, and in doing what is best about that—everything else seems all right, too. So I'm not being a martyr—just letting the instrument fulfill itself as an instrument. Nobody here seems a bit sorry that I'm not going!

April 26, 1962

Dear Emma and Joel,

Enclosed is a time schedule for all the activities which will be going on here during the week of your class. ...It seems wise to me to have a typed schedule available for each student with the time and place of each scheduled activity. Otherwise some of them will be likely to get mixed up. So herewith is enclosed a tentative schedule, about which I would appreciate your comments.

It looks like a wonderful class, and so many of the old time students will be with us. We have been having regular meetings to do the spiritual work preparatory to the class, and that is really doing something for us.

Thank you for your two dear letters. I have done some serious thinking and contemplating ever since I returned from Hawaii, with the net result that all kinds of public work are becoming increasingly distasteful to me. There are some people who are destined to do the greatest work away from the world, and I have felt that call more strongly than you have ever known—not that I would do such a great work, but that I would do what I am most nearly fitted for by temperament and nature. It seems that is being shown to me more and more. And, well, there is so much I would like to say, but perhaps never will. Will be seeing you soon.

With much love,

Lorraine

Joel's Chicago class immediately followed the California work. Every preparation was made to ensure the comfort of the students and the teacher at Joel's class in Chicago, but—despite all our experience in arranging for classes—we did not foresee the large number who would attend without making advance reservations. The meeting room we had reserved at the Conrad Hilton had a maximum seating capacity of 125, quite adequate for the seventy-five students who were already enrolled. When the class met, however, instead of seventy-five students, there were 225 who came and had to be squeezed like sardines into this small room—and baked sardines at that. Chicago was experiencing the hottest May in history and, to top it off, the air conditioning system broke down! None of these things, however, marred the atmosphere of the class and its message of deep mysticism, proving that consciousness knows no barriers.

Most of Joel's classes were for five or six days with the classwork in the evening, thereby making attendance possible for local students who were employed. This kept other students free during the day, many of whom spent the day studying and meditating. At this class, Joel initiated a new form of activity: class work during the day conducted by certain students who were beginning to be active in the healing work and in working with students in their local area.

When the tape recording work began back in 1951, Joel felt that would be the perfect way of presenting the undiluted message to the world and it proved to be a most effective instrument in serving that purpose. In recent years, I have become increasingly aware of the fact that mere passive listening, which can become a temporary happy respite from one's problems, is not enough. For students to awaken and unfold it is necessary for the teacher or group leader to have some feedback from them.

How can that be accomplished without its becoming merely an exchange of human opinions without a trace of that all-important spiritual uplift? How could there be a sharing of spiritual light without its degenerating into what might become an acrimonious argument, with each person vying to express the strongest human opinion?

After much meditation I found the answer in a basic principle of The Infinite Way. If God is individual being, then all that God is, is expressing as individual being— his being, her being, its being. Therefore within every individual is that same divine intelligence and wisdom only waiting to be recognized. It is the responsibility of the group leader not only to realize this truth for every person in the group, but also through daily meditation, establishing for the group the consciousness of a "free state of spiritual brotherhood *[whose]* only restraint is the discipline of the Soul".[2]

The method that came to me was a study group in which the students worked together on an assigned bit of material, reading it together, pointing out passages that had significance to them and explaining why. What it

2 *The Infinite Way*, op cit, p. 40.

was never to become was an airing of personal problems or discussion of human situations. Whatever problem might be considered must be on a completely impersonal level in which no personalities are involved and the application of specific principles is pointed up as the solution. Such a group serves the all-important purpose of awakening a student to the inner meaning of words. The study group would not supplant a tape group but supplement it and normally be held at some other time in the week or month.

One problem of using the tape recordings exclusively was that in presenting the message through a tape recorder there was no opportunity to develop teachers. Furthermore, without teachers the whole burden and responsibility for teaching was left on Joel's shoulders, a responsibility he realized he could not carry alone as more and more students found The Infinite Way.

While he recognized the value of the recordings in the unfoldment of consciousness, he realized that students needed the direct contact with a teacher-state of consciousness and that teachers must be developed. That is the reason he was so delighted when I was led to begin giving classes. In fact, he told me that I would never attract large numbers merely by playing tapes. In 1961, after Joel's Los Angeles work was completed, before I set out to go up the Pacific Coast to give classes in Portland, Seattle, and Vancouver, I asked Joel what value I could possibly be to the students because the complete message was on tapes. His response was, "You go to bring Consciousness."

Hoping to develop more students with a teacher-consciousness, Joel asked me to arrange to have KX and Eileen Bowden give a talk to students of up to an hour each day during the class week in addition to the work I would give. Eileen Bowden was to talk on her work with parents and I, on meditation. That work was especially difficult for me because of the demands made on me as manager of the class, which included smoothing over the many little problems that can arise with a large group. On the third day I gave up trying to do a good job of the class on meditation and said to myself, "God, it's no use. I just can't do it. You'll have to take over." Of course, God did just that and the message flowed.

May 23, 1962

Dear Emma and Joel,

As I watched you walk down the stairs and onto the plane on Monday, it just didn't seem possible that the two people who mean so much to me had come and gone, but even this brief, brief interlude with you was a rich blessing and for that I am grateful.

The last of the students has departed, or so I believe, and now I can settle down to the business at hand which is quite enough to keep me occupied more hours than there are in the day. A good night's sleep does wonders for me, and I am refreshed and ready to get going again, but not until I have written a letter of thanks and appreciation to you and then one of appreciation and gratitude to KX and Eileen. After that, work begins as usual: manuscripts, mail, calls, meetings, etc.

The whole week was a tremendous experience for me following that super effort in which complete exhaustion takes over, and in that moment when one is at the end of one's reserve and there is no possibility of stopping, Something greater than one's self comes into play. I saw it happen and marveled and glimpsed the infinite possibilities when the barrier of self is removed and there is only *I*. Only that made the work possible....

Everyone here is most enthusiastic about your whole week, and seems to have received so much which now must be distributed after it has been nurtured. My only regret is that the demands of the schedule made it impossible for me to do the gracious things befitting a hostess which I should like to have done for you, KX and Eileen. Perhaps I can find some way of making that up.

K.T. took me to dinner after the meeting on Sunday night, and in the midst of dinner took one look at me and said, "You can't even keep your eyes open. I'm going to take you right home," which he did and then left immediately. Then, however, the telephone began and it was well after midnight before my head hit the pillow.

Have a beautiful, joyous, and relaxing voyage—a journey that takes you "beyond the beyond".

Lovingly yours,
Lorraine

May 31, 1962

Dear Emma and Joel,

Enclosed are the July "Travelog" and the statement on the financial status of the class, plus all the bills I now have received. For those not received, I have the correct information as to their amount. Included is an account of expenses....

Yes, the mountain of work would have been staggering if I had let myself think about it, but I just take one minute at a time. If I go beyond that, I get weary at the very thought of it. One thing I'm doing is to cut my appointments down to the barest minimum and during the next three months we are cutting out the midweek meeting and centering all the activities during the weekend—Saturday, Sunday, and

Monday. That will free me for the rest of the week for the editing, healing work, and mail...

Guess the whole world and its wife will be in Hawaii for your class—all except me. I get a little tug at my heart, but quite obviously it is not possible for me to go away for a month or more with all that is facing us here. During this little jaunt east that Valborg and I are having, we expect to utilize several hours each day to get in those precious licks of work together. I had hoped to go down to Williamsburg—have such a yen to go there—but this added bit in Philadelphia makes that impossible.

With much love,
Lorraine

During this May, 1962, week of class work, Arthur Ceppos, head of Julian Press, flew out to Chicago to make arrangements for an American edition of *The Master Speaks, Consciousness Unfolding, God The Substance Of All Form, and Conscious Union With God.* These were to be carefully checked for any typographical errors, or necessary corrections and ready for publication within a few months plus completing the work on *Parenthesis.*

July 1, 1962

Dear Joel,

...When you write of your need for more help, I long to be there to serve in whatever capacity I can be most useful, to extend myself so that in some way I would be able to lift a tiny bit of the burden from your shoulders. There must be a way, and the "birthing" of that way must be the reason for some of the unrest I feel.

Right now it seems that this manuscript is the first "must", but perhaps that will taper off so that it will be possible to be of greater help to you in other areas. It is only the manuscript work that has kept me here this July. In fact, I'm still surprised I'm here, and if it were not for the forthcoming book on mysticism—and all the others in the offing—I'd be off on your trek around the world, too—or at least to Europe.

Strange that for so many years the things I would like to have done, I could not do for lack of money, and now that the money always seems to be available, it is the matter of time. Do you see why I seek for an ever greater realization on the subject of time? Pending that deeper realization, I pray to be a ready instrument, to have no desires to do this or that, but only to be sufficiently receptive to recognize the next step when it is presented and to be responsive to whatever it may be.

If there is anything further that I can do or that you want me to do—whatever it is or wherever it takes me—please let me know....

With love,
Lorraine

July 4, 1962

Dear Joel,

...You have said so often that you learn more when you teach than the student ever does. It has been interesting to observe that, and Monday it struck me with double force as I was trying to explain to a student why we do not deal with the subconscious mind as do other teachings. Out of the blue it came: the theory of a subconscious presupposes a past which is the cause of the present, which is true in the human picture, but not in spiritual identity. According to The Infinite Way, there is no past and there is no future in the final attainment: there is only now—consciousness embodying all that ever was and ever will be in an eternal state of being unfolding to our awareness. It may not sound like anything, but it was as illuminating to me as a flash of light...

Independence Day, my Independence Day! Yes, just seven years ago today, I turned in my resignation from my position at school in order to devote myself to this work. The ensuing years have gone by very fast, so fast it is as if time has stood still, and yet it is as if there had never been any other years because the past has been almost so completely erased in the fullness of the present. There have never been any of the temptations of Lot's wife in any of this—not a single backward glance! Instead it was as if Inevitability knocked, and I recognized it—there was no choice.

You greet me as Brother. Thank you, but you will always be to me the master.

With love,
Lorraine

July 13, 1962

Dear Joel,

Parenthesis[3] is beginning to take shape. Going back to it after a month's interlude of work on other things was like going back to another world and required a little period of reorientation. Now, however, I am in the full swing of it and begin to see the form shaping up. The other morning while meditating, this came to me as the possible structure of the book:

I. The Circle—or The Circle of Eternity (The basis of mysticism, the principles, etc.)

II. Rising out of the Parenthesis (Steps on the   spiritual path

3 Joel S. Goldsmith. *A Parenthesis in Eternity* (New York: Harper & Row 1963).

and spiritual teaching leading to illumination.)

III.   Living in the Circle (The fruitage of illumination, etc.)

Nice? I think so. Tell me what you think about it. Part I is in pretty good shape—still needs something—but the rest remains to be worked on. The material is beginning to get together, and when it is all together it will have to be viewed as a whole.

Well, I don't think there is any point to my passing on all the things I have heard.... My probably overzealous desire to "protect" The Infinite Way finally was released in the realization that God is fulfilling Itself as this activity and provides every safeguard necessary for its fulfillment, and so there is no need for me to usurp the prerogatives of God because I couldn't even if I wanted to. I have enough work to do on myself without being concerned about anyone or anything else. And so with this as a daily realization, plus my work for you, I am at peace—most of the time.

And your personal life? It could never fail, because you could never have one. As it is, you have about as ideal a situation as it is possible to have within the confines of a human pattern of life. Of course problems will arise from time to time, but basically you have the ingredients of about as satisfactory a relationship as this human experience has to offer. You have told me what a lonely way this is, and experience has confirmed that for me. Perhaps it is better to live alone and experience that aloneness than to feel that awful void in the midst of people—but that's just my way of rationalizing my own situation, and finding comfort in that rationalization.

It does not matter to me that I am busy beyond all words. That is my joy, really the great joy of my life. The work is fulfilling and satisfying, but every so often there steals over me a feeling that maybe, because of all this busy-ness, I am missing the great Thing, the great Realization. The other

Wiseman was so busy—so busy in being about the Father's business—that he almost lost the Master—and yet when he gave up all hope, the Pearl was found right there where he was.

Maybe that is to be my way, too—the way of the true karma yogi, to work with all my heart and soul for the sake of the work, and to be satisfied with that—and perhaps someday, out of that, fulfillment will come. Even while writing this, I feel guilty because of my deep, deep gratitude for the measure of light that has already come, but in comparison with that, the distance yet to be traveled is so great—there is so much you have yet to teach me, if you only will. Always that Soul-hunger gnaws away at me. Sometimes I think ulcers must be tame *[compared with it]*.

With love,
Lorraine

August 9, 1962

Dear Joel,

...In the last couple of months in working very seriously with the *I*, I've been realizing more clearly than ever before that there is only the one *I*: my *I* is your *I*, my Self is your Self, and with that it has come to me so strongly that the little "I," the one we put in quotes in the books, is also universal and yet one—the "I" of Jim, John, or Mary is the "I" of me. By that I mean that all the "I"'s we see about us as persons—good, bad, and indifferent—are really only the one "I," the one great dragon of personal sense, appearing as many people, but really only a false sense of the one true *I*. Therefore, they do not really represent people, but only our false sense of the one *I*. The pictures we entertain of people are only our own personal sense out-picturing itself. Isn't that another way of expressing the story of Cain and Abel?...

The healing work has been good lately, and I feel that it is because of this unfoldment, the crux of which centers in a deeper understanding of your teaching, that there are no human beings in reality: There is only *I*.

With love,

Lorraine

After a little over a month at home following *The 1962 Princess Kaiulani Closed Class* in Hawaii, accompanied by Emma and Daisy Shigemura, Joel was off on an extensive tour around the world which included a program of lectures and class work. He was scheduled for work in London, Stockholm, The Hague, Hamburg, Munich, Lausanne, Capetown, Durban, and Johannesburg, and a last stop in Hong Kong. I longed to be going along with them, but the work which always came first did not permit my indulging this longing.

August 17, 1962

Dear Emma and Joel,

I just telephoned you at the Statler Hilton, but evidently it was too late. I wanted to send my love to you to take along with you on this long trek on which you have embarked, but, of course, you know it goes with you without my telling you—I guess I just wanted the joy and reassurance of hearing your voices once again....

Sometimes, Grace takes us into the "green pastures" of spiritual refreshment beside the teacher—and how blessed in that I have been—and at other times It keeps us close to the task It has set before us. So I'm learning to accept whatever It gives me to do with equal equanimity and joy, whatever it may be—and try to silence all longings for anything but for the grace to serve as an instrument.

I am driven. Always that has been so, but never like this. The impulsion to work every moment is so strong that it is as if something is standing back of me and pushing and pushing me, and as if the very breath I breathe were dependent upon working with it. Yet, there is no strain, even with a scant four hours of sleep—just absorption; no me—just the work!...

Well, much joy and fulfillment to you both.

With much love,
Lorraine

August 29, 1962

Dear Emma and Joel,

When your last letter came—your letter of August 21—I gave out one great chuckle! Just the day before there were to be no more books, and now two new ones right away, quick like a bunny! *[Philip Unwin, at lunch with Joel in London, wanted two more new books in addition to Parenthesis.]* Well, I'm glad, as you say, your spirits are on the up and up. That equanimity to which I referred comes in handy for me, too.

With much love,
Lorraine

September 6, 1962

Dear Joel,

...Yes, I think a book about healing would be right, and in that case you would perhaps let me use this recent work as a climax of the ultimate in advanced spiritual healing. Right now, the immediate job is *Parenthesis*, and it's growing and growing and growing. Every time I turn around something new pops up which is just a "must". So be patient with us....

I can hardly wait to hear the Wednesday night lecture in Manchester because yesterday, when you were giving it, I felt something tremendous moving. Today, too, I shall be there. The very time when you feel the Spirit eludes you, some of the greatest messages have come forth. Did you realize what you gave us the Wednesday of this last class in Chicago? It is one of the high points of the new book, if not the very highest! So it goes...

Following the beautiful chapter in part two of *Parenthesis* on "Initiation," it would be wonderful to have a chapter on "The Mystical Marriage." We don't have much on that. I don't know whether you could come forth with anything we don't already have, but it would be a nice try. How about it real soon? It could be called "Union," if you don't like the above title. It is touched on beautifully in *The Art of Meditation*, pages 146-148. Can you add anything to that? Maybe I'm asking the impossible, but with a good ex-Marine, that should only take a little longer, and what is likely to come forth from an ex-Marine and Joel Goldsmith, the Teacher? Earthshattering!

All is well here. Nothing earthshattering happening however.

With much love,
Lorraine

September 21, 1962

Dear Emma and Joel,

Your illuminating experience relative to the question of the opening of the Red Sea was a tremendous one. Such experiences are meat and bread for a thousand lifetimes! Just think how many thousand lifetimes you have had right here in this one life span in terms of illumination! What doors of consciousness this last one must have opened! Thank you for sharing it with me. Guess we need to hear over and over again that there is no externalized illusion, and then have it pointed up in a thousand different ways.

Much love,
Lorraine

Joel was on the platform almost continuously in 1962 beginning with classes in Honolulu and on Maui in January and February, followed by classes in Riverside, San Diego, Glendale, Pacific Palisades, and Los Angeles in California during March and April. After the Chicago and Tulsa work in May, Joel returned to Hawaii for classes in Honolulu and on Maui again, whereupon he took off for England almost immediately. There he conducted two classes in London and one in Manchester. As always, Emma was at his side, and, on this trip, they were also accompanied by Daisy. The three of them, Joel, Emma, Daisy, were to fly to South Africa, where Joel would complete his heavy program of work for 1962.

The refusal of the South African government to grant Daisy a visa because of her Japanese ancestry forced her to return to Hawaii. At the same time the granting of the visa was pending, a problem had arisen in Hawaii that made Emma decide to return to Hawaii with Daisy.

October 23, 1962

Dear Joel,

Well, what shall we say? Never a dull moment in The Infinite Way? Things certainly have been happening fast and furiously for you, and the scene shifting moment by moment.

When Emma called me last night, I had not even had an opportunity to open my mail which was waiting for me when I returned home from a very full day at the office, and which had in it your two letters. You can imagine my surprise to hear her voice! I was even more surprised that you were not right at her side to take over when she finished speaking. Couldn't imagine you two separated!

I'm sorry beyond words that I have this commitment in Detroit *[to give an Infinite Way Class]* so that I will not be able to see her—tried to persuade her to stay over and stop here on Sunday when I would be back, but I guess she and Daisy want to get home. It's a tough spot for you both. I well remember our conversation last December, and I can understand how you feel. I wondered why you never wrote to me about it, and that must have been the uneasy feeling I had. You have surely had the patience of Job, and the wings on your shoulders should really be quite visible by now. I won't even have to look carefully to see them. They'll be the dominant feature of your makeup.

The news that you will stop off here is, for me, a wonderfully compensating part of all this—scant compensation for you not to have your traveling companion, but a nice boon to me. It's been so long—so very long...

The Cuban crisis has cast a shadow of gloom across the nation. There is a heaviness in the air, and now, more than ever, the time to break the hypnotism of fear, the lust for power, and greed—yes, and sheer stupidity—has come.

With much love,
Lorraine

From Rome, Joel had flown alone to Cairo, Egypt, and then on to Capetown, a twenty-hour flight, with a brief stopover at the airport in Johannesburg. It was the first time since their marriage in 1957 that he had gone any place for public work without Emma at his side and it saddened him that she was not with him. In both Johannesburg and Capetown, he was greeted warmly by students with a reception at the airports. The next day he gave a lecture in Capetown to over two hundred students. All this time, too, he had been awake, meditating hour after hour because of the Cuban missile crisis.

What he most needed was a few days for rest before undertaking the taxing program that had been arranged for him. But this was not to be. The unending schedule of class after class in 1962 provided few of the intervals of quiet aloneness and inner renewal so essential to carrying on a worldwide spiritual activity. Before the class in Capetown was to convene for its first session, he found himself laid low with coronary thrombosis and landed in the hospital, an unfamiliar place for him.

His rapid improvement was remarkable. In a few days he was again answering mail, albeit from a hospital bed, for there was no stopping Joel. He persisted in carrying on the work, teaching a few students from his bedside, and eventually giving the classwork in Capetown that had been previously arranged. Presenting his beloved message and teaching it to those ready for it was his lifeblood. He could no more keep from doing that than the sun could keep from shining, even though clouds might sometimes obscure its light.

For me, it was an opportunity to give back to my teacher some of the spiritual support he had so unstintingly given me in all the years preceding. So everyday I wrote to him as did he to me, and meditated almost unceasingly.

November 2, 1962

Dear Joel,

All this week I've had an uneasy feeling about you as if you needed help, and lots of it. In fact, I have had that ever since you were in Cairo. Your letter of October 27, yesterday, was an indication of this, and today I learned that you were having a sojourn in the hospital. I trust it has been a more restful one than the one I had many years ago. Hospitals here have as much traffic in the middle of the night as Chicago's State and Madison in the middle of the day!...

Out of this experience a glorious new unfoldment will come to deepen the experience of the whole student body. Incorporeality is ringing in my ears! My simple little lessons to the students have emphasized and re-emphasized God appearing as individual being, and inextricably woven into that was the word "incorporeality" as the inevitable product of that "appearing." It couldn't be otherwise, could it, but it made incorporeality so real, so alive. I've been with you morning, noon, and night, and in the middle of the night. Your incorporeality shines like a bright light in my consciousness.

With love,
Lorraine

November 3, 1962

Dear Joel,

Just a good morning to you, or good evening, or hi! to you. I've been rereading your last letter and smiling a bit at the all-out receptions you were given both in Capetown and

Johannesburg. If you are going to take to your bed when you are thus greeted, we'll continue to keep your reception here cloaked in anonymity—quiet and unobtrusive. Of course, that is the only way we know how to do it here anyway. We have stereotypes of the English and Dutch as being reticent, undemonstrative, and stolid, and then they outdo all of the supposed outgoingness associated with Americans! Concepts! Concepts!

All goes well here. Something wonderful has taken over with me. It is the strange feeling of having come home. In this class work here, I'm really teaching—teaching as I did when I was in the classroom in school, completely absorbed in making a point, whatever one is given me to make. It has brought such tremendous freedom, just the kind I used to have. Back in those old days when I taught school, almost all the teachers made elaborate lesson plans before they presented their lesson, and I would always walk in cold, relying on the inspiration of the moment, which never failed me. It is like that now: the message is the all important thing—imparting its beauty and its glory—and I am unaware of anything but that. Sometimes I find myself hammering away, but it is something over which I seem to have no control. It just pours out in a steady stream.

There's still that uneasy feeling before I begin, and an increasing inability to do any kind of "preparation" except deep, deep meditation in which there is no thought of any message, but once I am talking, there is no "me": there is just the message. I don't know whether or not it will continue, but it has been quite an experience, and I am grateful to you for lifting me to this freedom. I'm standing close by every moment.

With love,
Lorraine

November 3, 1962

Dear Joel,

In my work for you, always the word comes: This is not a man: this is the Christ-consciousness revealed in Its fullness to this generation and to the centuries to come. That Christ-consciousness knows no limitation and no barriers to Its activity or expression. It is so clear to me that malpractice cannot operate on that Christ-consciousness, which forms its own vehicle of expression through the unconditioned mind. Just perfection!

I talked with Emma yesterday, and from her learned that you were very much on top, and again about your having deep spiritual unfoldments.... If it weren't for all this silly business about visas and other paraphernalia entailed with travel in foreign countries, I'd be on my way down there. Of course, I know that if you needed anyone with you, Emma would be right there beside you. I am resting in the assurance of the limitless, boundless, incorporeal nature of the Christ-consciousness. It's wonderful.

With love,
Lorraine

November 6, 1962

Dear Joel,

Your cable arrived late Sunday, but I am convinced that there is a mistake in it which changes its whole meaning. It read in part: "It is important because of my present condition will explain why I can carry out my American 1963 program." I would certainly doubt that you would go into a long explanation as to why you could do something you were already scheduled to do, so I assume they left out the "not."

Well, it is time you had a period of rest for renewal—your

sabbatical year, and not one where just a few minutes are snatched for that purpose, but a freedom from the responsibility of appearing at scheduled times on a platform.... This must be the time for that final realization. Now you are to go the whole way without a single veil remaining.

The practice has grown to such proportions that the last few nights there has not been any sleep possible at all---long distance calls from all over....   There was a point in consciousness I knew I had to reach, an elevation above every call of "this world," and after hours of restful, peaceful meditation, it was reached, and then the calls—all critical—came pouring in, so I knew why I had to have that quiet time, work or no work....

Our Monday noon meditations have not been attended by large groups, just a half to a dozen people, but those who come once come back again and again.   We have a full hour set aside with the understanding that people may come and go during that time as it fits in with their programs and that those who are there will meditate a while, come out of the meditation, and then go back into it if they want to do so. After the first fifteen minutes, I give fifteen minutes of instruction in meditation. This provides the keynote or theme for our 10 second meditations throughout the ensuing week. All of this work is leading students to doing some real work with the principles instead of just drifting.

You do know, of course, that I am always at your service, ready and waiting to do whatever I am called upon to do and to go wherever I am called.

No time and no space! I feel that at times when I am meditating for you, and an ever-deepening awareness of *I AM* is growing—*I AM* omnipresent, here and everywhere, only there isn't any everywhere, just here. I'm sticking like glue!

With love,
Lorraine

Joel's response to my letter came in an unpleasant cable in which he insisted that I had completely misunderstood him and I was to go ahead and carry out the directions for his American program for 1962. Later he saw the wisdom of totally reversing his plans.

A certain irascibility is evident throughout this period as Joel became increasingly concerned that what appeared to be his conflicting orders might not be carried out. He vented the full force of his aggravation over this on both Emma and me in a lengthy telephone call to each of us.

On November 14, however, he sent identical letters to Emma and me, in which he was quite contrite. It was as close to an apology as he could go without actually apologizing. In these identical letters to both of us, he emphasized his great love for Emma and his gratitude to and love for Valborg and me for our work. After this he sent innumerable letters to me outlining my role in The Infinite Way while he was still functioning here and after his transition. He indicated that because of my love for the Message, and my being the first to give up a successful professional career for Infinite Way work, I might as well resign myself to living and dying for The Infinite Way. He urged me to train someone to take over the responsibility for the Chicago Center in order to free myself for the larger work including teaching the message and taking charge of all the publications. Furthermore, I should instruct patients not to call me after 10:00 P.M. except in an emergency. After all, The Infinite Way was his and my life and our reason for living, so we really weren't persons but just The Infinite Way appearing as persons.

November 17, 1962

Dear Joel,

This has been a difficult week...of class work. The last night of our six weeks' class...I was overwhelmed...not only by an emptiness which gave me nothing to say, but a spiritual barrenness which left me desolate....

Never before have I asked for a sign, but this time I did, and not the kind of a sign most people might pray for in such a situation so that the class would come to a grand and glorious finale, but it was a prayer that no words would come forth from me as a person, that I would be unable to speak, but be dumb, and completely silent, that I would not fool them with pretty words which could so easily well up from the surface of the mind, that no word pass my lips unless the Spirit spoke through me and to me. If the Spirit did not speak, then I knew this must be the end of all such work for me. This would be the sign.

What came through was different from anything I had ever given before, and something I had not dreamed of talking about: it was on karmic law and sin! Something tremendous had taken over; and I knew I had not spoken it.... It seems that I had died, and was in that in-between realm before the resurrection has taken place: the stone was still firmly in place in front of the tomb.

Charles A. Beard once said that all history could be epitomized in four simple statements, one of which is that when it is very dark, the stars come out. Today there is the first glimmer of light and a few stars that are valiantly shining in the darkness! It isn't like the sun, but oh, how welcome those stars are.

Thank you for listening. I had to tell someone, and you are the only one who could be told.

With love,
Lorraine

November 20, 1962

Dear Joel,

Ever since my first appointment with you back in 1949, a perpetual song of gratitude has been singing in my soul, but today it is of a very special kind and quality because of the news of your complete and miraculous recovery.

How beautiful that there is such complete oneness with the doctor who attended you! Companionship of that kind is rich and rewarding, a boon given to few and given to them but rarely. I'm so grateful, too, for all the recognition and honor paid you. I love the people down under for their appreciation of you. Can it be that prophets are recognized sometimes even in their own day? The fruitage from your pen which you have sent me is of a high order. The one on "My consciousness do I not give to another" seems to be a "wisdom" of very great significance with a special meaning for me. The ditty about the white and black brotherhoods is a most succinct and cogent analysis of the problem, and may find a comfortable and congenial resting place in *Parenthesis* because there is something about these brotherhoods in the chapter on the function of the mind and its possible and frequent misuse.

And I dearly love the paper about your own search. It touched me deeply, went right to the heart, because in a few words, all the aspirations of a lifetime—and of a very special life—found expression. Thank you for sharing these wisdoms with me. As you know, I save everything you send me, making a mental catalogue of them, and every so often resurrect something special from the files for use in just the right spot.

I thank you, too, for your beautiful letter written to Emma and to me. I do understand your anger, but am grateful it was sufficiently mitigated by love and understanding to save us our heads, although the alternative of being strung up by the thumbs does not have too pleasant a ring. *[In Joel's letter, he had indicated that an ancient king would have done this.]*

You know that it would be my joy and great privilege to go
to Hawaii or anywhere else to work with you on the book or on
anything else. And I shall look forward to that possibility.

Love,
Lorraine

November 21, 1962

Dear Joel,

Your letter of November 14 has just arrived. I thought I
knew what humility was, but I guess that until now it was just
a word. The responsibility you give me fills me with awe and
wonder. All I can do is to pray that God's grace will keep me
true and steadfast always. You know where I stand. This
Infinite Way goes pretty deep with me. I do believe that there
is a divine Plan working in each one of us—even in the most
miserable of creatures—and I am sure that this Plan has
brought me to a place of very real freedom, so that there is no
one for whom or to whom I am responsible, and I am bound by
no human ties. Of course, there is, and always will be, the
great love that exists between Valborg and me, but that is not a
responsibility nor a tie. We leave one another free always, free
in a deeply spiritual bond of love. And no great human love has
been given to me, so that I am free of the encumbrances such a
relationship entails. That I thus stand so alone must be part of
the Plan.

Please help me to keep self out of the way so that it does
not become an impediment to being a good servant. I don't care
how many times you lose your temper with me, or even if you
"string me up by my thumbs", if only the work can be served.
Oh, that's not quite true—I care, but I'll survive those
temporary unpleasant situations. I'd never survive failing the
work.

All your directions have been carefully noted, and I shall endeavor to carry them into effect.... If the work and you are best served by my attending all the classes and by working closely with you next year, so it will be, and of course that will be my great joy. On the other hand, I am flexible, and if the work is better served by my remaining right here, that, too, must be accepted and will be all right. That will have to be your decision.

With love,
Lorraine

November 24, 1962

Dear Joel,

...I feel impelled to beg and plead with you to take it easy. Please, please do not drive yourself so hard. From what you tell me of your schedule, you must be working all the time, more actively than ever. Is this wise? Could you not use this time for some rest and quiet instead of letting every Tom, Dick, and Harry come to see you? You don't have to prove anything to the world: you have proved it all....

You are again saddling yourself with an impossible program, and just because you are an ex-Marine, you don't have to break your head proving it.... I know that there are countless students giving you spiritual support, as I am, but don't you think you are stretching it a bit? You know that even with some of us carrying the work during the daytime, you won't rest, because there will always be this one and that one you will just *have* to see, and so you will be pushing and pushing yourself again. Can't you use some sense? You are more important than all the classes in the world or all the thousands of people who would come to hear you, and only you know how much a class takes out of you—and I have a sneaking suspicion of how much that is. And Joel, you must save yourself for the days ahead when the new book is out and you will have the repercussions that will come when it hits the world with a bang. Then you will be busier than ever....

Again, let me tell you that I'm at your service, air-conditioned office or not, and will go wherever and whenever you want me to go. And I assure you that it is no hardship but my very great joy. Please do be careful.

With love,
Lorraine

November 25, 1962

Dear Joel,

Your letter of last Sunday, a week ago today, makes me think of a lot of things I have not thought about for a long, long time, for years and years. There is a rare beauty in this letter, maybe because it strikes such a universal chord. Your life surely has been a life of love, even though I have always felt that there was a void as far as your personal life was concerned, still something unfulfilled. Your love has been that impersonal love which is the only kind of love I really understand, although with me, there is little sense of loving even in that way. So many times I feel cold and hard.

I used to long much for what the world calls love—and it wasn't sex I wanted, but love—but my longing for God was so great that it overshadowed even that natural human desire. A man, who was at one time very important in my life, would have said that I was escaping, but I like to think that instead I exchanged the shadow for the reality.

The bond between us is surely one of the deepest kind of love, and yet I never think of it as human love because it needs no human satisfaction of any kind; it could never be imprisoned in words; it is above anything in this world. For me, it is a kind of love that is just happy to know that you exist; it needs nothing more....and it seeks nothing but the joy of seeing you happy and fulfilled. I suppose that is the love that grows up between the teacher and disciple when there is real discipleship, and when that relationship is real, the love is always pure. It is that spiritual bond of which you so frequently speak, and which is above every human consideration. Anyone who is privileged to experience that is blessed above all others. You have summed it all up when you say, "It is a feeling of incorporeality, since nothing of a corporeal nature is of any real interest."

Love has never been anything I expected of anyone and I am sure that that lack of expectancy has its roots in an unerring intuition that no one has it to give—at least to me—and so I have shied away from the pain of disappointment. For me, life has been a pretty hard school, and it has forced me to face life realistically and calmly.

It is not that I withdraw from people. In fact, few have been given as many pleasant hours with as many people as has been my lot, but no one of these people ever penetrates my wall, a wall of which most people are completely unaware. I guess you are one who has gotten a tiny step inside. I long to break down that wall, but it remains—an aloofness which is an armor I don, but which I cover over and try to make up for by an excessive outer solicitude. I do care about people and their troubles, and yet that concern is always one sided—my own troubles can never be shared.

So much for reminiscing! Now every day has become so full of activity that there is little opportunity for that kind of introspection, and it is years since I've indulged in this kind of luxury. It is only that your letter brought to a focus things very deep inside. I have not reached your high altitude of vision which is always able to see beyond the shell. Too often I see that shell and am sad at its emptiness. But I'm working at it, trying to get that broader vision, my good friend, and maybe some day I'll move up another notch on the ladder. I better had or your "littlest angel"—figuratively and not figurewise—will be trailing so far behind in your stardust she won't be able even to catch a glimpse of you. You are moving so fast these days. Please don't go so fast that you go completely out of my orbit. And please take care of yourself.

With love,
Lorraine

November 27, 1962

Dear Joel,

It is true that you and I should be able to compliment or insult one another, both of which are sometimes involved in real communication, without its creating any need for forgiveness, but I would never intentionally be guilty of doing the latter. That is probably because our relationship is, and always will be throughout all time, that of teacher and student, master and disciple.

For a free and naturally rebellious soul who chafed at any restraint, the lesson of obedience and respect for her spiritual superior has been surprisingly well-learned, and in spite of a flippancy which crops out at times, the reverence is there, a reverence which is all the deeper because it is not a blind emotional worship of a self-created image of a perfection impossible of attainment of this plane, but because it has its roots in a pretty realistic appraisal of you.

...It's natural to weep over the lost sheep, and always they are the ones from whom one had expected the most. They were so bloated with their own ego that they didn't know the great boon that had been bestowed on them. They couldn't be servants: they had to be masters.

Isn't that why esoteric teaching has always required a long preliminary period for the process of self-purification to be accomplished, that process wherein the neophyte learns humility and obedience? I've often wondered how successful it was and if its system of training really succeeded in submerging personal sense, or if it were not just suppression. It seems to me that through the principle of the impersonalization of good and evil, you have given the only way that the process of self-purification can really be accomplished.

Speaking of our own lost sheep, I like to think that...just as with T.K., no teaching and tender nurture such as you have given them can be lost. They may be the fallen away ones now, but in some future life experience, they will awaken again and be the spiritual light which you had groomed them to be here.

It's tough for you, but maybe some of the rest of us who have been able to remain steadfast were the O's and G's in another experience and some other master—it might have been you—worked with us and wept over us. How else did we learn? Certainly, we were not better—just at a different state of evolving consciousness because of what we have been through before. Surely John Bradford was right when he said, "But for the grace of God, there go I."

With love,

Lorraine

11:45 A.M.

November 28, 1962

Dear Joel,

...In your last letter you said, "Truly I *can* take you to heaven!" Will you? That is asking a lot of you because I don't think even you know how far that is for me to go and what a job you would have for yourself. I'm sure you think I know a lot more than I do and that I have gone much farther than I really have. You don't know how much there is for you to teach me.

When I first met you, you made me feel that I could make the jump into heaven in this incarnation, but the longer I work at this, the farther the goal seems to be from me. There have been miracles in my own life beyond anything one could dream up—the miracle of real financial freedom, a freedom so great that I believe no matter how much money were needed for any legitimate purpose, it would always be there, plus; a freedom from the body in that I'm rarely aware of it except that weariness comes sooner than it did; and freedom in relationships. All these things have come flooding in upon me, making this experience here as comfortable as possible, but these are not It.

Each day is so full that I don't think too much about it, but the longing is always there. I have touched It, that I know, and sometimes I am It, and there is nothing else. My deepest meditations are always formless. Only a few times has there been anything which might be classified as visions, and those experiences, the first of which dates back to 1954, are just as real today as then....

But you don't come to me as a form.... I don't do any of the things that other people can do so easily. You have said we must not try to make these things happen, and I don't, but it's strange. This is only mentioned so you will know what a novice you are dealing with. It would be useless to try to fool you by pretending to be farther along than I am. Do you still think you can take me to heaven? Sometimes I feel I'm already there with so many blessings.

> With love,
> Lorraine

December 8, 1962

Dear Emma and Joel,

It was wonderful to talk with you both today! A lovely way to greet the middle of the day. However, the all important question I failed to ask: How much weight did you lose, Joel?...

I practically dropped dead in my tracks, Emma, when you asked to see some of the finished chapters of *Leave Your Nets*. And here I thought you were my very dear friend! I look to you to be a buffer to that arch slave driver with whom you happen to be so closely associated! I'm afraid if I have two people driving me, that will really be the finish of me.

So that you will both understand, let me give you a brief summary of the situation as it now stands. We are continuing to work on *Parenthesis*, and it is far from being complete. We hope to be able to give the typist the first of the three sections of the book for final typing in a couple of weeks, while we will be working on part 2. I won't attempt to explain to you what is involved in compiling this book. All I ask is that you be patient and realize that we are doing the very best job possible, working with countless transcriptions—and I mean countless—weaving them into a tapestry of rare beauty and inspiration as we did with *Thunder*. This, I'm sure you must know. It involves far more than putting in punctuation and capitalization—that is a very insignificant part of the work...

Then, after *Parenthesis* is ready, the 1962 *Letters* have to be made ready for the printers. Thrown in between all this will be the proof on *The Contemplative Life* and the proofs of the 1962 *Letters* plus the monthly *Letter*—and each month has a way of inexorably rolling around.

If we were satisfied just to throw things together, of course, it would be a simple matter. In that case *Parenthesis* would have been finished long ago. It would have been a much shorter version and would have only superficially skimmed the subject, but I would like to make this a definitive treatise of this subject from The Infinite Way standpoint. That is not done at the drop of a hat. Good craftsmanship takes time as well as inspiration. Well do I remember how long I beat my head against a stonewall until the *pattern* and organization of the book were given me in a flash—but only after weeks and months of work. Until that moment, I did not know just where we were going or how. After that, things began to fit together as with a crossword puzzle.

You wrote me, Joel, that the two books by which you wish to be remembered were *Thunder* and *Parenthesis*. Then, let's take sufficient time to make it a glorious memory! So *Nets* will have to wait a bit, but everything will get done in due time....

Have a wonderful time and lots of fun.

With love,
Lorraine

December 29, 1962

Dear Joel,

I trust the miracle has occurred and that out of the emptiness and desolation—for such I have felt it was---the fulfillment has come. I'm thinking aloud when I say: I wonder if fulfillment can really come without the disintegration of all that one has cherished.

Remember the wings about which I wrote you? They're still growing and very much in evidence *[in you]*. There is much I would like to say and write, but it is not possible—just this one thing: you cannot afford to let people upset you. The price you pay for reacting is too high for you to indulge in such a luxury. I know from my own experience.

Years ago I was given a beautiful mantra which I used to chant rhythmically as I took my regular 6 o'clock morning constitutional along the deserted streets come rain or shine, heat or cold: "I take refuge in order; I take refuge in serenity; I take refuge in universality." To me the two most beautiful words in the English language—at least almost the two—are serenity and joy. So may those two words be fulfilled in you.

I hold you high in my consciousness in deep serenity. "I am come that your joy might be full."

Always deep thanks and gratitude,
Lorraine

On January 11, Joel telephoned me late at night to announce the cancellation of his scheduled 1963 work, which he hoped had come as "the propulsion of God." My response came in a letter of January 12:

No, you didn't awaken me last night.... I'm just human enough to believe that this *[cancelling the work scheduled for 1963]* was a difficult decision for you to make, and that you did not arrive at it without considerable Soul-searching, although probably you have risen so high that there was no possible alternative. Certainly, there should not have been because in remaining home, wisdom has surely prevailed. All along, in spite of the miraculous way you have come through a most debilitating and grueling experience, it has seemed so unwise and foolhardy for you to drive yourself simply to fulfill commitments made almost a year ago under different circumstances and conditions, commitments which you yourself have said must always be subject to change.

For you to remain at home, letting the Spirit have Its way with you, is a far greater service to The Infinite Way and to the world than for you to be ceaselessly traveling on the road. Out of this period will emerge a deeper message. That last hurdle you have been longing to make, that last leap which will forever separate and lift The Infinite Way above all other teachings—that is now!

I told our students this afternoon that just as in 1958 you cancelled your scheduled classes to wait for inner unfoldment—and how fruitful that year was that followed—so once again you were exhibiting the rare courage of a truly great spiritual leader and evolved Soul in heeding the Voice within....

You have taught us that when our lives are God-governed, there can be no such thing as disappointment. Today, I realize how deeply imbedded in my consciousness that lesson has become for much as I have looked forward to the month of February because of the promise it held of seeing you two, there was no sense of disappointment.

I have been counting the days in happy anticipation and had thought I couldn't live without the renewed spiritual inspiration being with you always brings. Knowing, however, that you are doing what is best for you—and that must always include what is best for the whole Infinite Way—brings a far deeper kind of joy, deeper than comes from any personal satisfactions...and surely the inspiration will come as the barriers of time and space are dissolved.... I shall miss being with you—miss more than you will ever know for you two are my very dearly beloved family. So it was from the beginning, sealed for all time to come....

Those difficult days of waiting in 1958 are a vivid memory. May the days that are to come be so filled with the outpouring of the Spirit upon you that the waiting is only a period of unalloyed joy, resting in that which you have always sought. And now, a silent toast to the great spiritual adventure that lies ahead!

And on January 21:

I am sure an inner propulsion from God Itself is forcing you into this period of quiet. You have always sought that one thing more, but the demands of your ministry kept you from having those necessary periods of silence and aloneness—big blocks of them. And so it is now, and now your disciples, those to whom you have given so much of yourself, are gathered around you spiritually in love and support. Perhaps we have been so well-taught that we will not yield to the mesmerism of the world, but will stay awake with you that hour, so that there will be no Gethsemane.

January 18, 1963

Dear Joel,

Did you have a very deep experience this morning from 5:00 on? It began for me about 9:00—5:00 your time—and I felt something must be happening within you, too, of which I had graciously been permitted to be a part. There had been a sense of barrenness, not being able to reach anything, just a deadness. As I sat down to meditate, I found myself saying, "Speak to me, God." It was a kind of pathetic begging, and the answer came very quickly: "Do you want to speak to yourself? *I* am always speaking to you. *I* am the very thoughts you think and the words you speak. And then you ask *Me* to speak to you?" From then on, It flowed in warmth, peace, and comforting assurance, and you were a part of It.

Just had to dash these few lines off to share this with you.

With love,
Lorraine

January 20, 1963

Dear Emma and Joel,

One of our students, Luella Overeem, who is a professional artist, made the enclosed calendar for me to use when I taught the January, 1963 *Letter*. It met with so much enthusiasm and such a tremendous response that everyone wanted a copy. So we had it printed and will sell it to our students here who want copies of it. I wanted you to see it before it was printed, but everything moved so fast, all done within about 10 days—that it was done before I knew it. I'm sending you the first copy, and will await your response. I hope you will approve. Personally, I think it is magnificent. Notice the excellence of the drawing and the ideas she has incorporated into it. If you should want any more copies, please let me know and I will be happy to mail them to you.

Love,
Lorraine

January 28, 1963

Dear Emma and Joel,

Thank you for your beautiful letter and also for your letter about our calendar. Seven or eight more were quickly dispatched to you as soon as I knew you wanted more. Every time I look at it, I see something new. For example, it was just brought home to me that the minute hand of the clock is "Realization" and the hour hand "Renew." If we have minutes of realization, the net result will be renewal. I didn't see that at first, and I don't think Luella Overeem did. She was surely an instrument when this came through her.

Well, it looks as if whether there are manuscripts galore or not so many manuscripts, the days ahead will be busy ones for me. To carry out your idea of my working with groups out in the field would keep me going. There is no doubt but that in the Middle West there are many groups that would want me to speak to them, but I'm pretty much unknown in Florida so I don't know how they would even dream of asking me to go there...Whatever comes, I am free to do it. That is the blessing—nothing to hold me any place!...

With much love,
Lorraine

February 5, 1963

Dear Emma and Joel,

Thank you for your beautiful letter of January 27 in which you tell of the real significance of Gethsemane.[4] It is really a tremendous revelation with overtones that go far beyond the words themselves.

The meditations this last week have been of a depth and a height that, on several different occasions, momentarily lifted me completely out of this world. It is very strange, too, that the great spiritual experience that pushed me out of public school work into a full time Infinite Way activity has been so alive in me these last few days that it is as if it were occurring now, this minute.

Just today, another letter came from you, one written in Capetown on November 22, and sent by slow surface mail—and it was really slow! It was a beautiful letter in which you wrote of your desire to have your books carry a line "indicating that they are edited by Lorraine Sinkler, and this should also be included in the new printing of the old books." This came as a surprise to me although in your letter you said that you had always desired this to be. Whatever you want to do about it is all right with me. Just let me know.

Thank you for your good advice on investments. That is

4 *The Spiritual Journey of Joel S. Goldsmith*, pp. 179, 180.

something about which I know nothing, so your advice is greatly appreciated.

With much love,
Lorraine

February 11, 1963

Dear Emma and Joel,

So glad you like our calendar! Luella Overeem is the mother of four children, two of whom are in college, one in high school, and the fourth in junior high school. She is completely devoted to The Infinite Way, and I have worked with her hour on end over the last two years. During that time she has had some tremendous spiritual experiences as well as some very tough human experiences knocking at her door. But throughout these, she has adhered to the principles and sought to live by them. I think the calendar itself is a testimony to the depth of her perception of them. I, too, feel that this work will go far and wide, fulfilling its purpose.

Milwaukee *[where I gave a lecture and a two session class]* was a beautiful experience for me. The weather was atrocious. Snow made the streets a sheet of ice, but even though the group was small, it was worthwhile. The response was excellent, and I'm sure, as was true when I went there in the fall, there will be fruitage....

Happy Valentine's Day to you two precious friends. Will you please have dinner on me, and let me be the silent, invisible hostess?

Much love,
Lorraine

March 15, 1963

Dear Emma and Joel,

...Valborg has been with me for the past month—ill at first as I told you, but she has been able to stay on for a few weeks so that we could work together. We have used this precious time to work night and day on *Parenthesis*. Yesterday, it was from seven in the morning until three the next morning, except for the necessary time out to take care of the calls for help that came in. So we are both ready for a long "breather."

And now I have news for you: *Parenthesis* will be finished and ready to deliver to you by Tuesday night, March 19!...

With much love,
Lorraine

April 5, 1963

Dear Joel,

Just a word about *Parenthesis*. Your last letter did not make clear whether you wanted me to send the manuscript to Harpers or whether you wanted to go over it a few more times.

Will you please return your copy of *Parenthesis* to me and I will annotate it so that you can see exactly where the material came from. This you should know. We did not have it ready when we sent the manuscript to you, but have been working on it and we could transfer that information to your copy in a few hours and return it to you immediately.

Of course, you know how grateful I am that you are satisfied with this manuscript. Your cable was right: it was done joyously. There was the daily adventure of seeing what God would call to my attention each day: finding the right transcription, but always culling so that the end result would be a unified whole. And then the morning the three divisions of the book unfolded, it became clear how all the mass of material being assembled could be woven into one complete whole garment. All that was pure joy—hard, hard work, but with no heaviness, only joy. Now I pass that cup of joy to you while I drink of the cup I cannot ask to pass from me. Strange that for me there should be no joy at the end of the journey. So it was with *The Art of Spiritual Healing* and also *The Thunder of Silence*. Why? Is it to learn more fully the lesson of the true Karma Yogi of the *Baghavad Gita*? I am trying.

With Love,
Lorraine

April 6, 1963

Dear Joel,

That I should ever in any way be angered or irritated by you—and sometimes I am—always fills me with remorse. I hit the bottom of the pit. The problem is always with the editing job. It's a tough spot for a disciple to be in. The disciple is not to question the master, and yet an editor has to. If I didn't continually risk your displeasure, and I seem to have made 100 percent score of that in the last few months—by screwing up my courage and sticking out my neck I would be acting like a craven, fawning coward. So consequently, I'm often in hot water with you. Walking the razor's edge is simple compared to this....

And yet, yesterday morning an experience came such as I have never had before in all my life. I was in meditation, and I felt that I was on the edge of the cliff—figuratively—and that it was now or never for that complete surrender to come.... Never have I felt so soft and pliable and yet so strong. A tremendous upheaval in consciousness is taking place. Please be with me.

Lovingly yours,
Lorraine

April 7, 1963

Dear Emma and Joel,

Yes, *Parenthesis* was God's from beginning to end. Think what Divinity within you brought forth such a message! I think of the travail of heart and soul you endured to bring forth each priceless jewel in this great book. In it there must be hundreds of hours of your class work, and I know in part the terrific price you paid to bring forth each one. Only you know the full price. *[This letter was returned with a marginal note from Joel in which he asked me why I should not experience the same pain in my rebirth.]*

You are right: only divine inspiration made possible the assembling of this material and its editing. That divine guidance was always there. I wish I could tell you of the infinite ways in which it appeared. Each morning brought a complete surrender of this work to God and a realization that in consciousness it already is complete. Then, during those days when Valborg was with me, we would work a while, stop to meditate as some call for help would come as a pause in the work, and then go forward with renewed zeal and enthusiasm. Valborg was marvelous. She is the one who was inexorable in her demands for perfection to the last little detail.

Do you know what really made it possible for me to perform my part of it? It was that December with you in Hawaii in 1961 when I sat in your office all day long, mostly in silence, absorbing and absorbing like a sponge what emanated from your consciousness.... All that month I was refueling for a fifteen-month nonstop flight into realms beyond imagination. So thank you for girding me with the strength, wisdom, and vision to be a small instrument in your very great work. You will never know how lovingly and tenderly each jewel has been fondled as it passed through my hands. I love this book so dearly.

[Joel reassured me that his work for me never stopped.]
With much love,
Lorraine

April 11, 1963

Dear Joel,

What a tailspin I took! Such rank hypnosis—even the cliff itself, all but the self-surrender. That was real.

You know the old story with me—how tired of it you must be—any deviation from principle fills me with terror that you will feel it is no use trying to teach me anymore. What a paradox that a person who feels so relatively secure in facing the world should have such a deep sense of spiritual inadequacy! It is dormant sometimes for months or years on end, and then there it is.

Perhaps all this is necessary to awaken me more fully, and at last I am sufficiently awake not to crawl into a mental corner in shame and disgust at myself for the fall *[from Grace]*. Maybe when we are just partially in the thrall of hypnosis, the opportunity of awakening is less likely, but when it comes to a focus as it did with me, it was either awaken or—!

I was seeing people—many people—as less than the Christ. Not you, but others, even though the whole experience seemed to be related to you. Being so close to you, what was in my consciousness hit up against your consciousness to be rooted out by your clear vision, just as darkness turns to the light.

A Roman circus is tame to battles that go on in the arena of consciousness. This has been a shattering experience, tearing me apart even though all this time I knew I was doing it to myself. That was the struggle.

Thank you for your beautiful and forceful letter which

arrived today by slow surface mail. I am more grateful to you than I can say, but you do know, don't you? The overturning has been pretty complete, the cleansing and scrubbing out process thorough. I am more grateful than any words for your patience with me. It has not left me where it found me. There has been a working through and greater clarity. Oh, well, you know so well what has been taking place within because you've been right there with me, watching.

Thank you.

> With love,
> Lorraine

12

Ascending Above the Horizon

Every inner experience Joel had was another horizon surmounted, and each one, while a confirmation of what had been given him at the very beginning, opened ever-new vistas of consciousness. Each unfoldment signalled a new horizon.

For me too, new vistas were opening up. Even more important, the seeds sown all these years of my searching, from the earliest days and culminating in my fifteen years of work with Joel, were sprouting and little seedlings were beginning to be visible, giving me the strength and courage to go forward on a spiritual ministry that encompassed the world.

It was hard to believe Joel when he asked me to get a cable address. He indicated that, although I lived in a particular place, I was not localized there.

Now the awareness of the infinite, unlimited nature of consciousness was becoming increasingly real as I found myself called upon to give classes and lectures far from my own locale. Furthermore, calls for spiritual help began coming from far-away places. All this only emphasized the need to go deeper and to be an ever better transparency for that Spirit within.

So it must be for everyone who walks the way of the mystical consciousness, for the revelations are infinite in number and always new, as that Consciousness, which is already unlimited and complete, opens up more and more to our awareness.

April 15, 1963

Dear Joel,

It is early Monday morning after Easter. All night long there has been such a feeling that for you it was a day of resurrection. Last night I felt a very strong call to work for you, and the resultant conviction that came was so powerful that sleep was banished for the entire night. The conviction expanded in depth and breadth around what is so often the theme of my meditations for you: This is the mind of the Christ, forming itself as perfect body and perfect condition.... This is the unconditioned mind, never under material or mental laws, walking this earth, untouched by the combined and concerted efforts of either human good or human evil.

"Whereas before I was blind, now I see. And I saw a new heaven and a new earth, and there was no more sea,"—no more sea to mirror forth the changing moods of the ever-changing atmosphere. I saw into the human mind, "the great red dragon," and witnessed it fall by its own nothingness. Milton's words from *Paradise Lost* rang in my ears: "How vain against the Omnipotent to take up arms."

The vision is clear and bright. Thank you. Now I know.

With love,
Lorraine

April 21, 1963

Dear Joel,

I'm so grateful to you for carrying me through this period of rebirthing. The experiences have been deep and fulfilling, even though a bit rough on "me." Your undeviating adherence to principle and your stern and unyielding holding me to that principle have been the greatest love and compassion there is. I'm sorry to have been such a nuisance, but I do thank you so very much for your guidance and support. The light that has come and the unfoldment are worth it all.

All these years, a transition in consciousness has been going on, but the last few weeks have brought about a sharp and quick overturning—although it seemed like an eternity while it was going on. A new kind of strength, courage, and fearlessness has entered in. There is no ecstasy, no emotion in connection with any of this: there is only a great sense of love for the whole world and almost complete detachment. Compassion for a struggling world is a thread running through the whole fabric of these days, a compassion born out of my own struggles. Love really is the Christ-way, a love that is strong and fearless, and yet gentle.

I've never had a conviction of the necessity for suffering (although most of my forward steps on the Path have been marked by periodic moments of anguish of spirit and soul) so I sought a deeper meaning than implied in the typical theological concept *[of the Cross]*. I saw the vertical bar as the influx of divine energy, wisdom, and strength—the individualization of the Divine—and the horizontal bar as the distributing point, the outpouring of that divine wisdom and force universally: individualization becoming universal. The point where the two meet is the point of tension, and any pain involved is resistance to universality.

This interpretation is probably not a new one, but it was new to me and had real significance. It made of the cross a beautiful, meaningful symbol of universal love, rather than an evidence of the sadism of mankind.

I would not trade the experience of these past few weeks for anything. Now I really know what you mean when you write in The Contemplative Life[1]:

> All alone you receive your particular temptation in the
> form of disease, accident, sin, death, poverty, or
> lonesomeness—all alone. You resolve all temptations
> within yourself. No one can take your temptation from
> you but you, and no one else can surmount the
> temptation. No one can be alone with you in your inner
> sanctuary in those hours preceding illumination.

It cannot be otherwise, can it? Yet I am sure that you were
standing close by, only for me there had to be that feeling of
being alone—so alone—before the light came. Thank you.

With love,

Lorraine

May 1, 1963

Dear Joel,

Thank you for your letter of April 27. I'm so grateful for
your instruction and I'm working with it so sincerely that
surely there must be some response to it in me....

In a great many areas, there is little or no reaction at all,
and these are areas in which most people react and markedly
so: the commonly accepted sense of sin never brings any
reaction. What an unholy sinner I must have been in previous
incarnations for there isn't a sinner I can condemn or to whose
actions I react. Disease, too, and impending death both find me
for the most part as cold as steel. But in other areas, ah, yes!
You are so right....

Within me there is a great deal of serenity which I
brought with me into this world. But "every knee must bend"
and the rubbish stored in the dark corners of the mind must be
routed out. That is where the "not peace but a sword" comes in.

1 Joel S. Goldsmith. *The Contemplative Life*, p. 69.

Whether or not it will be possible for me to destroy every vestige of personal sense while still on this plane, I do not know, but to this end I dedicate myself. Please help me with this "grand warfare".... This instruction could be the bridge I could not find, the missing link. This could be the one thing needful to make possible that final step. I feel as if I'm on the brink of discovery, the great Discovery.

With love,
Lorraine

May 31, 1963

Dear Emma and Joel,

Today I received the last financial accounting of the work in the East *[my classes in Philadelphia, Washington, and Cleveland]*. All three people did a beautiful job. They wanted so much to have everything perfect and beautiful that in some cases they went beyond what the activity justified in the way of expenses, not realizing that it is no tribute to me to do this because too many of the receipts go into expenses. However, there were several hundred dollars left, after expenses, and so I am enclosing a little sharing, as a small expression of my very great gratitude for your help during this strenuous period of lectures and classes. Without your teaching and work with me, this could never have been.

You can be happy that in these three cities you have such competent and dedicated representatives of The Infinite Way. They were really wonderful and gave me beautiful and very loving cooperation....

So glad to hear that the Bible lessons are continuing to meet with such a fine response. There is no doubt but that Virginia is doing a beautiful job. She could not miss with her beautiful consciousness.[2]

2 This refers to Virginia Stephenson who has since been carrying on a heavy Infinite Way lecture and teaching schedule with classes in the United States, Europe, Australia, and New Zealand.

Incidentally, she wrote and invited me to share her apartment at the Colony Surf *[in Hawaii]*. Wasn't that dear of her? It was a real temptation, but one I put behind me quickly. I wrote to her and explained it was impossible for me to accept her more than gracious and generous invitation *[because of deadlines to be met]*.

For years I have lived without a single desire, without really caring to have anything, and then when I fell from Grace into that trap of wanting something, I got my fingers so badly burned that I trust the lesson has been sufficient to last a good many lifetimes. So I'm living each day joyously and gratefully. It is wonderful.... Incidentally, the Instruction Tapes are magnificent! It will take another whole letter probably to tell you just how good they are. This was a much needed piece of work and I'm so grateful you have put this on tape.

Please don't be so busy that you neglect your rest. Do take care of yourself.

With much love,
Lorraine

June 9, 1963

Dear Emma and Joel,

We are having one of those hot, humid, sticky days that Chicago can have, just to remind us that it can be warm here and that the sun can shine—in between thunder showers! Sounds like Joel talking!

Thank you for your helpful and illuminating letters. Even before your letter about scheduling work outside of Chicago arrived, it came to me that this close scheduling was for the birds. The ideal thing for me is to have work in one city and then return home for a while before doing any more. That gives me a respite from that grueling kind of thing. Thank you for underlining that for me.... Thank you for sending the confidential material. As you know, I will cherish it and save it until the proper time for it to become evident, and then it will go forth to the world....

Thank you for everything, and bless you both.

With much love,
Lorraine

July 2, 1963

Dear Emma and Joel,

The enclosed letter is being sent to Eugene Exman *[the religious editor of Harper & Row]* today. I trust that it says all that you had in mind. Each day I grow more pleased and grateful for the outcome of this problem.... Your song is not sung—far from it. On that I'd be willing to place a very large bet. I'm counting on you to come through with work which will impart and teach the top of all mystical work. No one has evidenced the capacity to impart spiritual wisdom in the same measure that you have, and because of that, I am sure that you will complete your mission here. You are right: there is still unfinished business.

These days I am living in such a state of divine Grace that it is impossible to describe it.

With much love,
Lorraine

July 2, 1963

Dear Emma and Joel,

You said it! I am constantly in a state of amazement at the lack of perception of most people in the world. Chapter 10 of *The Contemplative Life* is a rare jewel. Do you remember that it came out of your last Open Class in London in 1960? Right afterwards, when I saw you in New York, you were fairly bursting with it, realizing that it was one of the high moments in the whole Infinite Way. Naturally, it found its way into a *Letter*.

At the time the *Letter* on "Meditation on a Life by Grace" came out, I longed to see it in a pamphlet, but now I am sure that it is better that people should have to read the whole *Contemplative Life* all the way through in order to discover this prize gem in the midst of so many others. To read it is an experience in another world....

People are always gushing about how lovely this is and that, while all the time their response makes it so evident that it has not made the slightest impression. Yes, as you say, "Just mush!"

Did you ever stop to think that "Meditation on Life by Grace" is the modern *Song Celestial*, the modern *Baghavad Gita*? In its emphasis on self-surrender and seeking only the *Me*, it restates that ancient wisdom for modern man. That has been your life always, and now you have stated it so clearly that all the world can see it—if they but have eyes.

With much love,
Lorraine

July 2, 1963

Dear Joel,

There are always "if's" in the human sense of life. But for you there are no "if's" because you are not living the human sense of life.

Saturday and Sunday I felt such a need to do special work for you, and it came through so beautifully.... I could feel you upheld by the Everlasting Arms which were lifting you above all that is in "this world," and yet they were maintaining you here as a light to the whole world. There was such a realization of Omnipresence that today I cannot for a moment accept any of these conditioning "if's." Thank you for telling me about them, though, and thereby giving me the opportunity of tossing them out. Anyway, I'm keeping up the work, although I feel mountains have been dissolved. There is nothing quite like this consciousness of Grace, is there?

Your mention of "glimpsing the horizon" has always been a perennial state with you. You have glimpsed horizon after horizon, and each has taken you and your students up to a new plateau. Because of Infinity, I wonder if that can ever really cease. There must always be a horizon, even though at times, as with me, during these last days, we feel we are already there, and there is no more horizon, no more earth or heaven—just *I*....

So grateful to hear about the widening circle of your Masonic work and also of your forthcoming lecture in the church in Hawaii. Who is better qualified to talk about religion for the Twentieth Century? Good horizons to you!

With love,
Lorraine

July 17, 1963

Dear Emma and Joel,

Thank you for all your letters and for the material enclosed. I'm so grateful to have this autobiographical material. The idea of a biography of you based practically exclusively on your spiritual unfoldment as evidenced in the progressive class work you have conducted and the unfoldments that have come to you has long been uppermost in my mind. It is the only kind of biography there could possibly be. I shall take good care of the material you have sent me....

What a joy it is to hear of your latest revelation and of the assurance that you have received of your ascension in this life-experience....

My Cleveland Class was a rich experience in unfolding consciousness. It was a beautiful and responsive group.... To you, I can only say that in spite of a very great uneasiness that always precedes the zero hour, when I am on the platform, I no longer exist. Something takes over, and the force with which the words tumble out almost shatters me at times. It's like a torrent trying to get through a narrow channel. Furthermore, I have little recollection afterward of what has been said. I haven't gotten used to it, but it is very plain that I have nothing to do with it. If only I could learn to trust It, it would save me the struggle beforehand.

With much love,
Lorraine

July 19, 1963

Dear Emma and Joel,

Your spiritual saga has been such a great inspiration to me. I've been living with it in every spare moment, reading it, at first avidly to savor of its riches, and now dwelling on one gem at a time.... To continue commenting on all the jewels in your spiritual diary would be pointless. Suffice it to say that some of its spiritual fire has spread to me just through this brief contact with it, and it has spread with the speed and force of a prairie fire that burns every barrier in its way. Thank you for giving me this opportunity to see the master-consciousness in operation. These papers, I know, you have sent to me for a purpose, and I will hold them until that purpose is revealed.[3]

3 Much of this material found its way into *The Spiritual Journey of Joel S. Goldsmith*, but there is much more that legal restrictions do not permit me to use.

In the meantime, they are serving a purpose in my experience. Thank you...

Enclosed is a bit of sharing from the fruitage of my Kansas City and Cleveland work. My deepest gratitude for your help and spiritual guidance which made it possible.

With much love,
Lorraine

July 26, 1963

Dear Emma and Joel,

Thank you for your two beautiful letters. I felt that all was not well on that Friday and Saturday and was forced into meditation most of the day and night.

A tough experience it was for you, but what a rich reward came in your unfoldment on karmic law. How strange these valley experiences are! Even though I, too, have experienced my share of them, I will never fully understand them. Perhaps that is because my whole nature revolts against any doctrine of suffering as necessary, and yet how often great wisdom comes out of such periods! Just another paradox on this strange Way we are walking!

To me, this whole subject of karmic law is like walking the razor's edge. There is the necessity, or so it seems, of making people in the Ten-Commandments-state of consciousness aware of the operation of the law of cause and effect as long as they are on that level, while at the same time the practitioner must realize that the son of God is never under any such belief, but eternally lives under divine Grace. As long as one is living out from world standards and world beliefs, he is unconsciously accepting the law of as-ye-sow. Is not the primary job of the spiritual healer that of lifting the individual out of those beliefs into spiritual consciousness? Really, is not the whole healing practice a dedication to proving the nonpower of karmic law?

In this connection, I think of what you have explained as the perfect way to nullify karma: Stop sowing! Just that simple. Can we ever come out from under the belief of karma as long as we believe we are the actor and the do-er? Is there any way to surmount the belief of karmic law other than to surrender ourselves as instruments of the Divine?

A flat world is effective and limiting to the ignorant. So also, karmic law is operative and limiting to the unillumined. Am I right in this, or am I missing the point in failing to see beyond the Absolute? In a relative world, it is a matter of levels of consciousness, but beyond the Absolute, there would be no levels—only the One.

It would be wonderful to have some time with you in Hawaii. You cannot possibly know how I would love it. So thank you for asking me to come. Perhaps when the current work is disposed of, that will be possible. If it is and is convenient for you, it will be a joy, and if not, that, too, is all right.

Your house and schedule of work both sound beautiful and stimulating. What riches the students there are privileged to enjoy! Maybe it's their karma, or maybe Grace has taken over.

With much love,
Lorraine

Joel heartily concurred in every point raised in this letter recognizing the inviolability of karmic law on the human level of life. He felt that the unfoldment that came to him on karmic law must have been comparable to having quintuplets.

August 4, 1963

Dear Emma and Joel,

When you say that the spiritual path is a difficult one I guess you're the one who speaks from experience! Yet, to know that all this suffering is part of a forward movement in consciousness, the great Initiation perhaps, must make it seem less futile, although nonetheless difficult. If Initiation reveals the hypnotic nature of appearances and their nonpower, and brings about eventually the destruction of all personal sense, would the degree of realization another individual might have in that area, even though he might not have the attained state of consciousness of the Initiate, be of help? In other words, I know that you have helped me, but is it possible for us lesser ones to help you, the teacher, the master, through this experience?...

Your explanation of karma, while it has in it elements of the oriental teaching on this subject, goes far beyond that, and releases man from the hopeless acceptance of present conditions as being a necessary evil which must be endured because of stored-up karma. Against this, I always rebelled, being the incorrigible optimist I am. But to see karma, just as are birth and death as part of the mesmeric picture of the human experience, this makes sense and carries with it the method of destroying it.

This takes me back to that momentous moment in 1956 in New York when, during the last session of the *First Practitioners' Class*[4] in the morning and of the *First Closed Class*[5] at night, you pointed out that all disease was the law, *[the material sense of law]*, but that the moment Grace was realized and brought to bear, there was no longer any law.

As I write this, a crazy idea flashes across my mind: I thought of going away a few weeks in September, taking my work with me, and going up into the north woods to work in a different atmosphere. The flash was this: Why don't I go do

4 First Steinway Hall Practitioner Class, Reel 4.
5 First Steinway Hall Closed Class, Reel 3.

that very same thing only in Hawaii instead of the north woods?... Would you have time to see me? Please know that if I should go, I would be happy to pay for my own transportation even though you so generously offered to take care of it. Well, all of this was just one of those quick flashes that came this moment and so I'll just wait and see. I only want to go there if it is the right thing for me to do at the right time. If you feel that later would be better, then that is fine.... Well, if all this sounds crazy, just tell me so.

With so much love,
Lorraine

August 7, 1963

Dear Emma and Joel,

The agony and the glory of your spiritual experience of July 30 have gone very deep, as deep as you were lifted high. All this must be tearing you apart, but out of the shreds the Phoenix is rising....

During the past year the teaching aspect of my activity has increased noticeably. Although practically born and brought up a teacher, I never cease feeling how strange it is that people should come to me in this capacity. Maybe that is because I fulfilled myself as a teacher years ago and do not have any desire for it. Other people hanker so after doing this, but not I. It has been interesting to see people coming to me for teaching and to watch the unfoldment that is taking place. Sometimes slowly and sometimes rapidly a transformation of consciousness begins to take place....

Lovingly yours,
Lorraine

August 15, 1963

Dear Emma and Joel,

...The paper of your talk on karma is beautiful, and of course something I love and heartily believe in. I read it very carefully and I wonder if you would like to underscore it further by adding a paragraph just above the last paragraph to the effect that karma operates only in the human picture, just as do all other human laws, but that as soon as one rises into Grace, as did the thief on the cross, there is no longer any karmic law. It operates on the human level of consciousness, but to those on the spiritual level, "against such, there is no law."

Also, in the first paragraph after "as ye sow so shall ye reap" could you add something about the whole idea of karmic law's being a part of the hypnotism of "this world"? You deal so beautifully with eliminating the word "I" from our life. Would you want to add a bit further emphasizing that the way to come out from under karmic law is to stop sowing through the application of the principle of impersonalization? As Paul said, "There is a sense of sin in me," but the sin is impersonal carnal mind, whereas the good is the activity of God shining through. We are not doers—only transparencies, and then we are not sowing. This may not be in accordance with your unfoldment, but it is just something that hit me as I read it.

With much love,
Lorraine

August 16, 1963

Dear Emma and Joel,

...For years I have dreamed of writing about you, Joel, as "The Most Unforgettable Person I've Ever Known", and those are the truest words I have ever spoken about you! Someday that will come through perhaps, as well as your biography, but not now. Better yet would it be to work with you on your autobiography—not the usual recounting of incidents from birth to fruition, but a spiritual odyssey. My files are bulging with material that could serve as biographical material for the story of your spiritual journey. It was sent to me for a purpose, and that purpose must be fulfilled. Someday! Someday!.

I have been so grateful that you have had these months at home, and much as I would like to have you back with us lecturing and giving classes, it is something no one who cares for you could urge you to do. That is too rough a life! Certainly I hope that if you are given the instruction to travel, the Spirit will reveal a little of that Omniscience, which It is, by arranging a gentle and reasonable schedule. It is hard to believe that It could have arranged for you such schedules as you have undertaken in the past—staggering, they were.

The Initiation experience that has opened the doors on a new phase of the work has surely endowed you with the wisdom to carry it forward. I'm never worried about your having the wisdom to meet any situation. All your life has been an exemplification of Omniscience pouring forth in infinite measure.

I'm getting all excited about going to Hawaii. Can't let anything interfere with that, except your work.

With love,

Lorraine

My dream of writing about the most unforgettable person I ever knew was fulfilled in 1973 when Harper & Row published my book, *The Spiritual Journey of Joel S. Goldsmith*. Into it were put many of the special gems in the form of notes and papers Joel had sent me for my use "at the right time." It truly is his spiritual odyssey and reveals much of Joel's soul unfoldment.

August 30, 1963

Dear Joel,

Of your mission, there can be no doubt. This mission of the revelation and demonstration of the Christ in this age will not fail, and since you are the instrument, how can you fail? That Wisdom that chose you knew what It was doing, and It will carry you through this valley experience into the fullness of life. There is some hurdle to be jumped, but the ultimate fulfillment can never be doubted. I have never believed that your life is not a life of complete Grace. The fruitage of that Grace is too evident, and your life is a testimony to the activity of that Grace in your experience. All this week this has been singing in me. The music is clear and sharp. It is so.

Your letter to me was so very kind and comforting. Thank you...I am working harder on myself than I have ever before, knowing full well that only a deeper touch of the Christ can do the job. So the work is to attain that greater depth. Thank you for your light.

With love,
Lorraine

Joel encouraged me to come to Hawaii as soon as possible because, after a year of intensive work, he and Emma were going to England about the middle of October for a period of refreshment. So, on September 17, I was off on another trek to what had become my spiritual home.

While I was in Hawaii in October, an invitation

came from the one person I knew in Florida for me to give a class there. I hesitated to accept, thinking that no one would come, but Joel assured me that students around the world knew of my work as editor of the writings and that there would be many students who would attend such a class.

Even though my trip in September and October turned out to be the last time I would work with Joel in Hawaii and was the shortest of all trips there, it was perhaps the most fruitful. There were the usual long periods each day with Joel, culminating in one special day when Joel meditated and talked to me ceaselessly from morning until night. That day Joel, undoubtedly sensing his impending transition, gave me the greatest gift of all: a complete freedom from any dependence whatsoever on a person as a teacher. This great master had revealed the Master within in Its fullness. The love remained, even stronger than ever, but the dependence was gone in a total reliance on That which would never leave me and which had used Joel as the instrument for my own awakening all the years of my working with him. That Presence which had always been with me now revealed that I needed no instrument but could receive whatever instruction was needed directly from It.

It was at this time that Joel shared with me more fully his evaluation of his experience in South Africa the preceding October and December, when he, himself, had been laid low by a coronary attack. From this attack he had recovered in a relatively short time and was able to continue his work at home in Hawaii. Even there he was far from inactive, carrying on a world-wide healing practice, meeting with individual students who continued to come to Hawaii for special work with him, and giving classes to students who came there from all over the world.

In retrospect he recognized the experience in South Africa as an initiation in which he found himself at the very gates of hell, if not in hell itself. For so long, he had in a large measure transcended the physical sense of body and was living as pure consciousness, but now he found himself very aware of his physical sense of body with its attendant pain. Most of all, he experienced a sense of failure and even moments of concern as to what might lie ahead. Out of it came, as it always does for those who have selflessly given themselves to the world, a resurrection and the realization that there is nothing to be overcome, not even death: it is only to be seen through.

He expressed his surprise to me that he should have had to go through this initiation even though every great spiritual master has testified to its necessity. He felt that the realization of the principles of impersonalization, never ascribing good or evil to a person, and the nothingization of all appearances as hypnotic suggestion, should have obviated it.

On this point I heartily agreed with him and still feel that with sufficient dedication and selflessness the ascension, a total rising above this material sense of world, would come as gently as a summer breeze. Then nothing in this world could hold us in shackles any longer. Joel felt that his having experienced this and thus being able to communicate it could save others this descent into hell and that they could awaken more painlessly, joyously, and gloriously.

October 16, 1963

Dear Emma and Joel,

Home again after such a beautiful month! I wish you could know the treasures I have carried back with me—enough to digest for years and years to come. I trust you received the note of gratitude I left for you on the dining room table containing its tangible expression.

Los Angeles kept me busy morning, noon, and night. I began with appointments at 8:00 in the morning and never finished seeing people until late at night. Mail and everything like that had to wait. It was a strenuous time. There is surely a tremendous interest out there in your work.

Tuesday, Virginia Stephenson took me over to Pasadena for the afternoon and evening group there, and nothing would do but that I talk to them. It was a very fine group and I had the pleasure of hearing Virginia talk a bit: beautiful, clear, direct, and impersonal. She is a grand person. This was the first time I really had an opportunity to know her and I found her clarity of vision a great joy....

Home here looks good, too. There is work ahead, and in the forthcoming days I shall be assimilating the work you have given the past couple of months. Much has already come through in regard to its significance, and more of that, later.

The work for you has been going well, Joel, so I feel all must be well. Do try to make this a tiny bit of vacation, and don't work too hard. Much joy to you during these weeks in London.

With much love,
Lorraine

October 17, 1963

Dear Joel,

The long paragraph on healing in your letter, explaining so clearly what our response to a call should be, is very helpful. Thank you for it. It seems to me that the whole secret is in taking no account of the "man of earth" as you pointed out.

The article you sent me on "The Secret of The Infinite Way" was an outpouring that came through you as you were talking to me one day the last week I was there, and, as you began to feel what was happening, you said, "Let's get this down," and turned on the Stenorette. It is to be used as a special article or maybe as a "Note from Hawaii" in the January *Letter* which will open with a lead article, the first on the healing principles which you said were to be the theme for the whole year.... You remember you thought this would be particularly good for 1964 since *Parenthesis* would be out and students would be working with that so that an emphasis on the healing principles would make for a good balance.

Could you give me some further instruction or information on initiation?... My own sense of initiation from my own experience... is of its being a heightening of consciousness which occurs during moments of crises and which brings a deepening of consciousness and a more universal wisdom....

With much love,
Lorraine

October 21, 1963

Dear Emma and Joel,

...Right after the letter to you in which I asked about initiation was posted, I had my answer.... Of course, initiation would have to be an inner experience as it was with you and as it has been with me, and much more came to me about its real meaning as a "dying" to one level of consciousness and a rebirthing in a higher one.

So far it is apparent to me that your work of the last couple of months is lifting us above words and thoughts, above metaphysics into the mystical consciousness. It has become increasingly clear how the principles serve as the ladder on which we climb up to the Experience Itself, and why an understanding of these forms the basis of the attainment. But the principles are the "letter" *[of truth]* and they are dead without the Experience, an Experience which is essential to all healing and spiritual teaching. There can be no resting in the metaphysics of The Infinite Way: its mysticism must be attained.

The larger message, and the one which gives real meaning and purpose to life, is the lifting of human consciousness universally—or perhaps I should say dissolving human consciousness universally—in the Christ-consciousness. That places this teaching in an entirely different category from any other teaching. It is not a message just for a few, but for the world, to bring the Christ to the whole world. This I know has always been your goal, but I think in this work you make clear the method of attaining the goal.

The real meaning of Christ-consciousness as the consciousness that does not react to the outer pictures has become indelibly engraved in my consciousness during the past months. You have borne home to me the reason It does not react: It has no distorted mental images to which to react. That is the secret and for me the great secret.

Much love,

Lorraine

October 27, 1963

Dear Emma and Joel,

Well, this last week has come and gone, every minute filled to the brim. What loomed ahead of me as an eternity has come to an end with the speed of light.

The class itself *[an Infinite Way class I gave in Chicago]* was far and away the best work that has come through me. Throughout it, my prayer was that the students be given the bread of life and not a stone, and so powerful was the word to me that I was almost shattered and certainly completely overwhelmed the last day. The vision was so tremendous that unfolded before my eyes and the world so far away that to be brought back to it from time to time during the final hour was almost unnerving. I'm sure you understand what I mean.

After all this, I should be happy and satisfied, but strangely enough I feel nothing—nothing at all. It is as if I witnessed something going on outside of me, and I stood there watching.... And now let me add my very grateful thanks to you both for your wonderful help during this week. Your consciousness was there with us, blessing every one of us.

With much love,
Lorraine

October 29, 1963

Dear Joel,

Thank you so much for your letters. So grateful for your sharing something of your last experience with me. As, yes, the Buddha is also finding fulfillment and fruition of his mission in The Infinite Way. All your experience has pointed to that.... It was this that I saw on the last day of my class *[in Chicago, last week]* that so overwhelmed me with its magnitude. For a moment there was no one there, and as I looked up above the heads of the class into infinity, I saw a flame of Light and not people, but worlds—planets—being drawn up to that Light and merging with it until there was only the flame—no people, no worlds, just a flame of Light. And I felt the full import of The Infinite Way and of your work. I couldn't speak for a few seconds, and it was even harder when I looked at that beautiful class and realized that they did not know. They were still trying to lift themselves above their own personal problems and personal sense, and the sadness was almost unbearable. The words don't really come. All I can say is that I can never be the same again, and maybe this was given to me just for me. There is no way to evaluate the work you did with me yet, but the above and the class here and in Los Angeles are some of the fruitage of it.

The method of attaining this vision of yours? It is inherent in the vision, inseparable from it. Never before has it been so clear to me how senseless it is to try to heal cancer or discord. I see with every realization, every treatment, the sum total of nothingness being revealed as just that. Your teaching rings in my ears, "Error is not nullified one by one, but universally with every treatment."

With love,
Lorraine

November 7, 1963

Dear Joel,

I am sure that because it does not emphasize healing, *Parenthesis* will have a wider appeal. Many people are not primarily interested in healing *per se*. They are hungering and searching for the kind of satisfaction that can be found only in the life of the Spirit. Such persons as these will seize upon

Parenthesis as the answer for which they have been seeking since time began.

This I can understand because I so well remember saying to you in my early days in The Infinite Way, "I want none of this healing business." But your answer satisfied me, and still does, "No, but healing is the proof of the principle." That principle will be proved in proportion as people turn away from healing as their first and foremost objective and strive for that mind which was in Christ Jesus. When they stop being interested in healing, they will be able truly to "seek ye first the kingdom of heaven" and then the other things will be added. As long as people turn to the teaching only for healing, how can they kid themselves into believing that they are really seeking God? But when they do turn wholeheartedly for the purpose of attaining the God-experience, the ills of the flesh will drop away for lack of feeding.

How well I understand you! Certainly in the new heaven and new earth, there will be no more tears, but until that state is achieved in its fullness, tears can never be far from those who go deep within. There will always have to be that empty space, not really empty, but filled with yearning. I have often pondered the function of tears. It has been said: "These tears, O thou of heart most merciful, these are the streams that irrigate the fields of charity immortal." It is those streams of compassion that will take you up that extra notch. I stand very close to you - ever watching.

With love,
Lorraine

On their way home from London, Joel and Emma stopped in New York, where I met them on my way home from giving my first week of classwork in Florida with 35 students *[the beginning of what became a yearly event up through 1981 - with some 400 students attending in Palm Beach, Florida].*

Joel and Emma arrived in New York on that tragic day in the history of our country when President Kennedy was assassinated. That weekend, even though the whole city was closed down in mourning, Joel conducted his scheduled two-hour class on Sunday. It was a magnificent two hours. In our time together, however, there was the sense of Joel's withdrawing from the world. It was plain that he was reaching toward the next horizon.

December 10, 1963

Dear Emma and Joel,

You must have wondered if I had dropped off the earth or had taken to orbiting around the moon because it is such a long time since I have written to you. I'm still very much here, but I've been so overwhelmed with work that accumulated while I was away that I am just now beginning to come out from under.

First and most important of all is to tell you what joy it was for me to be with you in New York. Those five days were so very wonderful—a respite from the mad rush of which there are so few these days.... I always treasure every moment I can have with you, and this time I was singularly blessed. Thank you for the blessedness of those days....

Would you be interested in having a section called "Tape Department" in the monthly *Letter*? I have long thought of such a possibility and would include in it a brief outline in the nature of a resume in which recent tapes could be included. It should be sufficiently brief to make it possible to include two or three excerpts in each *Letter* without taking up an undue amount of space, and thus whet the appetite of the reader. Yet they should have enough in them to give the student something with which he can work. If you are interested, let me submit something along this line to you and see what you think of it.

Enclosed are two pages from last Saturday's "Panorama," the weekly feature magazine section of *The Chicago Daily News*. You will note that the two marked pages deal with books to purchase for Christmas giving and you will also note under the heading of "Religion": a book called *A Parenthesis in Eternity* by one Joel S. Goldsmith. Also please note that the suggested books, of which there are only a few, are not arranged alphabetically, and that Mr. Goldsmith's book leads the list. Furthermore, he finds himself in such good company as Hans Kung, Niehbuhr, and Paul Tillich! The list was compiled by our friend David Meade.

Also, do you have a copy of *The Phenomenon of Man* by Teillard du Chardin?... If not, I would like to send one to you since Adela Rogers St. Johns has linked your conclusions to his. It is a book, Stuart Brent, spent six consecutive weeks reviewing because he considered it of such major significance. So please let me know.

Enclosed are the Study Guides I made for our students to use with *The 1962 Stockholm Tapes*. If you would like to have more of these to use or more of our Weekly Bulletins, I will be glad to send them to you.

With much love,
Lorraine

Joel often spoke of the importance of the monthly Infinite Way *Letter* as an instrument for the unfoldment of consciousness. Each month, one or more specific principles was emphasized to encourage students to go forth and make those principles a living experience through daily practice. The idea of incorporating a Tape Recording Department as a regular feature in the *Letter* met with enthusiastic approval from Joel. Later, sample Tape Departments were submitted and Joel was quite ecstatic about them and most grateful for this idea.

December 20, 1963

Dear Joel,

The sense of the passing of years, and still the vision unfulfilled, is the deepest of frustrations. It is the vision that keeps us soaring, even though unattainable. That is the needling that will not let us rest in our present achievements and pushes us on and on into the infinity that is.

Certainly, you have more—far more—than your share of accomplishments to your credit, and yet there is always, and always there must be, that hungering for more. You, as would any intelligent person, pooh-pooh the idea of sitting up in heaven strumming a harp for eternity. And yet, what is the difference between that and *attaining* the vision? Is it not basically the same idea only on a higher level of fulfillment? Life is in the living of it, and what is living without the vision? And if the vision is attained, where is the vision? Perhaps the real fulfillment is the zest one experiences in reaching for that vision.

It is like the man who left this life-experience and found himself transported into a new and glorious world. In this new world he had every luxury: a magnificent home, expertly trained servants to wait upon him, and every creature comfort. For days he luxuriated in these sumptuous surroundings until, satiated, he turned to the major-domo and said, "Now for some work!"

"Oh," the reply came back, "There is no work here!"

"No work? Why that would be hell."

"Well, where did you think you were?"

Well, this is all on a very relative level, but it is an expression of something that has been a part of me for a very long time. Kahlil Gibran said so much when he said in substance, "Pain is the breaking of the shell of your awareness." How true! Someday when we are in the full awareness of our perfect being, we will be that Infinity expressed in Its fullness. But until then, the joy must be in beholding Infinity unfolding to our awareness.

With much love,

Lorraine

January 1, 1964

Dear Emma and Joel,

Happy New Year! I can do no better this New Year on this new day than begin it with a letter to you. First of all, let me tell you that my beautiful new ribbon knit arrived and it is so lovely. Thank you, thank you....

For a long time I have been considering a more adequate set-up for my work at home, and quite out of the blue the opportunity has come to rent one of the two bedroom apartments in this building. It would be ideal for me. Now the only consideration is the rental of my own apartment for which I hold a lease until next November. These lake front apartments are rarely vacant, and this one is in just the right location, but apartments such as mine are not so easy to sublease now with all the new high rise buildings. Of course, rentwise, this is the best buy on the Lake Shore.

This is surely a quiet New Year, and it was so good to have it that way. I enter it with my mail practically caught up and all my work in good order which is a most wonderful feeling. I also enter it with a heart filled with love and gratitude for you both.

> With love,
> Lorraine

January 5, 1964

Dear Emma and Joel,

Yes, 1963 was quite a year for you. The major achievements you have listed for that one year would be enough for a whole lifetime, or better, for most people.

I'm looking forward to hearing the tapes of the London work—have only received the first two I ordered so far and they give no indication of what is to come, and the earthshaking revelation that came to you. You brought it out in New York, but I always like to hear it as it comes through with the elevated consciousness of the revelation itself. I have been working toward having a few days, maybe three or at least two, all alone for meditation and rest and refueling. I would love to sit down during those days with the transcription of the 1963 work to read as I listen to the tapes from beginning to end.

Last night I couldn't sleep, and almost dreamed up a whole "The Most Unforgettable Character I've Met," but I didn't get it down on paper. The idea was there, though, and surely was flowing.

Nineteen sixty-four is not at all clear to me. Nothing looms as imminent.

> With much love,
> Lorraine

January 12, 1964

Dear Emma and Joel,

So glad you are going to be in California. I will arrange my schedule here so that I can be out there with you....

Be sure to let me know as soon as possible when you will be in Chicago. In fact, just on general principles, I think I will check about available dates. This time we want to have plenty of room—!!!

This last Saturday afternoon we had a most interesting experience during our two-hour tape session. Ordinarily, I play one whole reel of one side of a tape—anything anyone wants to hear, but this time, I selected the tape, "Flesh and Flesh"—and played a little of it, the section that completed the elucidation of some particular principle or portion of principle, and then asked if they had caught that point, and replayed that portion of it again. It took over an hour and a half—almost three hours —to complete the tape, but I wish you could have heard the enthusiasm! Results: five orders for the tape! We're going to try that on Saturday, for a while at least.

This year I seem to have launched forth on a concerted campaign to awaken our students, and break this tendency just to drift and have a pleasant restful Saturday afternoon. I'm watching it with detachment and interest.

With much love,

Lorraine

Joel asked me to leave the second and third weeks in May free for lectures and work in Chicago. Furthermore, a trip to Europe was in the offing following the Chicago work. My response to this news was sent in a letter of January 9, 1964:

If you are going to be in California for any length of time, I might fly out there. Also, I would love to go to Europe, but do not want to go unless it is agreeable to you and unless the work is sufficiently ahead to make it possible.... The copies of the letters to students that you have sent me are most illuminating.

                                        January 15, 1964

Dear Emma and Joel,

Well, where to begin? Sometimes there is so much happening that I wonder where, but I guess by answering one letter after another....

It has been hard for me to keep my feet on the ground since receiving your last letter. They are trailing in that cloud in which my head is firmly anchored! I'm delighted at the prospect of going to Europe with you both and will be glad to fit into your schedule, doing whatever you have for me to do there. I hope you and God and all the Powers that be will forgive me for being just a little excited about it. I am trying to be very calm and cool, but my heart is beating very, very fast—even skipping some beats in its hurry....

I received that registered mail with some of your early gems, and will guard them carefully. Beautiful, beautiful! I see something. Again, how can I ever thank you both for your love.

                    With much love,
                    Lorraine

February 4, 1964

Dear Emma and Joel,

Well, I'm moved! What a job! Even with all the wonderful help I had it is a big, big undertaking. Now the living room and bedroom are liveable, and the study or office has been used as a catch-all until I get time to go out and get new furniture for it. Anyway, I can now wade over to my typewriter and here I am sitting at it looking out over calm, peaceful Lake Michigan with the Drake Towers in the distance. It is a perfect spot for work, more perfect than any dream could have conjured up! The arrangements at the Conrad Hilton are made as per my last letter....

With much love,
Lorraine

February 14, 1964

Dear Emma and Joel,

Thank you for your very dear letter and for your most generous gift. Since my office is practically bare except for boxes which have not yet been emptied, it will be a joy to select something and call it my Emma and Joel piece. I do want to get out and do a little shopping, but I must get a little better caught up on the work before doing any such gallivanting. I can't tell you what a joy it is to sit here typing and be able to glance up and see an unobstructed view of Lake Michigan with Navy Pier in the distance—a continuous marvel....

With much love,
Lorraine

Every experience with Joel seemed better than the one preceding it, probably because each was marked by an ever-increasing degree of receptivity, making it possible for me to go deeper in consciousness. So the two weeks on the West Coast in Los Angeles and San Francisco brought greater awareness and a sense of urgency to prepare for whatever lay ahead. These joyous days included hours and hours of talks and meditation with Joel with a sense of peace, quietness, and completeness—fulfillment—prevailing.

Joel spoke very seriously of the importance of our work together, the full value of which would be revealed in the frame work of passing time. He recognized that my being drawn to him and his work was a part of the divine Plan: his consciousness unfolding as what was necessary for the work given him to do: my consciousness unfolding as the teacher necessary to prepare me for the work I was to do on the books and in fulfilling a world-wide ministry.

I remember walking up the hill with Joel to the St. Francis Hotel in San Francisco, and Joel saying, "I never can remember which is correct: between Mrs. Jones and I or Mrs. Jones and me? Which is it?" And the schoolteacher in me, so long ago left behind, responded not with a discussion on grammar and grammatical rules, but with a simple, no-fail gimmick that anyone could follow. And we both laughed. So many times it was like that with Joel—no launching forth on deep spiritual subjects, but just a nondirective, nondidactic beingness that made his teaching all the more potent. And there was that closeness in which neither student nor teacher dons a protective covering—not even tissue paper between that total oneness.

March 13, 1964

Dear Joel,

Welcome home! Imagine it looks good to you even after so short a trip as this last one. How are you doing? Have been sticking close and will continue to do so.

For me this last trip was really *it*. Never have I had such a beautiful experience, and that's saying a lot because there have been so many beautiful experiences with you and Emma. It seems that this time I reached a plateau beyond and above anything heretofore attained, a livingness, a depth—oh, there are no words to describe it. It just is.

I was so grateful for so much of the audible teaching: "Fatalism has to do with good and evil.... Prayer is really self-surrender.... Everything known yesterday is as nothing to what can be known today.... Givingness is receptivity.... I stand at the door and knock."

But of all the things you told me, as you gave me one long last penetrating look, your last words to me seemed to be indelibly engraved on my Soul: "*I* is fulfilling Itself at every level of your life." In the calls for help, that is all that comes—just *I* fulfilling Itself. Those parting words sing within me and are like a benediction and a mantra that repeats itself continuously. And, of course, it is the silent teaching that went on all the time that made it possible for me to *hear*. This is the "pearl" such as connoisseurs have never dreamed of. Thank you, thank you.

With much love,
Lorraine

March 19, 1964

Dear Joel,

Yes, California was a good experience—for me, one of the

best, if not the very best. But I can see what you meant when you talked to me about organization creeping in. I suppose it is because people are so accustomed to organization and doing things that way that they simply do not realize the signs when they appear. Most of all people love to be affiliated with something, and to participate in all the fanfare that goes with it. Well, such is the human mind! You probably remember the story that was told about three Americans who had to bail out of an airplane. Before they reached the ground, they had had an election, and one had become president, another secretary, and a third treasurer! The organizational man!

Your work is too clear for me ever to accept any lack of fulfillment for it. You could not have been the instrument chosen for this work, and then not be given everything necessary to fulfill it—the physical vehicle as well as the unfoldment. You have had more evidence of this than probably anyone has ever had in all the centuries that have come and gone. Now, too, surely the unfoldment and the discernment to establish it securely in human consciousness will follow. How long it took the realization of supply to come through to you! There were hard days, and bitter ones, before that principle was revealed, and after the principle had been glimpsed, months and years followed before the fruitage was there in its completeness.

So now, something new is coming forth into form. This body-problem is, in some way, a part of the hypnotism that must be seen through before what is to be revealed can take form—else it would not plague you so, but would have been met with all the work that has been done. As you have said over and over again with emphasis: "He performeth the thing that is appointed for me to do." You wouldn't have been appointed to do this if Omniscience did not recognize the potential transparency. That could never be because Omniscience really is Omniscience.

Perhaps out of this you will discover why barrenness and unhappiness are the accompaniment of spiritual attainment. Always, even at my lowest ebb, I have felt that joy must be a part of this Path—"My joy no man taketh from me"—but I know only too well that barrenness—or perhaps frustration is the word.

Last night in working for you, such a clear picture of the nonpower and nothingness of malpractice revealed itself. It could never touch the Christ-identity because it is aimed at reaching a person, a human being with a material sense of body, but all it is doing is trying to touch that which is only a mental concept, and which is nonexistent; and so of course it can't do anything! The conviction that came with this was a full guarantee of immunity from the "mess" (abbreviation for mesmerism) of this world.

With love,
Lorraine

March 28, 1964

Dear Emma and Joel,

I've just finished a Saturday afternoon session in which I played, "Rising Out of the Parenthesis" from the *1962 Hawaiian Village Open Class*, and I can tell you that it was a top experience.... It is enough to remake anyone's life, if practiced. And amazingly enough, we had been working with that very principle for the past three weeks: God's grace operates only in the immediate now, and to live in either the past or the future is to forget God's grace....

The "Secret of Zen" given you on March 17 is really it. *[Written on a little scrap of paper from a blank sheet in an old diary which he sent to me just as it came through, that there is no person to have a problem.]* I'm so grateful to you for sharing it, and you know that I keep it safe and secure in my files for reference.

What you wrote reminds me of the experience I had at a student's summer home over a year ago. One student asked, "How come Moses was able to lead the Hebrews out of Egypt after his revelation of I AM THAT I AM?"

And I, too, thought, "Yes, how come?" But having been well-taught by a teacher *par excellence*, I did as he would have done, just waited. Then it rushed in: "Oh, that was because he didn't have any people, he just had I."

The following day when someone sought to commiserate with this student at the prospect of having some 180 people for a wedding reception for her daughter, her response was, "Oh, I'm going to be like Moses. I'm not going to have any people: I'm just going to have I." And that she has carried with her ever since.

We're really working these days—on *Letters* and *Letters* and *Nets*—not leaving them but very much in them.

Much love,
Lorraine

April 8, 1964

Dear Emma and Joel,

It seems ages since I've written to you, but I guess you know that I've been busy—not vacationing! ...The enclosed check is a bit of sharing from the proceeds of this last weekend session and a small way of saying, "Thank you."

I have been giving a great deal of consideration to working out a time when Daisy, K.X., and Virginia could talk to the students during the class in May. We agreed in California that it would not be possible in the short time you are here for class, but I'm still thinking about it. Perhaps we could have one of them speak on Friday afternoon (your lecture is in the evening) another on Saturday morning (the first session of the class is on Saturday afternoon at 3:00 p.m.) and the third on Sunday morning at 9:00 (the last session of your class is at 11:00 a.m.). It would not need to be scheduled, and I do not know if Eileen will be there. Let me know what you think of this, and if you think it is too crowded, I will drop it, but I did want to make every effort for the students to hear these people. I will say nothing to them until I hear from you about it.

With much love,
Lorraine

Note: Joel was very happy with the idea that I was willing to arrange the program so that these teachers could be presented on the platform.

April 27, 1964

Dear Emma and Joel,

...When I listened to the second reel of the *Oahu-Maui Series,* I almost jumped out of my skin because of your reference to *Parsifal.* I quickly went to my desk and looked at a note I made on Good Friday, March 25, and this is what it says:

Tonight I gave myself a treat and played the Good Friday music and finale from Wagner's opera *Parsifal.* Wagner's majestic and poignant music and also through the music the stainless purity of Parsifal, able in his sinlessness to release Amfortas from the penalty for his sin, were borne in upon me with tremendous force. And then in a flash it came: They are not two men. They are one! The one, the man who came down to earth, and the other the same man in his return journey to heaven, but still only one! One under hypnosis, and the other free of any spell hypnosis could cast, a pure and undefiled son of God.

Isn't it interesting that I should have caught the message that you must have given sometime during that week, and caught it in almost the same words? So it is that the student is never far from the teacher's consciousness even though to the world thousands of miles may separate them. Thank you for such illumination.

With much love,
Lorraine

April 24, 1964

Dear Joel,

...*Nets* is coming along well—so gorgeous—and we expect to have it for you and for the publisher when you arrive in May.... In fact, I'm making every effort to have every bit of the work in such form that it can go forward just as if I were not off on a safari. The only problem is that you will have to put up with me in my old clothes because shopping is just out of the question. I shall have to be satisfied to wear a substantial covering of the "garments of righteousness"—if I dare be so brazen as to believe I might qualify for any such gorgeous raiment.

If there is some work you want to have finished at once, let me forego this trip to Europe and stay home to do it. The work I do for you, particularly this editorial work, which will be here long, long after you are gone from this plane, as a testament to one man's light, is far more important than any trip abroad would be to me. That a few more people might be helped through this trip is relatively unimportant in comparison to having your work preserved in all its beauty and correct form.

Don't you know that it is because I have this vision of the permanence and importance of your work that I watch over it so tenderly? Anything that might come to me in the nature of pleasure or some other form of good is so unimportant. There is within me the feeling of "To this end was I born, and for this cause came I into the world." I am sure that I was born to be like the "other Wiseman," finding the Christ in this work for you—a true karma yogi. To me, it is given to attain whatever measure of realization Grace gives me through the work.

With much love,

Lorraine

EPILOGUE:.....AND SO IT CONTINUES

In May, accompanied by Emma, Joel left Hawaii on the journey that was to end all earthly journeys for him. After stopping for classwork in Portland and Seattle, he arrived in Chicago for his last class in the United States, where he found 525 students waiting to hear this illumined consciousness pour itself forth as spiritual food.

At the close of the public lecture and after each of the class sessions, hundreds of students came up to the desk for a brief word of greeting and farewell, some of them later commenting that they sensed a transparency about him not of this world. There was an aura of "Touch me not; for I am not yet ascended to my Father."

A few days after the class in Chicago, Joel was off for Manchester, England, beginning what had been planned to be an almost three-month schedule of travel in England and Europe, with lectures and classes along the way. On this trip, he was accompanied by Emma, Daisy, a few other students, and me. But he was not to complete this trip, for in London on June 17, 1964, came his graduation in that final initiation for which he had waited so long, and which brought his transition into a new experience.[6]

Emma had called me at five o'clock in the morning, "You'd better come." Throwing on some clothes, within minutes I was at his side. Subsequently, at Emma's request, Daisy Shigemura and Tom Jones came in to join in the vigil. The next few hours were but a timeless moment as the realization of the ever-presence, ongoingness, and continuity of life flooded my being—life never confined in the shell of a body. Before me lay the

6 The Spiritual Journey of Joel S. Goldsmith, pp. 185-190.

shell but all I was aware of was the boundless, illimitable nature of Life. When the hotel physician arrived a couple of hours later, we retired to the living room, silently waiting and listening. At 7:40 the words came to me, "Release the shell, Lorraine, I am everpresent." A few minutes later Emma came in and announced that he had gone.

A few days before, after the last of three afternoon classes I had given in London, Joel came down into the room adjoining the classroom for the traditional afternoon English tea. When Joyce Burns Glen and I went over to speak to him, he said, "I hear that now I can go on." ...Sensing what he meant I countered, "Oh, Joel, how can you talk that way?" Now, a few days later, this very visible man had become invisible.

Later that memorable day, Walter Eastman, Gertrude and Roland Spencer, Tom Jones, Daisy Shigemura, and I met with Emma in Emma and Joel's suite to decide upon a course of action. It was decided by this group that I should write a foreword to the July *Letter* to inform students of Joel's transition and to explain that the activity of The Infinite Way would be controlled by Emma Goldsmith. Then Emma turned to me, "Will you continue the work in Europe and fulfill Joel's schedule of classes and lectures?" It was a request to which I acceded and a responsibility I agreed to undertake.

Months before, Joel had arranged to give classes not only in England, but in The Hague, Holland; Stockholm, Sweden; Hamburg, Munich, and Stuttgart, Germany; and in Vevey and Zurich, Switzerland. It was then that Joel had promised to show me Europe through his eyes and vast experience. Now I was to embark on this tour alone, and not only alone but with the challenge of carrying on the work of the great teacher himself.

The first stop at The Hague, which marked the beginning of this trek through Europe, did not bode well. The leader of the group and her daughter met me at the airport and, while driving me to the hotel, asked inquiringly, "And what do you propose to do? Play Joel's tapes?"

"Oh, no," I responded quickly, "I'm going to talk."

What seemed like an eternity of silence greeted that remark, and then came these far-from-encouraging words, spoken with a certain grim resignation, "You know, we people of Holland are very critical." This inauspicious beginning, however, was completely reversed in our first group meditation, and as the class proceeded, what had been resignation gave way to a feeling of outgoing love and oneness, which continued wherever I was called upon to conduct classes.

So it was that the spiritual path I had striven to follow was not to give me the rest that comes with a retreat or withdrawal from the world. It was a way of life in the world: and yet, even in the midst of the greatest activity, the spiritual work was always going on. The little self never wants to give itself up, yet that is the work. Whether in me or in someone else, wherever the specter of that false sense of self loomed before me to cloud my vision, it had to be destroyed. Where better could whatever vestiges of self still clinging to the disciple be revealed than in the arena of the day-to-day living of the spiritual life out in the hurly-burly of the world's activity? Its challenges and demands provided far sterner discipline than any tasks or sacrifices artificially imposed from without. There, the many little "I"s the aspirant all-unknowingly embodies, which show forth as the conflicting sides of the human personality, come to the fore only to be dissolved in the one all-embracing *I*.

For those who seek to attain the goal of liberation, a teacher with the clarity of vision to penetrate beyond the veil of personality to spiritual identity is indispensable, one with whom the failures as well as the triumphs could be shared. To such a teacher, one could bring the faults that keep surfacing until the dross of human consciousness is burned away by the light within which the attained spiritual consciousness of the teacher reveals. What perfect trust that entailed! It was that childlike trust to which Jesus referred when he said, "Except ye...become as little children, ye shall not enter into the kingdom of heaven." Only absolute trust, integrity, and honesty could characterize the relationship of guru and disciple. It was trusting in a person who himself had not surmounted every trace of humanhood, but who had attained sufficient of that penetrating light which would enable him to see through the fog to the Reality obscured by lifetimes of accumulated experience in the realm of duality.

Such a teacher was my teacher. Out of the roots he had so carefully nurtured came the blooms unhampered by the weeds of personal sense, the remnants of which could no longer impede the steady movement forward. As the guru undeviatingly held the disciple in the light of his consciousness, the disciple, slowly, sometimes gently and easily and sometimes painfully, began to cast off the veils hiding the essential unity to merge with the light of the one indivisible Consciousness.

Just as the guru was always open to receive more enlightenment, maintaining a deep humility and dissatisfaction with himself in the light of the vastness of what lay ahead to be attained; so, too, the disciple saw humility, an indispensable concomitant of the spiritual path, increase and grow in her, as she gained deeper insights.

Joel had one motivation, and only one: an all-encompassing passion to attain ever greater heights of awareness and to share that awareness with those who exhibited any sign of receptivity. His letters show his sadness at the lack of comprehension of those with whom he would share. But this disciple was well-matched with her guru, for to her, too, there was one overriding goal, and from that nothing could deter her.

The master had indeed pushed his disciple forward, as he always did, to stand or fall on her own conscious awareness or to fly on the wings he had so carefully nurtured as he watched over her unfoldment. The fifteen years of ceaseless, untiring work had firmly established the roots, with little saplings appearing and growing strong enough to withstand the winds of the world and remain immovable throughout all the challenges that followed. These had been years of dedication and devotion to the work carried on under the guidance of this loving but stern taskmaster, who penetrated her very soul and to whose light she held up whatever weaknesses she became aware of to be dissolved in that greater light.

Joel was no longer visible, but not really gone, for truly the disciple's consciousness had become so at-one with the master's that there was no separation, no going or coming, just a merging in the oneness of the one Consciousness of *I AM*. Never again would she need her beloved teacher, not that she had in any way the feeling of having fully attained the goal, which still loomed as a beacon far ahead of her, beckoning her on. But there was a realization that the Master within, that *I* that is the identity of the disciple, would never leave her, but would walk with her all the way.

It was no longer my teacher and I. My teacher had opened up to me the limitless nature of Being, my being, and I knew that the *I* within me was the one and only teacher. All these years were only that I might understand that there was no teacher external to my own being. The *I* that appeared as Joel, the teacher, was the one *I*, the *I* of me. It was only in my unillumined and unenlightened stage that *I* had to appear as something external to me. In conscious oneness there was no separation, only that one *I*, Consciousness, manifesting and expressing in infinite form and variety as whatever was necessary on the way to a realization of the Self-completeness of that one *I*. It was an in-depth confirmation of the first glimmer of realization that came to me on September 28, 1949, the realization that nothing could be taken from me and nothing could be added to me. That *I* that *I* am was already infinite and Self-complete, and It would never leave me, nor forsake me, but would be with me throughout all time and eternity.

Always, the message in all Scripture is "Seek Me." Seek that *I* within you that is the Master in your heart. "Seek me with your whole heart and ye shall find Me." To each who seeks, the way opens.